*ESOP*s

The
Handbook of
Employee
Stock
Ownership
Plans

Gerald Kalish

PROBUS PUBLISHING COMPANY
Chicago, Illinois

This publication is designed to provide accurate and authoritative information in regard to the subject matter covered. It is sold with the understanding that the publisher is not engaged in rendering legal, accounting or other professional service.

Library of Congress Cataloging-in-Publication Data Available

ISBN 1-55738-090-2

Printed in the United States of America

1   2   3   4   5   6   7   8   9   0

To the memory of William J. Kalish

CONTENTS

Preface   vii

Foreword   ix
John D. Rockefeller IV

Introduction   1
David Binns

One: Overview of ESOP Legal Requirements   9
Gergory K. Brown

Two: Planning for an ESOP   53
Gerald I. Kalish

Three: ESOP Valuation Considerations   71
Paul J. Much

Four: Lending to ESOPs   93
Robert F. Schatz

Five: Financial Aspects of ESOPs   113
Robert W. Smiley, Jr.

**Six: Accounting for ESOP Transactions by
the Plan Sponsor**   141
Rebecca J. Miller, CPA

Seven: ESOP Administration: A Practical Guide   167
Karen Bonn

Eight: The Use of an ESOP for Corporate Finance 195
R. W. Pricer

Nine: Unions and Employee Ownership 217
Deborah Groban Olson

**Ten: Communicating the Message of Employee
Stock Ownership** 253
Shela C. Turpin-Forster

**Eleven: Ownership, Motivation, and Corporate
Performance: Putting ESOPs to Work** 271
Corey Rosen

Appendix A: Major Federal and State Laws 291
*Compiled by William J. Merton, Alan J. Hawksley,
and Helen H. Morrison*

Appendix B: Key Organizations 303
Compiled by Corey Rosen

Appendix C: Suggested Readings 309
Compiled by Corey Rosen

Index 319

PREFACE

My purpose in organizing and editing this book is amply expressed in its title. It is a handbook and guide to employee stock ownership plans, rather than an exhaustive technical treatment of ESOPs.

It is my hope that interested readers—whose backgrounds may be business, labor, professional, academia, or government—will find this book to be a valuable source of authorative current knowledge and thinking about ESOPs.

To be effective, a book of this nature should offer a broad perspective. The experiences of a broad range of experts is more informative than that of a single expert. I have chosen some of the best known ESOP experts to contribute to this book. All have been actively involved in the evolution of employee stock ownership plans.

Each chapter of this book stands alone and is complete in itself. While this produces some overlap in certain of the chapters, it eliminates the need for the reader to refer to other chapters, and it provides valuable reinforcement of important concepts.

Finally, I would emphasize that this book is a guide and not a rule book. The statements and opinions of the guest authors are, of necessity, general in nature and are not intended as a substitute for legal counsel or other professional assitance in planning, designing, implementing, or maintaining an employee stock ownership plan.

Acknowledgements

I would like to express my appreciation to the contributors who participated in this project. They are all eminently qualified ESOP experts, and without their contributions this book could not have been published.

In addition, Gregory K. Brown, Esq., of Keck, Mahin & Cate gave generously of his time to comment on several of the chapters. Mary Wolf served as Editorial Assistant and deserves much credit for her organizational and editorial efforts in moving this project from the planning stage to publication.

Gerald I. Kalish

FOREWORD

Every so often, an idea emerges that suggests a way of promoting a number of previously conflicting goals. Certain concepts have a powerful ability to change the context in which we think about a problem. I believe that ESOPs, or employee stock ownership plans, are such a concept.

My first experience with an employee stock ownership plan dates back to 1982, during my second term as Governor of West Virginia. In that year, a remarkable story unfolded. The employees of Weirton Steel made the decision to purchase their mill, and created the nation's largest employee-owned corporation. I still vividly recall the fear that struck when National Steel announced in March of 1982 that it would be closing its Weirton mill. Eight thousand people were threatened with unemployment. I remember well the initial skepticism about the idea that something called an "ESOP" might be able to save the plant and maintain this community lifeline.

Fortunately, despite the skepticism, the mill's employees and the citizens of Weirton refused to be downed by defeat or overwhelmed by the awesome task of rescuing their plant. They courageously decided to push forward with the employee stock ownership model.

As Governor of West Virginia, I worked closely with the employees and Weirton's community leaders to make this plan a success. I saw first-hand enormous courage and hope. A publication was created to keep every single worker fully informed of the process of forming an ESOP. Speakers were sent out to every corner of the community to explain ESOPs and their potential. Billboards proclaiming "We Can Do It" and "Let's Save Weirton" sprung up around town. Green ribbons, symbolic of a fresh beginning, appeared on car doors, shop windows, trees, and telephone poles.

Perhaps most significantly, the employees of Weirton did not let short-term financial losses deter them from their goal. When the workers gathered on September 23, 1982 to vote on the proposed ESOP plan, all present were aware of the conclusions of a recently published feasibility study. While generally optimistic about the future of Weirton's ESOP, the report made it clear that wages and benefits had to be cut by 20 percent. In a straight up or down vote, the employees overwhelmingly agreed to make the concessions and approved the proposal to buy Weirton Steel.

Since then, Weirton has become a shining example of successful cooperation between labor and management. From the shop floor to the board room, worker participation in decisions affecting the mill's operation has flourished. Weirton has become one of the nation's most profitable integrated steel mills. It has shown profits for 22 consecutive quarters, at a time when most of the steel industry has experienced much grimmer returns. Recognizing the crucial role of research and development, Weirton has pushed to improve and expand its products. Confronting the hard realities of a rapidly changing industry, it has been steadfast in its commitment to plant modernization. Weirton Steel is truly inspiring proof of an ESOP's potential.

In recounting this amazing story of Weirton's success I recognize that the circumstances in that West Virginia steel town were, and still are, relatively unique. The chain of events leading to Weirton Steel's recent prosperity cannot be precisely imitated elsewhere. But since Weirton was formed, I have followed experiences with ESOPs throughout the country. After carefully studying these pioneering models, I have come to the conclusion that the ESOP approach is generating tremendous benefits in many places besides Weirton, benefits that should be much more widely understood and promoted.

Throughout the United States, and indeed across the globe, thousands of companies have established employee stock ownership plans. Since 1974, when Congress enacted the first of some twenty tax measures designed to encourage employee stock ownership, the number of American employee-owned or partially-owned companies has grown from some 1,600 to 8,100. The number of employees owning stock in this country has jumped from 250,000 to more than eight million.

Those who follow the legislative history will recall that Congress originally intended ESOPs to be a technique for broadening stock ownership. Lawmakers wanted to encourage corporate leaders to more widely distribute asset ownership to citizens who otherwise might not have the financial means to acquire such assets.

The continuing spread of ESOPs has contributed significantly to that aim. Within ESOP firms, the distribution of stock ownership has tended to be far broader than in the general population. According to a General Accounting Office study, close to 90% of the corporate stock in this country is owned by just 10% of citizens. *Half* of one percent of Americans own almost half of all stock. By contrast, the median rate of employee participation in stock ownership in ESOP firms is about 71 percent. Without question, ESOPs have been a powerful and effective lever to share wealth and ownership more fairly with those who sustain that system.

Recently, ESOPs have come under a great deal of criticism just because in some cases employees are not getting the magnitude of benefits critics think they should. I am certainly not opposed to discussing these concerns. I wholeheartedly support exploring ways to improve the operation and management of a program that has proven so effective. But I urge the critics to keep in mind General Accounting Office statistics indicating problems with the use of ESOP incentives to be marginal, existing in only 3% of cases. In the overwhelming majority of instances, the tax code requirement that ESOPs be for the exclusive benefit of employees is tightly enforced, and workers have access to honest, objective information about the stock they will be acquiring.

Skepticism has its place. But our response to any problems with ESOPs should be proportioned to the scale of the difficulty. Given the spectacular success of most ESOPs, I believe we should focus on improving what laws there are rather than eliminating the tax incentives for ESOPs altogether. Rather than tear down what we've already accomplished, we should explore ways to build off the ESOP approach a strategy for promoting broader goals of productivity, worker dignity, and cooperation between labor and management.

I was amazed recently to read the results of a survey by the Yankelovich polling firm indicating that only seven out of a hundred American workers think that if they make any extra effort in the workplace it will translate into a real gain for them. These workers believe that the benefits will go to the stockholders, the managers, or their boss, but not to them. By contrast, nine out of every ten Japanese workers think that if they work harder, *they* will benefit.

Given the link between performance and reward, America simply cannot afford not to recognize the importance of employee ownership. By providing an identification between the worker and the company, significant employee ownership encourages greater motivation, commitment, and productivity. Knowing they have a financial stake in the company's future, employee-owners are likely to work harder, suggest new ideas, and take a greater interest in the quality of their product. Example after practical ESOP example proves this.

As any good manager knows, though, loyalty, creativity, initiative, and drive cannot be motivated by impersonal incentives alone. ESOPs are one example of the new thinking we need. Only when employers make sincere efforts to treat their work associates more like partners than hired hands, only when employees are convinced that they are working with rather than against their employers, will more people be willing to make the kind of effort that keeps society productive.

In the case of Weirton, workers were given honest, objective information from day one. They had three Union representatives on the Board of Directors. The company set up intensive, three-day training programs to teach employees to run employee involvement teams on their own. It installed television monitors throughout the plant to keep employees informed of developments, and it shared detailed financial and production data (good and bad) with employee-owners. Management at Weirton shared company profits, company ownership, and company control.

At the core of Weirton's success is the recognition of a simple fact about human nature. At the workplace no less than outside it, an investment in human dignity will more often than not be returned a thousandfold. Managers who recognize the value of sharing responsibility, trust, and autonomy will see their employees respond positively. Combined, freedom, hard work and an emphasis on human dignity can revitalize the American workplace. They can light the way to a world of Weirton Steels.

John D. Rockefeller IV

August 18, 1989
United States Senate

Introduction

David Binns

David Binns is the Executive Director of the ESOP Association, a Washington, D.C. based trade association representing the interests of ESOP companies and professionals who provide services to ESOP firms.

INTRODUCTION

Employee stock ownership plans, or ESOPs, are innovative, exciting, and controversial. Based on a simple idea—providing employees with an ownership stake in the company where they work—ESOPs nevertheless defy easy classification. ESOPs play a unique role in employee compensation and corporate financial transactions as both employee benefit plans and techniques of corporate finance. Fueled in part by attractive tax benefits, ESOPs are increasingly being used in leveraged buyouts, ownership transfers, corporate restructurings, stock buybacks, and even as a means of preventing hostile takeovers or plant closings. ESOPs also figure prominently in innovative employee benefit design and compensation techniques and are having a significant impact on labor-management relations and workplace operations in many companies.

Whether one is approaching ESOPs for the first time or has had some previous exposure to ESOPs, this handbook may have some surprises in store. Simply put, ESOPs can be different things to different people and can be used in many ways for a number of reasons. The flexibility of ESOPs coupled with their successful record in benefiting companies and employees alike has made employee ownership a viable option for many corporations.

The ESOP as we know it today has largely developed over the last two decades. Given such recent development, some observers may be surprised to learn that ESOPs are already well established on the American corporate landscape and are, indeed, one of the fastest growing trends in American business. ESOPs can be found in companies ranging from small, closely held businesses to some of the country's leading corporations. Companies owned in part or in whole by their employees are located in nearly every state and can be found in almost every type of business classification. In some companies, ESOPs own just a small percentage of the total shares outstanding, although increasingly, ESOPs own significant stakes or the company outright.

Although employee ownership has been around since the late nineteenth century, when worker cooperatives first began to appear on the scene and the idea of employee stock ownership first gained some popularity in the 1920s, only with the development of the ESOP has employee ownership been established on a large scale in mainstream American businesses. Not only are ESOPs the most prominent form of employee ownership today, but their use has also transformed the perception of employee ownership from that of playing a minor role in small cooperative companies to that of clearly benefiting a great many American corporations and even the economy at large.

What has caused this trend toward employee ownership? The answer lies partly in the pioneering work of two key individuals and partly in changing economic and political realities that have made ESOPs appropriate for many corporate applications.

The ESOP concept originated with the theories of Louis Kelso. Kelso's first book, *The Capitalist Manifesto*, written with the philosopher Mortimer Adler, argues that capital ownership is an important means of supplementing wage income for workers and that widespread employee stock ownership is the most effective means of broadening the ownership of capital in an advanced industrial economy. Kelso reasoned that in an ecomony in which capital (i.e., machines and technology) is responsible for an increasing proportion of overall economic production, it is necessary for more people to own capital. The problem with modern economies, Kelso said, is that a very small percentage of the population owns significant amounts of capital, and the vast majority of people do not have sufficient income to acquire capital. Thus, to maintain a healthy free-

market economy, it is necessary to broaden capital ownership.

It wasn't until the 1970s that Kelso achieved his next
major success—convincing Louisiana Senator Russell Long
of the merits of the ESOP concept. Senator Long, who at
that time was the chairman of the Senate Finance Committee, began to push for ESOP legislation and used his
powerful influence to include recognition of leveraged
ESOPs in the landmark Employee Retirement Income
Security Act of 1974 (ERISA). Having successfully worked
to establish ESOPs in the law, Senator Long continued to
champion the ESOP cause. Before Senator Long retired in
1986, Congress passed 19 different pieces of legislation
promoting the use of ESOPs.

Along the way, Senator Long gained growing bipar-
tisan support for the ESOP idea. Attractive to conserva-
tives as a means of creating more capitalists and to liberals
as a means of spreading the wealth, the ESOP concept,
though not without critics, is increasingly considered a viable means of promoting corporate economic growth while
simultaneously benefiting working Americans.

From the beginning with the passage of ERISA, ESOPs
have been treated differently under the law than other
employee benefit plans. As with all qualified employee
benefit plans, ESOPs are subject to regulation under
ERISA. ESOPs, however, have two important attributes
that distinguish them from other plans. First, other plans
are required to invest their assets in a diversified portfolio,
but ESOPs are required by law to invest primarily in the
securities of the sponsoring employer. This assures that
ESOPs will indeed transfer significant amounts of corporate stock to employees. In addition, ESOPs are unique
in that they can be used to borrow money for the purpose of
acquiring employer securities. This ability to "leverage" has
enabled ESOPs to be used not simply as an employee
benefit plan but also as a technique of corporate finance
designed to create more employee shareholders.

It is this dual role as both an employee benefit plan
and as a technique of corporate finance that has resulted in

the highly flexible—and complex—structure of ESOP law today. Indeed, most of the ESOP legislation passed in the last 15 years has promoted the use of leveraged ESOPs. Much of the recent growth of employee ownership has been fed by the increasing popularity of leveraged ESOPs, and prospects for continued growth appear quite good.

But beyond the many tax advantages ESOPs provide for companies and employees alike and separate from the important role that ESOPs play in promoting wider distribution of capital ownership is another aspect of employee ownership that should be considered by anyone seriously thinking of establishing an ESOP. To state the obvious, ESOPs provide rank-and-file employees with significant amounts of stock ownership. This can have important ramifications for the way ESOP companies do business.

ESOPs are often promoted as a means of giving workers "a piece of the action," and ESOP advocates claim that employee- owners will have a greater incentive to improve productivity since they will share in the fruits of their efforts. Many companies have, indeed, shown impressive productivity gains after establishing an ESOP, but it would be a mistake to assume that every ESOP will result in improved corporate operations. Companies not willing to adapt to the special dynamics of employee ownership and to put forth the extra effort often needed to make the ESOP successful may not be able to realize all of the benefits ESOPs can provide.

Employee ownership offers great possibilities for improved corporate operations, but the effective operation of an ESOP is not necessarily a simple task. ESOPs are most definitely not for everyone. Corporate stockholders, particularly in closely held companies, uncomfortable with the idea of sharing ownership with their employees, would be well advised to think twice about installing an ESOP.

This handbook provides an excellent means of determining whether an ESOP is suitable for you. ESOPs can mean different things to different people, but their very diversity and the successful track record of thousands of ESOP companies makes them worth a closer look. Read on to find out why ESOPs are one of the fastest growing trends in American business today and how they can benefit your company.

ONE

Overview of ESOP Legal Requirements

Gregory K. Brown

Gregory K. Brown is a partner in the Chicago law firm of Keck, Mahin & Cate and specializes in employee benefits and executive compensation.

Greg is a member of The American Bar Association, The Chicago Bar Association, Midwest Pension Conference, National Center for Employer Ownership and the ESOP Association of America, including its Legal Advisory Committee. He is the co-author of "ESOPs" Bureau of National Affairs, *Tax Management Portfolio*, 354-3d (1985), "Compensation Opportunities and Problems—The Economic Recovery Tax Act of 1981," Chicago Bar Record (September-October, 1981, Volume 63 No. 2) and "Costs and Benefit Factors" Illinois Institute for Continuing Legal Education Pension Practice Handbook, 1983.

Mr. Brown received his J.D. degree from the University of Illinois in 1975 and a B.S. in Economics from the University of Kentucky in May, 1973.

ONE

Much has been written about employee stock ownership plans (ESOPs) as either a tool of corporate finance or as an employee benefit. Little of what has been written about ESOPs has bothered to define exactly what an ESOP is or is not. Simply stated, an ESOP is a qualified retirement plan designed to invest primarily in employer stock. Contributions may be made on a discretionary basis or on a committed basis to amortize ESOP financing and may be made in either cash or stock. Distributions are also made in either cash or stock.

As a qualified retirement plan, many of the general qualified plan requirements attach to an ESOP, including the following:

- The plan must be reduced to writing and have a domestic trust.[1]
- The plan must meet the nondiscriminatory coverage rules of the Internal Revenue Code, which generally require that nonunion employees who have reached age 21 and have completed 1 year of service will participate in the plan.[2]
- The plan must meet one of several alternative vesting schedules reflected in the Internal Revenue Code. That is, participants must vest entirely in their benefits after 10 years of service (5 years for those working after 1988) or must vest on a graded basis over a period not exceeding 15 years (7 years for those working after 1988).[3]

11

- Distributions must generally commence no later than 60 days after the plan year in which a participant retires or reaches normal retirement age, whichever is later, and in any event must start by April 1 following the date the employee attains age 70½ years.[4]

USES AND APPLICATIONS

Defining what an ESOP is and the general requirements that it is subject to is merely a beginning. Before considering the more technical legal aspects of ESOPs, it is worthwhile to describe the various uses and applications of ESOPs. Through an ESOP, a company can:

1. Borrow at 80-95 percent of prime.
2. Deduct principal as well as interest.
3. Compel the government to purchase stock for cash and give it back to the company's employees.
4. Sell all or part of stock tax free.
5. Sell a controlling interest and retain voting control.
6. Create a buyer for a sale of the company and dictate the terms of the sale.
7. Provide a market for the company's stock without the expense or exposure of a public offering.
8. Deduct dividend payments.
9. Transform a retirement plan from a cash drain to a cash generator.
10. Provide liquidity to pay estate taxes.
11. Provide a takeover defense.

TYPES OF ESOPS

Enactment of the Tax Reform Act of 1986 established two principal types of ESOPs: stock bonus plans and leveraged

ESOPs. Each plan is designed to invest primarily in employer stock, but the two plans operate very differently.

A stock bonus plan usually involves employer discretionary contributions on a continuing basis. That is, no contribution by the employer is required for any particular year, but contributions must be made on a substantial and recurring basis for the plan to maintain its tax-qualified status. Contributions are made by the employer in either cash or stock. Occasionally, a stock bonus plan is combined with a money purchase pension plan pursuant to which contributions are made in either cash or stock or both but on a formula basis. For example, each year the employer contribution will be equal to 10 percent of the aggregate participant compensation for that year.[5]

On the other hand, a leveraged ESOP involves the use of debt financing to either redeem the shares of existing shareholders or to provide working capital to the sponsoring employer, who can then make capital improvements or perhaps buy the stock or assets of another company. In a typical leveraged transaction, the following would occur:

1. The employer would establish an employee stock ownership plan.
2. Debt financing would be provided either through a loan to the employer which would, in turn, lend the proceeds on substantially the same repayment terms to the ESOP, or the lender would lend the money directly to the ESOP with a corporate guarantee.
3. The ESOP would use the loan proceeds to either buy the shares of existing shareholders or to buy shares from the sponsoring employer.

The result of such a transaction is that the ESOP owns shares of stock in the employer corporation that it has purchased from either the employer corporation or its shareholder or shareholders; either the sponsoring employer or its shareholder has the loan proceeds from the sale of stock; and the ESOP owes money either directly to the lender or to the sponsoring employer. In future years, the employer will make contributions and other payments (perhaps dividends) to the ESOP to enable it to repay its debt obligation.

When the leveraged shares are purchased by the ESOP, they are held in an unallocated *loan suspense account*. The shares held in this account are released on a pro rata basis as principal and interest payments are made on the loan. As shares are released on such a basis, they are transferred from the unallocated loan suspense account to be credited to participants' accounts at least once each plan year.[6] Usually, the shares released from the loan suspense account are allocated to participants' accounts, pro rata, based on the participants' relative compensation. For example, a participant who earns $50,000 would have twice as many shares allocated to his account as a participant who earns $25,000. Some plans offer to allocate shares on the basis of other factors, such as years of service and/or a combination of years of service and compensation, but such plans must monitor the allocations on a yearly basis to assure that the allocation formula does not result in prohibited discrimination in favor of highly compensated employees.[7] The term "highly compensated employee" includes those individuals who for the current or the immediately preceding year:

1. Own 5 percent or more of the employer corporation.
2. Earn in excess of $75,000.
3. Are officers of the employer corporation and make more than $45,000.
4. Earn more than $50,000 and are among the 20 percent highest paid employees of the employer.[8]

The shares allocated on an annual basis to employees' accounts may be subject to a vesting schedule, as described previously. All employees must be vested upon reaching normal retirement age (usually age 65), and most plans usually provide for full vesting upon the employee's death or disability while employed.[9]

SPECIAL ESOP REQUIREMENTS

Although ESOPs are qualified retirement plans subject to the general requirements for all tax-qualified plans, the very different nature of ESOPs from regular qualified plans requires that special provisions be applicable to ESOPs. These special provisions concern the timing and form of distributions, the put option, voting, the meaning of employer securities, the need for an independent appraiser, and diversification requirements.

Timing and Form of Distributions

Distributions from ESOPs may be made in the form of either cash or stock, except that the retiring employee has the right to demand that stock be distributed to him.[10] Certain financial institutions are excused from the stock distribution requirement as are employers whose charter or by-laws require that substantially all (i.e., 85 percent or more) of employer stock must be held by active employees and/or qualified retirement plans, such as ESOPs.[11] Furthermore, distributions to an employee retiring on or after reaching normal retirement age under the plan or who separates on account of death or disability must either be made or commenced within 1 year after the end of the plan year in which the employee retires, dies, or becomes disabled.[12] Employees whose termination of employment occurs by reason of resignation or dismissal must begin to receive their benefits within 5 years after the end of the plan year in which their termination occurs, unless the employee is reemployed before that time.[13] In either case, the employee may elect to defer the distribution until a later date, and no distribution need be made while the ESOP still has outstanding acquisition indebtedness.[14]

Distributions must be made at least as rapidly as equal annual installments over a 5-year period, unless the participant exercises an election to lengthen the distribution period. For certain large balances (i.e., those in excess of $500,000) this 5-year requirement is lengthened by 1 year for each additional $100,000 in the employee's vested account balance but may not be lengthened beyond 10 years.[15]

Put Option

An employee who receives nonpublicly traded stock in his ESOP distribution may require that the employer (but not the ESOP) repurchase his shares at an appraised fair market value.[16] If the employee receives a single-sum distribution of his entire vested account balance under the ESOP, he may require that the employer repurchase his shares during the 60-day period following his distribution, or he may wait until the ESOP fair market value appraisal is announced, in which case another 60-day period will commence. The employer may satisfy its obligation by either paying the entire amount in cash or by paying a portion in cash and providing the employee with a written promissory note specifying a reasonable rate of interest and providing adequate security.[17]

If the employee is receiving installment distributions of stock, the employee also has the twin 60-day periods in which to exercise his put option for each installment payment. The employer must satisfy that put option within 30 days after the employee's exercise for each installment.[18]

Voting

If the sponsoring employer has a registration-type class of securities under Section 12 of the Securities Exchange Act of 1934, the plan must provide that the employee may direct the trustee as to the voting of all shares allocated to his account on all issues put before the shareholders.[19] If the stock of the employer is not a registration-type class of security, then more limited voting rights apply. In such cases, the employee is entitled to direct the trustee as to how to vote the shares allocated to his account on all matters requiring the approval or disapproval of shareholders for corporate transactions involving mergers, consolidations, liquidations, recapitalizations, reclassifications, sales of substantially all assets, and such others as the IRS may prescribe.[20] On all other matters, the trustees have complete discretion (subject to their ERISA fiduciary duties described later) to vote the shares, and the trustees have discretion to vote all unallocated shares in a loan suspense account.

A special provision permits a plan to provide for "one person, one vote" procedures whereby each participant is entitled to one vote and the trustee will vote all shares in accordance with the wishes of participants. This approach obviously has a more egalitarian, democratic appeal not tied to the participant's relative capital interest.[21]

Employer Securities

For purposes of the shares that may be purchased by a leveraged ESOP and for many of the tax incentives described later, the ESOP must invest in *employer securities*. In the context of a publicly held company, the term employer securities means any common stock of the employer. In the context of a company that is not publicly traded, the term employer securities means common stock of the employer that has maximum dividend rights and maximum voting rights. In either case, the term employer securities may also mean certain noncallable convertible preferred stocks that, when purchased by the ESOP, provide for a reasonable conversion formula into common stock.[22]

Independent Appraiser

Prior to enactment of the Tax Reform Act of 1986, there was no legal requirement that shares of a corporation not publicly traded be independently appraised on an annual basis.[23] However, ESOP shares acquired after December 31, 1986, must be independently appraised on an annual basis. Proposed regulations have been issued by the DOL regarding how the independent appraiser is to perform such annual valuations, with heavy emphasis on the general principles of *Revenue Ruling 59–60, 1959-2 C.B. 237*. That ruling provides for the consideration of the following factors:

- Nature of the business and the history of the enterprise from its inception.
- The economic outlook in general and the condition and outlook of the specific industry in particular.
- Book value of the stock and the financial condition of the business.
- Earning capacity of the company.
- Dividend paying capacity.
- Whether or not the enterprise has goodwill or other intangible value.
- Sales of the stock and the size of the block of stock to be valued.
- Market value of stocks of corporations engaged in the same or similar line of business having their stocks actively traded in a free and open market, either on an exchange or over the counter.

Diversification

The assets of an ESOP invested in employer securities are not subject to the general diversification requirements applicable to qualified plans. Many older workers are concerned with having "all of their eggs in one basket." As a result of the Tax Reform Act of 1986, shares of stock of the employer that are acquired by an ESOP after December 31, 1986 (including, for example, shares purchased with dividends paid on shares purchased before January 1, 1987), are subject to a diversification requirement.[25]

Pursuant to the diversification requirement, an employee who has attained age 55 and completed 10 years of participation (not service) may elect annually to diversify, during a 5-year period, up to 25 percent of his account balance (reduced by any prior amounts diversified) and in the next year to diversify up to 50 percent of his account balance (reduced by any prior amounts diversified). The plan must allow the employee a choice of three investment funds not involving employer stock or may provide that the employee's diversification election will involve a distribution of the stock to the employee, which would then be subject to the general put option requirements described earlier. No diversification need be provided if the fair market value of the employee stock allocated to a participant's account is less than $500.[26]

SPECIAL ESOP CONSIDERATIONS UNDER ERISA

The provisions of the Employee Retirement Income Security Act of 1974 as amended (ERISA), include certain general standards for fiduciary conduct, prohibited transactions provisions, and certain exceptions to those standards and provisions.[27] In general, a *fiduciary* is anyone who has discretionary control over the investment of plan assets or over the administration of the plan or renders investment advice to the plan for a fee.[28] This normally includes the sponsoring employer and its board of directors, the trustee or trustees of the plan, any committee that has administrative authority under the plan, and any investment manager of the plan. Certain custodians of plan assets are also included.

A fiduciary is generally required under ERISA to meet the following standards:

1. It must act for the sole and exclusive purpose of providing benefits to participants and beneficiaries of the plan and defraying reasonable expenses of the plan.
2. It must act prudently.
3. It must diversify plan investments unless it is clearly prudent not to do so.

4. It must act in accordance with the written plan documents.[29]

Since an ESOP is a corporate financing vehicle as well as an employee benefit plan, the exclusive benefit rule is normally interpreted as requiring that actions be in the "primary" benefit of the participants and beneficiaries of an ESOP.[30] Furthermore, while an ESOP is excused from the ERISA diversification requirements, it is not excused from the requirement to act prudently.

Difficult Issues of Exclusive Benefit and Fiduciary Prudence

While the special nature of ESOPs is expressly acknowledged in ERISA, there are few clear answers to the typical questions that arise, particularly as to the applicability of the exclusive benefit and prudence rules of ERISA. These rules apply to ESOPs but do not provide clear answers to the following types of questions:

- Is it "prudent" for a newly created ESOP to invest in the stock of a new employer?
- Must an ESOP dispose of employer stock if it is dropping in value or the employer has suffered an economic downturn?
- Under what circumstances must an ESOP fiduciary sell employer securities to a person who has tendered for them?
- May an ESOP acquire employer securities on the open market while the sponsoring employer is in a tender offer situation?
- Under what circumstances may an ESOP fiduciary convert a diversified profit-sharing plan or other plan into an ESOP?
- May an ESOP fiduciary follow an ESOP trust provision that prohibits the sale of employer securities by the ESOP?

Many newly formed corporations start out as speculative enterprises. Unless an ESOP fiduciary can invest in the stock of such a company, the company can never maintain an ESOP. Furthermore, if an ESOP were required to dispose of employer stock whenever the stock was declining in value or the employer suffered an economic downturn, the ESOP might not have stock available to distribute to its participants and beneficiaries. Indeed, such sales might be contrary to the underlying purpose of the ESOP—to invest primarily in employer stock. Accordingly, it could be concluded that an ESOP fiduciary should not be treated as *per se* acting imprudently because it acquires employer stock that has speculative value or holds stock that has decreased in value. The issue is not free from doubt, however.

Some public companies establish ESOPs with a large block of employer stock as a device designed, in part, to retain current management's control of the corporation. Such a use may backfire. While a large block of stock in the hands of a friendly fiduciary might be a deterrent to some types of corporate raiders, it might encourage others. A large block of employer stock might deter the type of person who tries to force his way onto a company's board of directors as a result of acquiring less than 20 percent of the company's stock; the ESOP's holdings might serve as a counterweight against such a person. On the other hand, a person who wishes to acquire the entire company might be attracted by the ESOP's holdings. He may reduce his cash needs for the tender offer by tendering a stock-for-stock exchange for the ESOP's holdings and cash for the nonESOP holdings. The suitor might believe that the ESOP's fiduciaries are required under the prudence and exclusive benefit rule to tender the ESOP stock if a favorable tender offer is made.

While it might be prudent for an ESOP fiduciary not to tender shares already owned by an ESOP, it might not be prudent for the ESOP to use its available cash to purchase shares on the market during a hostile takeover attempt.[31]

This is particularly true if the fiduciary intends not to tender in response to the takeover offer. If the ESOP investment decisions are controlled by an employer (or a committee appointed by the employer's board) that is fighting the tender offer, the purchases could be viewed as a maneuver to thwart the takeover that is not in conformance with the prudence and exclusive benefit requirements. This is particularly true since the price of the target company stock will generally rise during a tender offer and will usually fall if the tender is not successful, thereby jeopardizing the ESOP's economic investment.

An employer could attempt to alleviate some of these problems by putting into the ESOP trust agreement a flat prohibition on the sale of employer stock held by the ESOP. However, such a written prohibition is probably inconsistent with the statutory requirement that a fiduciary carry out its responsibilities in a prudent manner.[32] That is, if it were imprudent not to sell the stock, a fiduciary's prudence responsibilities would supersede the document provisions, and the trustee may have to seek instructions from a federal district court.

In *Eaves* v. *Penn*, the court held that the prudence rule applies to the acquisition of employer stock by an ESOP, despite the fact that the diversification requirement is waived by ERISA. This holding may be limited to situations in which the conversion of diversified assets into stock of a troubled company is involved.[33] If the diversified assets of a profit-sharing plan were converted into the stock of a "blue chip" sponsor, it is questionable whether a court would reach the same conclusion. Indeed, it is possible that the conversion cases represent the outer limits to which the courts will push the prudence rule in connection with ESOPs. Thus, while it is not per se illegal to convert profit-sharing plan assets into employer stock as a part of an ESOP, the responsible fiduciary for such conversion must take into account the "prudence" requirements associated with such a decision and suffer the consequences if it acts imprudently. Accordingly, before an ESOP is established as a "poison pill" device to thwart an unwanted suitor or an existing plan is converted to an ESOP, great care should be taken in designing the plan and assigning fiduciary responsibility to ensure that the plan is treated as an employee benefit plan truly in the interests of the employer and its shareholders and employees.

Prohibited Transactions

Not only does ERISA impose the prudence and exclusive benefits standards upon fiduciary conduct, but it also prohibits a fiduciary from making certain transactions between a plan and "parties in interest" because of the conflicts of interest involved in such transactions. The term *parties in interest* includes all fiduciaries; the sponsoring employer and its parent, subsidiaries, affiliates, employees, officers, directors, and 10 percent shareholders thereof; and service providers to the plan.[34]

The following transactions between a plan and party in interest are generally prohibited:

- Sale, exchange, or leasing of property.
- Lending of money or other extension of credit.
- Furnishing of goods, facilities, or services.
- Transfer to or use by or for the benefit of a party in interest of plan assets.
- Acquisition by a plan of employer stock or real property to the extent that it exceeds 10 percent of plan assets.[35]

Furthermore, a fiduciary must not:

- Deal with the plan assets in its own interest or for its own account.
- In any transaction involving the plan, act in its individual or other capacity on behalf of a party whose interests are adverse to the plan's interest or those of the plan's participants and beneficiaries.

- Receive any consideration in connection with the plan transaction from a third party dealing with the plan.[36]

Certain statutory exemptions are provided from the foregoing prohibitions, and administrative exemptions may also be sought.

ESOP Exemption from Prohibited Transactions

ESOPs are exempt from the prohibited transactions and other fiduciary rules that prohibit sales of employer securities to the plan. A party in interest may sell employer stock to a plan if the plan is an eligible individual account plan such as an ESOP, the security sold is an equity security of the company, no more than "adequate consideration" is paid for the security, and no commission is charged to the plan with respect to such acquisition or sale.[37]

In the case of securities traded on a national exchange, *adequate consideration* is defined as the price of the security prevailing on such exchange.[38] In the case of a security not traded on a national exchange, if a recognized market for the security exists, adequate consideration is a price not less favorable to the plan than the offering price as established by bid and ask prices quoted by independent parties.[39] If no recognized market exists, the fair market value is the value as determined in good faith by the trustee or named fiduciary in accordance with plan provisions and Department of Labor regulations.

Proposed regulations have been issued in this regard, and the Internal Revenue Code now requires valuations by independent appraisers. Under the proposed DOL regulations, the procedural and substantive standards for adequate consideration are generally in accordance with the principles established by *Revenue Ruling 59–60*, as described earlier.[40]

An important case to consider in matters of valuations is *Donovan* v. *Cunningham*.[41] In that case the ESOP purchased, in two separate transactions, nonpublicly traded stocks from the chairman of the board. The price was based on an appraisal that both parties believed provided a fair value for the stock at the time, 13 months prior to the first transaction and 20 months prior to the second transaction. The court rejected a test based on subjective good faith, stating that "a pure heart and empty head are not enough" (p. 1467). The court found that the trustees had not taken into account changes in the facts on which the appraisals were based and, therefore, had violated their duty of prudence in using the appraisal value for the purchases. In so finding, however, the court rejected very strict standards urged by the Department of Labor. Instead the court indicated that the standard is one of prudence.

Furthermore, Department of Labor correspondence in several recent ESOP transactions indicates that fiduciaries must observe "procedural prudence." This means that the fiduciaries must engage in meaningful negotiations with the selling shareholders or corporation regarding the terms and conditions of the stock purchase and, for this purpose, should be represented by independent legal and financial counsel. Furthermore, in a complex transaction involving many different investors with several classes of securities, a valuation opinion must not only address the issue of fair market value but also overall fairness from an economic point of view to the ESOP and its participants and beneficiaries.[42]

Exempt Loans for ESOPs

A statutory exemption exists for loans by a party in interest to an ESOP.[43] The exemption covers more than just direct loans to an ESOP. It also covers purchase money transactions, the assumption of a debt obligation of an ESOP, and a loan guarantee by a party in interest, including an unsecured guarantee and the use of assets by a party in interest as collateral for a loan to an ESOP. Any such loan must be used to acquire employer securities and must be primarily for the benefit of the ESOP participants and their beneficiaries. Although independent fiduciaries need not arrange or approve an exempt loan transaction, the applicable regulations state that such transactions will be subjected to special scrutiny to ensure that they are made primarily for the benefit of plan participants and their beneficiaries.[44]

Determination of whether a loan to an ESOP is primarily for the benefit of its participants and their beneficiaries is based on all the facts and circumstances. For example, the interest rate on the loan and the price paid for the securities must not be viewed as draining off plan assets. The terms of the loan must be at least as favorable as would be the terms of a comparable transaction between independent parties.[45]

The proceeds of the loan must be used within a reasonable time to acquire employer securities to repay the loan or to repay a prior exempt loan.[46] If collateral is given by an ESOP for a loan, the collateral must be limited to the securities acquired with the loan or securities acquired with a prior exempt loan that was repaid with the proceeds of the current loan.[47] A lender can have no right of recourse to the ESOP's assets other than the collateral given for the loan, contributions made to meet the ESOP's loan obligation, and earnings attributable to the collateral and the investment of such contributions. Apparently, employee contributions as well as employer contributions can be used to meet the ESOP's loan obligations.[48]

The regulations appear to provide that payments of an exempt loan cannot exceed the sum of the contributions made to meet the loan obligation and earnings attributable to the collateral given for the loan and the investment of such contributions.[49] As a result of the Tax Reform Act of 1986, dividends used to repay ESOP acquisition indebtedness may be deducted. While the regulations appear to indicate that payments made with respect to an exempt loan by the ESOP during a plan year must not exceed an amount equal to the sum of employer contributions and earnings received during or prior to such year on ESOP collateral (i.e., loan suspense shares), the Tax Reform Act indicates that a plan will not fail to be treated as a leveraged ESOP merely because of the use of dividend payments to repay ESOP acquisition indebtedness.[50] Thus, to the extent that any conflict does in fact exist, it appears that dividends on all leveraged ESOP shares, both allocated and unallocated, may be used to repay ESOP acquisition indebtedness.

In the case of a default, the value of the assets transferred in satisfaction of the loan cannot exceed the amount of the default. In addition, if the creditor is a party in interest, only assets sufficient to meet the loan's payment schedule can be transferred upon default. That is, a default on a direct loan from a party in interest cannot accelerate the entire loan. If a party in interest merely guarantees a loan, the loan may contain a provision for acceleration upon default. Although no more than reasonable interest can be charged, a variable interest may be reasonable.[51] As to what a reasonable rate of interest is, the following factors must be considered:

1. Amount and duration of the loan.
2. Security and guaranty involved.
3. Credit standing of the ESOP and the guarantor.
4. Prevailing interest rate for comparable loans.

Presumably, a lender is free to charge less than the reasonable rate of interest or no interest at all, particularly in light of partial interest exclusion available on ESOP loans made by qualified lenders.

An exempt loan must be for a specific term and cannot be due on demand, except in the case of default.[52] An exempt loan may provide that the ESOP has a right of prepayment. There appears to be no dollar limit on the term of an exempt loan except commercial reality.

As mentioned before, whether or not securities acquired with an exempt loan are used as collateral for that loan, they must be held in a loan suspense account. The securities in the suspense account are not allocated to the accounts of participants until the securities are released from the suspense account. Securities held in a loan suspense account must be released from the suspense account as the loan is repaid.

Generally, the number of securities released must equal the number of encumbered securities held immediately before release for the current plan year multiplied by a fraction. The numerator of the fraction is the amount of principal and interest paid for the year. The denominator of the fraction is the sum of the numerator plus the principal and interest to be paid for all future years. This may be expressed as the following equation:

$$\frac{principal \ and \ interest \ paid \ for \ plan \ year}{\begin{array}{c} principal \ and \ interest \ paid \ for \ plan \ year \\ + \\ principal \ and \ interest \ paid \ in \ future \ years \end{array}}$$

The number of future years under the loan must be definitely ascertainable and must be determined without taking into account any possible extensions or renewal periods. If the interest rate on the loan is variable, the interest to be paid in future years must be computed by using the interest rate applicable as of the end of the plan year. Under a special rule, the number of securities to be released from encumbrance is determined solely with reference to principal payments; generally, the loan must provide for annual payments of principal and interest at a cumulative rate that is not less rapid at any time than level annual payments of such amounts for 10 years.[54]

Finally, the securities acquired with an exempt loan may be subject to a right of first refusal by the company and must be subject to a put option where the shares are not publicly traded. A call option by the company is not permissible.

To be a leveraged ESOP that can use the exempt loan provisions, the plan must designate itself as an ESOP and specifically state that it is designed to invest primarily in employer securities. A plan that is designated an ESOP at the time a party in interest loan is made to it but that does not satisfy all of the ESOP requirements (such as the requirements relating to voting rights, distributions, put options, diversification, etc.) at such time may, within certain IRS guidelines, be retroactively amended to satisfy the requirements.[56]

SPECIAL ESOP INCENTIVES

In light of the sometimes cumbersome ERISA fiduciary requirements, why are shareholders, lenders, and employers inclined to use ESOPs? The answer is simply that many ESOP tax incentives outweigh the cumbersome ERISA requirements. Incentives have been created for ESOP lenders, ESOP employers, and ESOP shareholders.

Partial Interest Exclusion

An extremely significant incentive affecting ESOP loans provides for a 50 percent exclusion from the interest income received by certain ESOP lenders. A bank, insurance company, mutual fund, or other corporation actively engaged in the business of lending money may exclude from income 50 percent of the interest received with respect to a securities acquisition loan.

A *securities acquisition loan* is a loan to an ESOP or to an employer corporation, the proceeds of which are used to acquire employer securities by the ESOP. However, interest on loans between corporations that are members of the same controlled group or between the ESOP and the employer whose employees are covered by the ESOP is generally not eligible for the 50 percent exclusion, even if the lender is in the business of lending money.

The economic effect of the partial interest exclusion is that taxable lenders are making loans at anywhere from 80 to 95 percent of the interest rate that would otherwise be applicable. Even many large financial institutions that do not have appetites for tax breaks are offering reduced rates on ESOP loans since they may sell the loan to a taxable lender and retain the banking relationship with the sponsoring employer.

Tax-Free Rollover

Another extremely important incentive to ESOP transactions is the tax-free rollover provision provided to certain selling shareholders. Under the tax-free rollover provisions, a taxpayer may elect to defer taxation of gain realized in the sale of employer securities to an ESOP if he reinvests the proceeds in qualified replacement property during a defined replacement period.

Several requirements must be satisfied for a sale to be eligible for nonrecognition treatment. First, the employer stock sold to the ESOP must meet the definition of qualifying securities; be issued by a domestic operating corporation that has no readily tradable stock outstanding; have been held by the seller for a period that would otherwise qualify him for long term capital gains treatment; and not have been received by the seller as a distribution from a qualified retirement plan or a transfer pursuant to the exercise of a qualified or nonqualified stock option or stock purchase plan (unless full value was paid).[58]

Second, immediately after the sale, the ESOP must own at least 30 percent of the total number of outstanding shares of each class of stock (other than noncumulative, nonconvertible preferred) or 30 percent of the total value of all outstanding stock of the corporation (other than noncumulative, nonconvertible preferred).[59]

Third, the seller must purchase "qualified replacement property" within the period beginning 3 months prior to the date of sale and ending 12 months after that date. Qualified replacement property consists of any securities issued by another domestic operating corporation that does not, for the taxable year in which the securities are issued, have passive income exceeding 25 percent of such corporation's gross receipts and has more than 50 percent of the corporation's assets used in the active conduct of a trade or business. Financial institutions are treated as operating corporations for this purpose.[60]

Fourth, the selling shareholder must have a statement of purchase notarized within 30 days after the purchase of securities that he designates as *qualified replacement property* and must file a copy of his election with his federal income tax return for the taxable year or years for which such election in made. Note that the term qualified replacement property does not include tax-free municipal bonds or mutual fund shares.[61]

If these requirements are satisfied, any gain realized on the sale to the ESOP will be recognized only to the extent that the amount realized on the sale exceeds the seller's cost basis for the qualified replacement property. The seller's basis in the qualified replacement property will be an amount equal to his cost reduced by the amount of the gain that is not recognized on the sale.[62]

The ESOP must generally hold the employer stock received in a tax-free rollover sale for at least 3 years. An excise tax is imposed on the employer sponsoring the ESOP if, within 3 years after acquiring the employer stock in a Section 1042 sale, the ESOP disposes of or distributes employer stock that has been acquired in such a transaction and (1) the total number of shares in employer stock held by the ESOP after the distribution is less than the total number of shares of employer stock held immediately after the sale, or (2) the total value of employer stock acquired in the sale that is held by the ESOP after the disposition is less than 30 percent of all employer stock then outstanding. The tax generally is equal to 10 percent of the amount realized by the ESOP on a disposition or distribution. The penalty tax will not apply to distributions or sales of such stock made by reason of a participant's death or disability, separation from service for any period that results in a 1-year break in service, or retirement after attaining age 59½. In addition, an exchange of such stock in a reorganization for stock of another corporation will not be treated as a disposition for purposes of the excise tax.[63]

Note also that a plan that engages in a tax-free roll-over transaction must contain provisions reflecting the "prohibited allocation rule." [64] Under this rule, no portion of the assets of the ESOP attributable to the employer stock acquired in the sale can be allocated directly or indirectly for the benefit of the seller, family members of the seller, or any other person who owns more than 25 percent of the class (other than nonvoting, nonconvertible perferred) of any stock or the total value of such stock. The ESOP may not allocate other assets to these individuals in lieu of such assets. An exception is created for lineal descendants of the selling shareholder to the extent that the allocations, in aggregate, do not exceed 5 percent of the stock sold in the transaction. Furthermore, such prohibited allocation extends until 10 years after the last allocation of stock involved in the sale to the ESOP.

Dividend Deduction

Prior to the enactment of Section 404(k) of the Internal Revenue Code allowing a deduction for dividends paid to an ESOP, the pass through of cash dividends was not common in ESOPs. Usually, the ESOP retained the dividends for reinvestment or for the retirement of ESOP acquisition indebtedness. Section 404(k) allows for a deduction in the year in which a cash dividend is paid or distributed to a participant or beneficiary. The statute does not seem to limit the deduction to dividends paid on shares of stock allocated to a participant's account and, while it is not entirely clear, it is possible that dividends on stock held in a loan suspense account may be allocated in a nondiscriminatory manner to participants and beneficiaries and paid to them in cash.[65]

Furthermore, the Tax Reform Act of 1986 permits a deduction for dividends used to repay ESOP acquisition indebtedness. This is a significant provision, since the deduction limitation on a leveraged ESOP is 25 percent of covered payroll. For an employer with a rather small payroll in relation to the value of the employer securities purchased, the 25 percent of payroll serves as a low ceiling on the amount of ESOP acquisition indebtedness that could be incurred. On the other hand, if the employer has sufficient cash flow, dividends may be paid on employer stock held by the ESOP and used to repay acquisition indebtedness, in which case employer payments that are deductible could exceed 25 percent of covered payrolls. For this purpose, it may be useful to have the ESOP hold noncallable convertible preferred stock for dividend purposes and the nonESOP holders hold common stock. In this way, nondeductible dividends to the nonESOP holders would not be required.[66]

Estate Tax Exclusion

An ESOP may provide a very ready market for the shares of a deceased shareholder. Acquisitions of employer stock from the estate can be debt financed and then repaid with pretax dollars. None of the redemption provisions under IRC Sections 302 and 303 normally apply. Further, a definitive value of the company's stock for estate purposes may be established, which may be a double-edged sword in that a high valuation for purposes of an ESOP sale may trigger higher estate tax values for company shares held by any nonESOP shareholder at death.

Two new incentives have been added by DEFRA and TRA 1986. An ESOP may now, with an appropriate administrative prohibited transaction exemption, assume the federal estate tax liability of a deceased shareholder of a closely held company to the extent that the ESOP acquires employer securities from a deceased shareholder's estate. This assumption of estate tax liability is only permitted in the case of an estate that qualifies for the 14-year installment payment of estate taxes under IRC Section 6166, where the stock constitutes more than 35 percent of the decedent's adjusted gross estate. The employer is also required to guarantee the ESOP's obligation to pay the tax.

TRA '86 added IRC Section 2057, which allows an estate to sell employer securities to an ESOP and receive a 50 percent estate tax deduction for the proceeds from that sale. This benefit is not available for shares sold to defined contribution plans other than ESOPs. The estate tax deduction is effective for sales after October 22, 1986, but prior to January 1, 1992, and creates substantial interest for ESOPs to purchase employer securities, usually at a discount, from shareholder's estates. The tax deduction is not available for sales of stock that the shareholder received from a qualified retirement plan or a stock option or other stock incentive plan. Also, with certain de minimis exceptions, the stock cannot be allocated to the ESOP accounts of certain relatives of the decedent or any 25 percent or more shareholder of the company.

After enactment of TRA '86, however, it appeared that the statutory provisions contained a number of loopholes, which Congress agreed to close at the next opportunity. Those loophole-closing provisions were enacted by the Revenue Act of 1987. This act codified *Notice 87–13, 1987–4 I.R.B. 14*, but further limits the deduction. In general, the 50 percent estate tax exclusion remains intact, except that the maximum estate tax saving is limited to $750,000. The deduction cannot exceed 50 percent of the taxable estate. The employer securities that qualify for the exclusion are restricted to nonpublicly traded securities and must have been held by the decedent at his death for the shorter of 5 years or the period beginning on October 22, 1986, and ending on his date of death.

To qualify for the deduction, the employer securities must be held by the plan for 1 year after purchase, and the ESOP must make the purchase with its own funds (i.e., funds accumulated in that plan while it was an ESOP). Excise taxes are imposed on the employer for failure to comply with the holding period and allocation rules. The estate tax deduction is technically also available for sales to PAYSOPs and TRASOPs, although these plans are unlikely to have the liquidity necessary to purchase much stock.

The rules codifying *Notice 87–13* generally are effective if enacted as part of TRA '86 (for example, the requirement that the decedent must have owned the employer securities at his death). Other limitations are generally effective for sales after February 26, 1987.

Transfers of Reversions

If plan assets remain after a defined benefit plan has been terminated and all of its accrued benefits distributed, those assets may revert to the employer sponsoring the plan. To discourage employers from using this reversion mechanism, IRC Section 4980 imposes a 10 percent excise tax on such reversions.

However, prior to 1989, IRC Section 4980(c)(3) provided an exception for the direct transfer of all or a portion of such reversion to an ESOP if the following requirements are met. First, within 90 days of the transfer (which period may be extended by the IRS), the ESOP had to use the transferred amount to purchase employer securities or to repay loans used to purchase such securities. The securities so acquired had to be held by the plan until they are distributed to participants in accordance with plan provisions.

Second, any portion of the transfer not allocated to participants' accounts in the year of transfer must be credited to a suspense account and allocated no less rapidly than ratably over a period not exceeding 7 years. When allocated to participants' accounts, such amounts must be treated as employer contributions except that, for purposes of IRC Section 415, the annual addition attributable to an allocation may not exceed the value of the securities at the time they were first credited to the suspense account. An employer may not make additional contributions to the ESOP until the amount allocated to the suspense account has been distributed.

Finally, the transfer of the reversion to the ESOP avoided the excise tax only if at least half of the active participants in the defined benefit plan from which the assets reverted are also participants in the ESOP (as of the close of the first plan year for which an allocation of securities is required).

The special provision for transfers to ESOPs applied to amounts transferred after March 31, 1985, and before January 1, 1989, or amounts transferred after December 31, 1988, pursuant to a termination which occurred after March 31, 1985, and before January 1, 1989.

In *Notice 88–58* (May 16, 1988), the IRS has announced guidelines regarding approvals of transfers of plan assets and liabilities from defined benefit plans to defined contribution plans, other than those to which the ESOP exceptions of IRC Section 4980 applied. Generally, a transfer of excess assets from a defined benefit plan to a defined contribution plan of the same employer constitutes a reversion of the assets to the employer followed by a contribution to the defined contribution plans. Thus, a reversion of excess assets from a defined benefit plan, whether received by the employer or transferred to a defined contribution plan, is included in the gross income of the employer. However, the notice acknowledges the exception to this general rule contained in IRC 4980(c)(3) for ESOP transfers. Furthermore, any excess assets transferred from a defined benefit plan to a defined contribution plan and allocated to participants' accounts or annual additions for the limitation year in which allocated under that defined contribution plan will be subject to the limitations of IRC 415. These income tax consequences are also noted in IRS *General Counsel Memorandum 39744* (July 14, 1988).

The Revenue Act of 1987 changed the timing of pension plan terminations and the reversion of excess plan assets. The reversion change provides that no defined benefit plan provision for reversion (or increasing the amount that may revert) made after December 22, 1988, will be effective before the end of the fifth calendar year following its adoption, thus, possibly restricting the ability to recover excess assets under amended plans. This change affects ESOPs attempting rollovers of excess assets (to avoid the 10 percent excise tax), where defined benefit plan amendments will be required. Such amendments must be made during the 12-month window to avoid the 5-year delay.

TRA '86 imposes new limitations on the use of a corporation's net operating loss (and certain other tax credit) carry-forwards following a more than 50 percent change in ownership within prescribed time periods. However, if any transaction results in an ESOP's ownership of at least 50 percent of the fully diluted equity of the corporation, these limitations generally will not apply.[67]

CORPORATE AND EMPLOYEE TAX CONSIDERATIONS

The maximum deduction that an employer can take in any year is subject to the greatest of one of three alternative general limitations:

1. In the case of an unleveraged stock bonus ESOP, the deduction is limited to 15 percent of compensation paid or accrued during the taxable year for the participants.[68]
2. In the case of an unleveraged stock bonus ESOP combined with an unleveraged money purchase ESOP (or combined with other types of pension plans), the aggregated deduction is limited to 25 percent of aggregate compensation.[69]
3. In the case of a leveraged ESOP (whether or not combined with other plans), the deduction may be the sum of an unlimited amount of interest payments plus 25 percent of compensation if the contribution is used to repay principal of the loan incurred by employer securities.[70]

Note that the 25 percent of compensation limitation on the reduction of loan principal can be exceeded where the employer has sufficient cash flow to use dividend payments to repay loan principal.[71]

Also having an effect on how much may be contributed and deducted are the contribution limitations of Section

415 of the Code. The annual amount of employer contributions, forfeitures, and employee contributions that may be allocated to the account of any participant in an ESOP each year may not exceed the lesser of 25 percent of his compensation or $30,000. In the case of a leveraged ESOP, employer contributions used to repay ESOP loan interest as well as forfeitures of leveraged employer stock are disregarded. Furthermore, to the extent stock is allocated to an employee's account as a result of the retirement of ESOP acquisition indebtedness, the $30,000 limit is increased by the lesser of $30,000 ($20,000 after 1988) or the amount of contributions used to release stock for allocation to the participant's account for that year.[72]

As described earlier, there are specific requirements for the timing and form of ESOP distributions and for an employee's right to require an employer to repurchase employer stock distributed to the employee. The taxation of distributions to employees is complex. Much of it depends on whether the distribution is a lump-sum distribution or an installment distribution. When a participant receives a qualifying "lump-sum distribution" from an ESOP, he may elect a tax-free rollover of his distribution into an individual retirement account or another qualified retirement plan, or he may be eligible to elect to be taxed immediately under special 5-year forward averaging rules.[73] Under these rules, the lump-sum payment to the participant is separated from the participant's other taxable income and is taxed as if it had been received evenly over a 5-year period.

A lump-sum distribution need not be paid in a lump sum; conversely, a distribution paid in a lump sum will not necessarily qualify as a lump-sum distribution. Several basic requirements apply. For example, the entire account balance credited to the participant must be distributed within 1 taxable year to the participant or beneficiary of the participant. If the employer maintains several plans, the participant's entire account balance will be determined by aggregating certain plans. As a result of this aggregation rule, the distribution of the participant's entire ESOP account in a lump sum may or may not be a distribution of his entire account balance. Earlier distributions, such as current distributions of dividends by an ESOP, and later distributions attributable to a participant's election of a diversification right or amounts attributable to the participant's last or subsequent year of service will not prevent a subsequent lump-sum distribution from being eligible for 5-year averaging treatment.[74]

Furthermore, a lump-sum distribution must be paid upon the participant's death, attainment of age 59½, or on account of separation from service. Finally, a distribution to the participant will not be treated as a lump-sum distribution unless he has participated in the plan for at least 5 years. (This requirement does not apply in the case of the participant's death.)[75] No restrictions apply to how often a participant may elect 5-year forward averaging until he attains age 59½. After that age, only one election is permitted.[76]

An ESOP trustee must withhold income tax from a lump-sum distribution unless the recipient elects otherwise. However, no withholding is required to the extent that the distribution consists entirely of employer stock.

It should be noted that the amount that needs to be included in the lump-sum distribution for 5-year averaging is the trustee's cost basis for the shares. To the extent that the shares have appreciated in value since the time they were acquired by the ESOP trustee, such appreciation is referred to as *net unrealized appreciation*.[77] However, the participant may wish to include the full appreciated value for 5-year averaging purposes, in which case he may elect out of the use of net unrealized appreciation. In the case of installment distributions from an ESOP, the employee normally will be taxed on the full value of the stock distributed in each installment. However, any net unrealized appreciation on employer stock is only that attributable to an employee's nondeductible contributions.[78]

CORPORATE LAW CONSIDERATIONS AND ERISA

A variety of corporate transactions may affect the operation of an ESOP. These transactions may involve corporate mergers, consolidations, or even hostile takeovers.

It should be noted that the establishment of an ESOP after a hostile tender offer is made may violate applicable state corporate law. In one case, the court held that the directors of a target corporation violated their duty of loyalty to shareholders by establishing an ESOP in the face of a tender offer and thereby could not shield their actions under the "business judgment rule" normally applicable to the decisions made by corporate directors.[79]

Establishing an ESOP in light of a hostile takeover may also violate the exclusive benefit rule reflected in both the ERISA fiduciary provisions and in the Internal Revenue Code tax-qualified retirement plan provisions. In this case not only may the plan not be a qualified plan eligible for the special ESOP incentives, but the entire transaction may have to be undone to avoid prohibited transaction problems.[80] On the other hand, the establishment of an ESOP prior to the launching of a hostile takeover does not violate corporate law and probably does not violate the exclusive benefit rule. The act of merely placing a block of stock in friendly hands should not constitute a violation of the ERISA or Internal Revenue provisions.[81]

The sponsoring employer who sets up an ESOP to place a block of stock in friendly hands should not take excessive security from such an arrangement. The responsible fiduciary will be subject to the ERISA fiduciary conduct rules and must act in the best interest of participants and beneficiaries at all times. The trustee may be required by these rules to tender shares in a hostile takeover situation if it reasonably believes that such a tender is made in the best interest of enhancing the retirement benefits of the plan's participants and beneficiaries. For this purpose, the trustee may need to retain separate legal and financial counsel.[82]

If the ESOP plan documents include a prohibition against the sale by the ESOP of the target company stock, the trustee may need either to resign, ignore the prohibition, or seek court instructions in order to fulfill its duties under the ERISA fiduciary requirements.[83] Some ESOPs provide that the participant will direct the trustee as to whether or not to tender the shares of stock allocated to his account. Presumably, the trustee will have discretion over the shares held in an unallocated loan suspense account and over allocated shares for which no direction is received. On the other hand, the plan document may provide that the trustee will tender such unallocated shares and shares for which no direction is given in the same proportion as the allocated shares for which direction is given. Such an automatic rule may not allow the trustee to comply with its ERISA fiduciary duties.

At least two courts have indicated that having management trustees of an ESOP or other qualified plan that holds employer stock in the face of a tender offer may not be a good idea.[84] In these cases, the courts have suggested that the trustees should resign and an independent trustee should be appointed or at least that the trustee should seek independent legal and financial counsel and act in accordance with the interest of participants and beneficiaries. In assessing automatic rules that dictate the manner in which shares are voted, including a pass through of tender directions to participants and beneficiaries, one court has indicated that the trustee may or may not be able to follow such a provision, particularly if it believes that the participants and benefic-iaries have acted under undue influence, without full information, or are not acting in their own interest.[85]

Another question that often comes up is whether the trustee of a publicly held company may pay a block premium to an unwanted shareholder when the corporation does not want to make a "green mail" payment to that shareholder. Such an action would likely violate the adequate consideration requirements of ERISA, and would therefore be a prohibited transaction if that shareholder

holds 10 percent or more of the employer stock or is otherwise a party in interest.[86] Furthermore, a real question of
whether such an action is prudent would certainly arise
regardless of whether or not the shareholder owns 10 percent or more of the stock. Thus, such use of an ESOP
should be avoided.

SECURITIES LAW CONSIDERATIONS

1933 Securities Act

On February 1, 1980, the Securities and Exchange Commission issued *Release 33–6188* on the application of the 1933
Securities Act to employee plans. The purpose of the release
was to provide guidance to the public and to assist employers
and plan participants in complying with the '33 Act. The
release discusses circumstances under which interests in
plans and related entities may be subject to the requirements
of the '33 Act. The release also provides an analysis of the
criteria to be used to determine when an offer or sale of a
security will occur, discusses the various exemptions from the
act's registration provisions, explains the act's application to
the various types of securities transactions in which plans may
engage, as well as resales of securities participants acquire
through the operation of the plan, and further describes the
methods of registration of securities under the act.

The interests of employees in a plan are "securities"
only when the employees voluntarily participate in and
contribute to the plan. Employee interests in plans that are
not both voluntary and contributory are not securities and
are not subject to the '33 Act, according to the release.

In *Release 33–6188*, the SEC also indicated that, if a
plan is considered an affiliate of the employer, any offers or
sales of employer securities by the plan would be subject to
the registration and antifraud provisions of the Securities
Act in the same manner as if the employer were engaging
in the transaction. Unless an exemption were available,
registration would be necessary.

While lengthy and intended to provide guidance, the release does point out that it should not be viewed as an all-inclusive treatment of the subject and that the SEC staff will continue to provide interpretive advice and assistance on request, as will the courts.

Another release (No. 33–6281), issued January 22, 1981, further clarifies the SEC's position on the application of the 1933 Securities Act to employee benefit plans and also describes developments under the act after *Release No. 33–6188* was issued.

Resales by Plan Participants

The distribution of employer stock by a plan to individual participants generally is not deemed to be a registerable event. The SEC stated that, generally, securities held by plans that register the securities held by them are freely tradable upon distribution to participants, unless the person acquiring the securities is an affiliate of the issuer. Thus, participants in a registered plan who do not have a control relationship with the issuer may resell the shares or other securities acquired by them under the plan without any restrictions. Affiliates may resell their shares publicly, either pursuant to an effective registration statement or pursuant to Rule 144 under the '33 Act. Affiliates also may resell the securities in a private transaction, provided it is understood that the purchaser is acquiring restricted securities subject to the same limitations on resale that applied to the seller.

The SEC also stated in *Release 33–6188* that nonaffiliates who receive unregistered securities from a plan could resell such securities immediately without any restrictions (such as registration or compliance with Rule 144) if the following three conditions were satisfied:

1. The issuer of the securities is subject to the periodic reporting requirements of Section 13 or 15(d) of the Exchange Act.
2. The stock being distributed is actively traded in the open market.

3.   The number of shares being distributed is relatively small in relation to the number of shares of that
class issued and outstanding.

In Release 33–6281, the SEC indicated that a relatively small amount would be involved when the total number
of shares distributed by a plan to its participants during a
fiscal year does not exceed 1 percent of the outstanding
securities of the class. With respect to resales by affiliates,
the SEC indicated in Release 33–6188 that, even when the
three conditions just described are satisfied, resales by such
persons would continue to be subject to registration in the
absence of an available exemption, such as that provided
by Rule 144. In this regard, the SEC also stated that if the
three conditions are met, the securities involved will not be
considered "restricted securities" under Rule 144. As a
result, affiliates may disregard the 2-year holding period
requirement of Rule 144 if they choose to rely on that rule
for the resale of their securities.

Securities Exchange Act of 1934

The Securities Exchange Act of 1934 was designed to regulate
the trading markets for publicly held securities. Among other
things, it requires issuers of such securities, subject to certain
exemptions, to make continuing disclosures concerning their
affairs through 1934 Act registration statements, shareholder
reports, proxy statements, and periodic and other reports filed
with or submitted to the SEC. It also imposes reporting and
other obligations on large holders of publicly traded equity
securities, including ESOPs, and provides for margin regulation of securities transactions.

The compliance requirements of this Act are beyond
the scope of this chapter. However, the 1934 Act raises at
least three significant questions with respect to the operation of an ESOP that should be answered for each ESOP
that is established by a publicly traded company:

1.   Under what circumstances is an ESOP required to

comply with the shareholder reporting provisions of Section 13(d)and 16(a) of the 1934 Act?

2. Are purchases and sales of employer stock subject to the short-swing profit recovery provisions of Section 16(b) of the 1934 Act?

3. Are borrowings by the ESOP to acquire employer stock subject to the margin requirements adopted by the Federal Reserve Board under the 1934 Act? (Regulation U, dealing with ESOP loans, usually applies here.)

Other Reporting and Disclosure Rules

Additional reporting and disclosure rules that should be looked at are the following:

1. Section 15(d) of the 1934 Act provides that if a registration statement pursuant to the 1933 Act has to be filed with respect to certain stock-related qualified plans, then the registrant must file "such supplementary and periodic information documents and reports as may be required pursuant to Section 13 of this title."

2. Section 16(a) of Reporting Rule 16a–8(a)(2) provides that "vested beneficial interests in a trust" must be reported by officers and directors and beneficial owners of more than 10 percent of any class of equity security, and they must report periodically on changes of ownership. The rules are exceedingly complex, and several exemptions may be available.

3. The 1934 Act's antifraud rules apply to both initial and subsequent sales. Section 10 of the 1934 Act prohibits the use of manipulative and deceptive devices in the trading of securities. Certain fraudulent and deceptive practices are crimes. Various other rules require an issuer and its affiliate to follow certain procedures in the repur-

chase of its stock, which might apply to the ESOP's trustee. Another section provides that a person who relies on a false or misleading statement contained in a document filed with the SEC may recover for reliance on such a statement. Other rules require insiders to disgorge profits made under certain circumstances. There are many unanswered questions under these rules. For example: Does a company have a duty to disclose material nonpublic information regarding the company? Does the employer or the ESOP have a duty to disclose complete information to a participant if it is known that the participant will immediately resell the employer securities in the public market?

MISCELLANEOUS ESOP MATTERS

Floor-Offset Arrangements

Some employers maintain *floor-offset* arrangements that combine defined benefit and defined contribution plan features. Under such arrangements, a participant's accrued benefit under the defined benefit portion of the arrangement is reduced by the benefit provided to such participant under the defined contribution portion of the arrangement. The defined contribution portion of the arrangement is an eligible individual account plan, and all, or substantially all, of the participant's individual accounts may be invested in employer securities.[87]

Such an arrangement offers the employee the opportunity to realize greater retirement benefits than the defined benefit portion alone could provide due to employer stock appreciation, but has the potential risk to employees that a sudden change in the employer's fortunes (e.g., insolvency) could adversely affect benefit security. Where an employer has an existing defined benefit plan and uses an ESOP to buy out a current shareholder, the use of a floor-offset arrangement for prospective accruals can preserve employees' pension expectations.

Although the IRS has ruled in *Revenue Ruling 76–259* that floor-offset arrangements may meet the qualification requirements of IRC Section 401(a), the Department of Labor has not ruled that the individual account portions of these arrangements qualify for the eligible individual account exemption from 10 percent limitation on acquisitions of qualifying employer securities.

The Department of Labor has for a long time considered that both plans should be subject to the 10 percent limit. The Revenue Act of 1987 modifies ERISA to add ERISA Sections 407(d)(3)(C) and 407(d)(9), which provide that in a floor-offset arrangement both plans are subject to the 10 percent limit. Thus, the assets in both plans are combined and the 10 percent limit is determined by reference to those combined assets. Presumably, the employer securities could be held in either of the plans.

The amendment applies to arrangements established after December 17, 1987. The 1987 Act, thus, does not deal with whether these floor-offset arrangements were previously acceptable; although an inference is created that any arrangement set up before December 17, 1987, can continue, whereas any arrangement established after that date would be subject to this more restrictive interpretation.

ESOPs and Plan Disqualification

If an ESOP is ruled not to meet the requirements of either IRC Section 401(a) or IRC Section 4975(e)(7), a variety of problems results. First, any sales to such a plan will not qualify for the tax-free rollover treatment provided under IRC Section 1042, since that section requires that the sales be made to an employee stock ownership plan within the meaning of IRC Section 4975(e)(7).

Moreover, any loan to an ESOP will not qualify for the partial interest exclusion provided in IRC Section 133 because that section requires that the plan be an employee stock ownership plan within the meaning of IRC Section 4975(e)(7). While the lender will lose the ability to get the partial interest exclusion, properly drafted yield protection language in the loan documentation will ultimately shift that burden to the employer.

Disqualification will also have a negative effect on both employer and employees. For example, plan contributions will no longer be deductible under the qualified plan provision of IRC Section 404 (with its special limitations for ESOPs) but may be deductible under the special provisions of IRC Section 404(a)(5). When a qualified plan ceases to be qualified, each employee will have included in his gross income amounts contributed on his behalf for that year (and subsequent disqualified years) to the extent the employee is vested at the time the contribution is made. As he vests in the previously nonvested contributions made on his behalf while the plan is disqualified, the value of his interest in the trust is included in his gross income. Amounts credited to an employee's account that are attributable to qualified years are not included in his gross income until distributed.[88]

NOTES

[1] Treas. Reg. §1.401-1(a)(2) and (3).
[2] IRC §410(b).
[3] IRC §411.
[4] IRC §§401(a)(9) and 401(a)(14).
[5] IRC §4975(e)(7).
[6] Treas. Reg. §54.49757(b)(8).
[7] *Rev. Rul. 84–155*, 19842 C.B. 95.
[8] IRC §414(q).
[9] IRC §411(a)(8).
[10] IRC §409(h)(1).
[11] IRC §409(h)(2) and (3).
[12] IRC §409(o)(1)(A)(i).
[13] IRC §409(o)(1)(A)(ii).

14   IRC §409(o)(1)(B).
15   IRC §409(o)(1)(C).
16   IRC §409(h)(1).
17   IRC §409(h)(4).
18   IRC §409(h)(6).
19   IRC §409(e)(2).
20   IRC §409(e)(3).
21   IRC §409(e)(5).
22   IRC §409(1).
23   IRC §401(a)(28)(C).
24   Prop. DOL Reg. §2510.318.
25   IRC 401(a)(28)(B).
26   IRS Notice 88-56, I.R.B. 1988-19(Q&A: 7).
27   ERISA §§401409.
28   ERISA §3(21)(A).
29   ERISA §404(a)(1)(D).
30   ERISA §04(a)(1)(A). See also DOL Reg. §2550.408b-3(c).
31   *Donovan* v. *Bierwirth,* 680 F2d 263 (2d Cir. 1982).
32   *Martin Marietta Corp.* v. *Bendix Corp.*, 697 F2d 293 (S.D.N.Y. 1982).
33   587 F2d 453 (10th Cir. 1978).
34   ERISA §3(14).
35   ERISA §407.
36   ERISA §406(b).
37   ERISA §408(e).
38   ERISA §3(18)(A).
39   ERISA §3(18)(B).
40   Prop. DOL Reg. §2510.318.
41   *Donovan* v. *Cunningham*, 716 F2d 1455 (5th Cir. 1983).
42   See letter dated September 12, 1983, from Charles M. Williamson, Assistant Administrator for Enforcement, Pension and Welfare Benefit Programs, to Gareth Cook, Vinson & Elkins, Houston, Texas.

[43] ERISA §408(b)(3), IRC §4975(d).

[44] Treas. Reg. §54.4975–7(b)(2)(ii).

[45] Treas. Reg. §54.4975–7(b)(3)(iii).

[46] Treas. Reg. §54.4975–7(b)(4).

[47] Treas. Reg. §54.4975–7(b)(4)(iii).

[48] Treas. Reg. §54.4975–7(b)(5)(ii).

[49] Treas. Reg. §54.4975–7(b)(5).

[50] IRC §404(k).

[51] Treas. Reg. §54.4975–7(b)(7).

[52] Treas. Reg. §54.4975–7(b)(13).

[53] Treas. Reg. §54.4975–7(b)(8)(i).

[54] Treas. Reg. §54.4975–7(b)(8)(ii).

[55] Treas. Reg. §54.4975–7(b)(4).

[56] Treas. Reg. §54.4975–11(a)(3)(iv).

[57] IRC §133(a).

[58] IRC §1042(a) and (c)(1).

[59] IRC §1042(b)(2).

[60] IRC §1042(c)(4)(B)(ii).

[61] IRC §1042(c)(4), General Explanation of Revenue Provisions of the Tax Reform Act of 1984, Joint Committee on Taxation, at page 876.

[62] IRC §1042(d).

[63] IRC §4978.

[64] IRC §409(n).

[65] IRC §404(k).

[66] IRC §409(a)(3).

[67] IRC §382(1)(3).

[68] IRC §404(a)(3).

[69] IRC §404(a)(7).

[70] IRC §404(a)(9).

[71] IRC §404(k)(2)(C).

[72] IRC §415(c)(6)(C).

[73] IRC §§402(a)(5) and 402(e)(4).

74 IRS Notice 88-56, and Prop. Reg. §1.402(e)-2(d)(1)(ii)(A).

75 IRC §402(e)(4)(H).

76 IRC §405(d)(1)(B)(iv).

77 IRC §402(e)(4)(J).

78 Treas. Reg. §1.402(a)(b)(1).

79 *Norlin Corp.* v. *Rooney, Pace Inc.*, 744 F.2d 255 (2d Cir. 1984).

80 IRC §§4975(b) and (f)(5).

81 IRC §401(a) and Treas. Reg. 54.49757(b)(3).

82 *Donovan* v. *Bierwirth*, 680 F2d 263 (2d Cir. 1982).

83 See, for example, DOL Reg. §2509,755, Q&A FR-10.

84 See *Donovan* v. *Bierwirth*, 680 F2d 263 (2d Cir. 1982) and *Danaher Corporation* v. *Chicago Pneumatic Tool Co.*, 7EBC 1616 (S.D.N.Y. 1986).

85 *Danaher Corporation* v. *Chicago Pneumatic Tool Co.*, Ibid.

86 ERISA §§3(14), 406, 408(e).

87 *Rev. Rul. 76–259*, 1976–2 C.B. 111.

88 Treas. Reg. §1.402(b)–1.

TWO

Planning for an ESOP

Gerald I. Kalish

Gerald I. Kalish, President of National Benefit Services, has over 15 years experience as a consultant in the benefit and compensation area for publicly traded companies, closely-held companies, and not-for-profit organizations.

He is a frequent speaker at seminars sponsored by trade associations, professional societies, and universities including The Profit Sharing Council of America, for whom he serves as a member of the Communications Committee; The National Center for Employee Ownership; The ESOP Association, for whom he serves as a member of the Communications Committee; Chicago Association of Commerce and Industry; the Illinois CPA Society; University of Wisconsin Extension. He has been a guest lecturer at DePaul University School of Law, Masters in Taxation Program.

Mr. Kalish is a frequent contributor to business and professional journals, and has authored and edited several books published by Probus Publishing Company, Chicago. These include: *Compensating Yourself: Tax, Benefit and Income Strategies for Business Owners*, 1985; and the chapter on employee benefits and executive compensation for *The Handbook of Cash Flow and Treasury Management*, 1988.

TWO

Every ESOP is different, each with its own unique set of corporate, financial, and personal dynamics. But all successful ESOPs have one common element: comprehensive planning prior to implementation.

UNDERSTANDING THE ESOP PROCESS

Planning for an ESOP begins with understanding the ESOP process itself. The steps involved are described in more detail in this and the chapters that follow. They include:

1. Initial planning
   A. Feasibility analysis
   B. Independent stock appraisal
   C. Repurchase liability analysis
   D. Plan design
2. Implementation
   A. Financing
   B. Documentation
   C. Submission to Internal Revenue Service for approval
   D. Changes to other benefit programs, if necessary
   E. Announcement to employees
3. Operation
   A. Annual stock valuation
   B. Plan administration
   C. Repurchase liability analysis

    D.   Annual audit, if required
    E.   Continuing employee communication
    F.   Changes as required by law or changing circumstances

While these steps are logical and straightforward, successful completion of the process involves the coordinated efforts of the ESOP "team": company management, legal counsel, valuation consultant, accountant, trustee, and benefit consultant.

WHAT CONSTITUTES A SUCCESSFUL ESOP?

Even before the planning process begins, consideration should be given to the factors that constitute a potentially successful ESOP:

1. A leveraged ESOP cannot be maintained by a corporation that elected S corporation tax status. Thus, an existing S corporation should carefully consider the implications of changing to a regular "C" corporation for tax purposes.

2. There must be sufficient payroll to amortize the loan if the ESOP is leveraged. In other words, the size of the potential ESOP transaction is dependent upon a company's payroll.

3. The company must be profitable. While some ESOPs have been used to save a failing company, most are adopted by companies that can afford to repay the loan to purchase company stock.

4. The business must be stable. This is an important factor not only from the obvious standpoint of loan repayment, but also because yearly fluctuations will be reflected in the annual stock valuations, resulting in adverse employee reaction.

5. Management should be committed to employee ownership. The real value of the ESOP as a

method of improving operating results will be lost without that commitment.

While all successful ESOPs do not fit this profile completely, most have undergone feasibility analysis, either formally or informally. This analysis has two objectives: to anticipate any impediment to successful implementation and to maximize the objectives in adopting the ESOP.

The remainder of this chapter focuses on the specific areas that should be addressed when planning for an ESOP.

COORDINATING THE ESOP WITH OTHER RETIREMENT PLANS

A major step in the ESOP planning process is determining the fate of an existing retirement plan or plans. An existing retirement plan can be converted, terminated, or maintained in conjunction with an ESOP. In addition, a supplemental non-qualified plan can be adopted to meet specific needs.

Converting or Terminating an Existing Plan

There are three factors to consider in converting an existing retirement plan to an ESOP or terminating an existing plan and replacing it with an ESOP.

Vesting considerations. The conversion of a defined benefit plan to an ESOP would be considered a plan termination requiring full and immediate vesting of participants' accrued benefits. Even the conversion of a profit-sharing plan or other defined contribution plan may still be considered a plan termination requiring full and immediate vesting of participants' account balances. The result would be an immediate, and possibly unmanageable, repurchase liability.

Legal issues. If the participants have the option of rolling over their benefits to the successor ESOP, it may be considered a "security" by the Securities and Exchange Commission, thus requiring either a registration or exemption. Aside from the security issues, using the converted plan's assets to buy company stock may be considered a breach of "the exclusive benefit rule" and fiduciary requirements of ERISA.

Employee relations. If an existing plan were converted, the employees' retirement benefits would depend solely on the performance of company stock. In addition, if a defined benefit pension plan were terminated, older employees could receive fewer benefits from the combination of the terminated pension plan and ESOP than they would if they received their expected benefits from the pension plan at normal retirement age if it were maintained.

Maintaining an Existing Retirement Plan

Two major tax issues must be resolved to determine the basis upon which another retirement plan can be maintained in conjunction with the ESOP.

The first issue is the extent to which the company can make tax deductible contributions to both plans. The limits are set by Section 404 of the Internal Revenue Code, which generally restricts the combined contribution to 25 percent of participants' compensation.

The second issue is the extent to which any one participant can receive allocations or benefits from one or more plans. These limits are established by Section 415 of the Internal Revenue Code. A participant in one or more defined contribution plans can not receive an annual allocation (contributions plus forfeitures) greater than the lesser of 25 percent of compensation or $30,000. Special rules apply to a leveraged ESOP. A participant in both an ESOP and defined benefit pension plan (even if terminated prior to the establishment of the ESOP) is subject to a compli-cated set of rules regarding multiple plan benefits.

Using a Non-Qualified Plan

Many companies are using non-qualified plans to supplement or replace benefits lost by employees when the ESOP is adopted. Because a non-qualified plan can be selective, it can:

- supplement retirement benefits for that older employee when a defined benefit plan is terminated;
- replace ESOP allocations that a selling shareholder (and his lineal descendent) can not receive if he elects the tax-free rollover provision under Section 1042 of the Internal Revenue Code; or
- replace retirement benefits for an employee whose benefits are limited under Section 415 of the Internal Revenue Code.

DESIGNING THE ESOP

Plan design involves determining plan provisions. Because an ESOP owns company stock, considerations are sometimes different than in the case of a traditional retirement plan. Following are some of the provisions that must be determined with their special ESOP perspectives. The answers to these questions can obviously have an impact in accomplishing the ESOP's objectives.

Which Employees Should Be Covered?

The ESOP must meet one of several statutory coverage tests to ensure that the plan does not discriminate in favor of the "prohibited group" (officers, shareholders, and highly compen-sated employees). Employees under the age of 21, those with less than 1 year of service, and union employees can generally be excluded. It may be desirable to include the latter group to expand the payroll base upon which contributions can be made. If so, the matter would have to be negotiated.

Who Should Receive an Allocation?

In most profit-sharing plans, allocations are made at the end of the plan year to those participants who are still employed and who have worked at least 1,000 hours or more during the plan year. However, some ESOPs allocate shares regardless of hours worked or whether or not employed at the end of the year in order to provide a larger payroll base to pay off the loan or to motivate permanent part-time employees.

How Should Financed Shares Be Allocated?

In a leveraged ESOP, shares are initially purchased with a loan. The shares are placed in a suspense account and released and allocated as the loan is repaid. The number of shares allocated each year can vary depending on which release method is used, as described in detail in Chapter 7.

What Vesting Schedule Should Be Used?

Vesting refers to a participant's nonforfeitable right to receive his account balance based on his service with the company. The actual vesting schedule chosen and the extent to which service prior to the effective date of the ESOP is recognized will have a direct impact on the repurchase liability, a concept discussed later.

When Should Distributions Be Made?

The degree to which the ESOP permits accelerated distributions, subject to legal considerations, also affects the repurchase liability.

Should Employees Be Allowed to Contribute to the ESOP?

Many companies allow employees to contribute to the ESOP either to purchase company stock or other investments. If company stock is purchased with employee contributions, a recent Securities and Exchange Commission rule may provide for an exemption from registration. In addition, employee contributions can be made on a pre-tax basis under a 401(k) option.

Who Should Be the Plan Administrator?

The plan administrator is responsible for running the day-to-day operation of the ESOP. It is usually the company itself or an administrative committee appointed by the company.

Who Should Be the Trustee?

The ESOP trustee holds title to the ESOP assets (shares of company stock) and is responsible for managing the assets, such as voting the shares. In most small ESOPs, the trustee is one or more of the management group. In larger ESOPs, in special situations involving outside investors or in complicated transactions, an independent bank or trust company is used.

PLANNING FOR THE REPURCHASE LIABILITY

There has been no area more neglected in the ESOP planning process than that of the repurchase liability. And ironically, there is no area that has as much potential to impede the financial success of the ESOP than this one.

Repurchase Liability Defined

The term "repurchase liability" refers to the legal obligation of the company, *not* the ESOP, to repurchase shares of non-publicly traded stock distributed to a terminated employee. In general terms, the employee can exercise a "put option" by requiring the company to repurchase his shares at fair market value during the 60-day period following the date of distribution. If the put option is not exercised, the employee can get another chance within 60 days after a new valuation is performed.

The need for cash will continue as the ESOP matures for two other reasons:

1. The Tax Reform Act of 1986 gave employees a "pre-retirement diversification right." This means that ESOP participants who are 55 years old with 10 years of plan participation must be allowed the option of diversifying their accounts in regular investments over a certain time period for stock acquired by the ESOP after December 31, 1986. Alternatively, these participants could receive cash distributions starting at age 55.

2. The Tax Reform Act of 1986 also requires faster distributions for stock acquired by the ESOP after December 31, 1986, than for distributions from other qualified retirement plans.

Indeed, as the ESOP matures, the repurchase liability increases as more shares of stock are allocated to the employees and, presumably, as the value of the shares themselves increases. Even with modest growth in the value of the shares, the repurchase liability—the need for cash—can be a significant obligation in the future.

For example, assume an ESOP acquires stock for $1 million with a loan that will be repaid in 7 years. If the value of the stock increases at the rate of 10 percent per year, it will be worth $2 million by the time the loan has been repaid.

How to Measure the Repurchase Liability

The repurchase liability can be managed if it is planned for before the need for cash arises. A repurchase liability study should be conducted before the ESOP is adopted and periodically thereafter to estimate and plan for this liability in advance.

In fact, many lenders require that such a study be conducted before a loan commitment is made. The lender's concern is not difficult to understand. The company's need for cash will have an impact on its ability to repay an ESOP loan.

A repurchase liability study is somewhat analogous to an "emerging liability study" that many actuaries provide for defined benefit pension plans to project the pension plan's benefit obligations for retirees. By making certain assumptions such as employee turnover, replacement, salary increases, increases in the value of the stock, etc., a repurchase liability study can assist with the planning process.

Figure 2.1 illustrates a sample company's projected distributions required to be made over the next 10 years from the ESOP.

How to Plan for the Repurchase Liability

ESOP companies have used some of the following methods or a combination thereof to meet repurchase liability requirements.

1. "Pay-as-you-go." The company simply meets the liability from current cash flow much the same way that early pension plans provided retirement benefits.
2. Plan distributions can be deferred to the extent permitted under the law. For example, many ESOPs defer payment to terminated participants (other than terminations for reasons of death, disability, or retirement) until the ESOP loan is repaid.
3. A cash reserve can be developed either within the ESOP or the company. This may include the company making cash contributions to the ESOP or putting aside funds using a "sinking fund" approach.

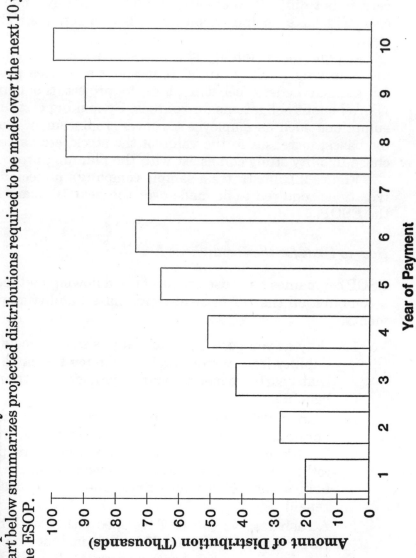

Figure 2.1
ESOP Repurchase Liability
The chart below summarizes projected distributions required to be made over the next 10 years from the ESOP.

4. The company can use the proceeds of "key-man" life insurance to purchase the stock. This approach is utilized in many cases in which a relatively large part of the liability is attributable to a few participants.

5. Dividends may be used to repurchase stock. The availability of tax deductibility dividend payments makes this an increasingly attractive option for many companies.

6. A public offering can create a market for the stock. This method has been called the ultimate repurchase liability solution since the company liability is eliminated.

USING THE TAX-FREE ROLLOVER PROVISION UNDER SECTION 1042

A shareholder selling stock to an ESOP can elect to receive favorable tax treatment under Section 1042 of the Internal Revenue Code. If the requirements are met, tax is deferred until such time as the "qualifying replacement securities" are sold; and tax may be avoided permanently if the shareholder continues to hold the "qualifying replacement securities" until his death.

General Requirements

1. The ESOP must own 30 percent or more of the total value of employer securities outstanding immediately after the sale.

2. The shares sold to the ESOP must be "qualified securities."

3. The securities acquired by the ESOP must not be allocated to the selling shareholder, his family, or to a major shareholder (one owning more than 25 percent in value of any class of outstanding securities).

4.   The selling shareholder must use proceeds of the sale to purchase "qualified replacement property" within a 15-month period beginning 3 months before and ending 12 months after the sale to the ESOP.

5.   If the ESOP sells the securities within 3 years of acquiring them, a 10 percent excise tax is imposed on the employer.

Procedural Steps

Even if all the technical requirements are met, care must be taken to meet all of the special administrative requirements necessary to effect the tax-free rollover:

1.   The ESOP company must consent to the election.

2.   The shareholder must execute a "statement of purchase" of "qualified replacement property" which must be notarized within 30 days after the date of purchase of any such securities.

3.   The shareholder must attach a "Statement of Election" with corporate consents and one or more "statement[s] of purchase" to his income tax return for the year in which the sale occurs, and file his return on or before the due date including extensions thereon.

Planning Considerations

There are several planning considerations involved with Section 1042:

1.   The selling shareholder does not have to elect Section 1042 tax treatment for all of his shares.

2.   A recent IRS Private Letter Ruling permitted a taxpayer to elect Section 1042 tax treatment under an installment sale with the ESOP extending beyond the replacement period, provided he rein-

vested the full sale price of the securities within the replacement period.

3. The selling shareholder may wish to forego non-recognition of gain under Section 1042 if he could receive comparable or maximum benefits under another company retirement plan or the projected value of ESOP allocation is greater.

4. "Qualifying replacement property" can include stock in a closely held company.

5. The shares of stock meeting the 30 percent requirement can be acquired from two or more taxpayers.

COORDINATING THE ESOP WITH SHAREHOLDER ESTATE AND BUY-SELL PLANS

The adoption of an ESOP immediately renders any existing estate plan and buy-sell agreement obsolete because any reference to the value of the stock involved was pre-ESOP valuation. Thus, all existing plans must be reviewed and revised. Part of this planning process should take into account the three estate tax incentives that are available in conjunction with an ESOP.

Tax-Free Rollover

The tax-free rollover provision under Section 1042 allows a stepped-up basis in the value of qualified replacement securities on the death of the owner.

For example, assume a shareholder sells stock costing $1,000 to an ESOP for $10,000 and takes 1042 tax treatment by buying replacement securities. He would pay no tax on the sale but will pay a tax on the $9,000 gain when he sells the replacement securities. If he leaves the replacement securities, now worth $15,000, to his heirs, the difference between the value at death ($15,000) and the gain on the original shares ($9,000) will never be taxed.

Estate Tax Assumption

An estate can satisfy a portion of its estate tax liability by transferring stock to an ESOP under Section 2210 of the Internal Revenue Code. The ESOP could assume the tax and could utilize the installment payment methods provided under Section 6166 of the Code to extend its payments over a 14-year period.

However, it provides little economic benefit to the estate which must still transfer assets equivalent to the tax liability. The real value is to the ESOP, which in essence borrows money from the government at more favorable terms than from a financial institution.

In addition, the ESOP trustee could not enter into a binding agreement with a shareholder prior to his death to acquire his stock and assume the estate tax liability under the fiduciary rules of ERISA. However, the plan document and shareholder's will can contain language permitting such transfer.

Estate Tax Exclusion

Unlike the other two Code sections which provide for a deferral of estate tax, Section 2057 provides for an absolute forgiveness of the tax.

Under this section, an estate can sell stock to an ESOP and deduct 50 percent of the proceeds provided certain requirements are met, as follows:

1. The deduction can not exceed 50 percent of the taxable estate, and may not result in a reduction in tax of more than $750,000.
2. The sale must occur before January 1, 1992, when the incentive expires unless extended by Congress.
3. The shares sold to the ESOP can not be allocated to the account of the descendent, members of his family, or other 25 percent shareholders and their families, or the company pays a 50 percent excise tax.

4. The stock must be that of a closely-held corporation with no readily tradable stock outstanding.

5. The ESOP must purchase the shares with "new money": not the proceeds of other securities sold in the previous year or funds transferred from other qualified plans.

Because of fiduciary rules, the shareholder could not enter into an agreement with the ESOP to guarantee the transaction. However, it may be possible for the shareholder to have a buy-sell agreement with the employer which allows the employer to transfer that liability to the ESOP with the trustee's consent.

THREE

ESOP Valuation Considerations

Paul J. Much

Paul J. Much is a Principal of Houlihan, Lokey, Howard & Zukin, Inc., the nationally prominent valuation advisory firm with offices in Los Angeles, San Francisco, Chicago, and New York. Mr. Much holds a B.S. in Finance from the University of Illinois and an M.B.A. from Northwestern University. With 17 years in the valuation profession, he has advised clients ranging in size from small closely-held concerns to major NYSE corporations and governmental agencies, including the Department of Labor, the Department of Justice, and the Internal Revenue Service.

THREE

An accurate stock valuation is the critical path in properly structuring an ESOP for a privately held company. Under ERISA, an ESOP can pay no more than "adequate consideration" for qualifying employer securities.[1] This chapter outlines some of the critical considerations in ESOP valuation including: (1) the requirement for independent appraisal; (2) the appropriate definition of fair market value; (3) the significant factors, both quantitative and qualitative, that should be considered in a determination of fair market value; (4) the importance of a current appraisal; (5) what to look for in reviewing an appraisal; (6) relative levels of value; and (7) the valuation issue of fairness and when it becomes important.

REQUIREMENTS FOR INDEPENDENT APPRAISAL

The Tax Reform Act of 1986 requires that valuation of non-publicly traded securities held by ESOPs be undertaken by an "independent appraiser." This requirement is effective in regard to stock acquired after December 31, 1986.

The appraiser must meet standards of both independence and qualification. To be considered independent, the appraiser can not:

1. Have a financial interest in the subject company.
2. Have a relationship with any party to the transaction, such as being an officer, director, partner, employee, employer, or relative.

A qualified appraiser has the experience and facilities necessary for the type of valuation needed, as well as a thorough understanding of the business principles of evaluation. The person or firm normally engages in such appraisal activity and, although not spelled out in law, it is suggested that the appraiser does valuation work on a full-time basis. A fiduciary of the ESOP may act as an appraiser if it can meet the requirements of being independent and qualified.

FAIR MARKET VALUE DEFINED

In the absence of Department of Labor valuation regulations, independent appraisers previously relied on *Revenue Ruling 59–60*, which has served as a general guideline for the valuation of closely held securities since 1959. Although this ruling specifically addresses itself to stock valuations for gift and estate tax purposes, the principles it sets forth may be applied to a wide spectrum of valuation questions, including those related to an ESOP. As set forth in the ruling, *fair market value* is defined as "the price at which the property would change hands between a willing buyer and a willing seller when the former is not under any compulsion to buy and the latter is not under any compulsion to sell, both parties having reasonable knowledge of the relevant facts."[2]

Regulation 29 CFR 2510.318(b), proposed by the Department of Labor in 1988, sets forth a definition of fair market value that is not substantially different: "The price at which an asset would change hands between a willing buyer and a willing seller when the former is not under any compulsion to buy and the latter is not under any compulsion to sell, and both parties are able, as well as willing, to trade and are well informed about the asset and the market for that asset."[3]

Normally, such prices are determined by supply and demand factors in a market that functions with reasonable effectiveness. In the absence of such market transactions, fair market value can be determined through analysis.

When fair market value is determined through analysis, the appraiser, in essence, simulates what would likely occur in an actual transaction. The hypothetical willing buyer and seller are assumed to be well informed about the property and the market for the property. This simulation further assumes that the buyer and seller are both shrewd traders. When they reach a negotiated fair market value, each feels that he has gotten a little bit better than his own estimate of fair market value and, therefore, each is willing to consummate the transaction.

The proposed DOL regulation focuses on "adequate consideration" and clearly states that what is meant by that term, for nonpublicly traded securities, is fair market value. This regulation also addresses situations in which the Department would view a valuation as not reflecting fair market value. These include valuations that:

1. Rely on a value determined at a date other than the date of the plan transaction.
2. Rely on a value not supported by written documentation.
3. Are performed for a different purpose or by parties who do not demonstrate a sufficient level of expertise.

Under the proposed regulation, the fair market value assigned to an asset must result from a determination made by the plan trustee or named fiduciary in "good faith." The good faith requirement focuses on the fiduciary's conduct in determining fair market value. All conflicts of interest between the fiduciary making the valuation and the plan and plan sponsors must be negated. The fiduciary must determine the fair market value based on a prudent investigation of the circumstances prevailing at the time of valuation and the application of sound business principles of evaluation. If the fiduciary is not independent or experienced, the fiduciary must rely on an outside appraiser who is.

The proposed regulation also would establish the minimum contents required in a written valuation. The written valuation would need to include documentation of the appraiser's qualifications and independence and a statement of the methods used in determining value and the reason for that value in light of those methods. Other issues needed in the written statement are discussed in the next section.

IMPORTANCE OF REASONABLE JUDGMENT AND QUANTITATIVE SUPPORT [4]

Valuation of closely held securities requires consideration of many pertinent factors. The Department of Labor's proposed regulation lists factors to consider in determining the fair market value of a closely held security. This list is similar to the one in *Revenue Ruling 59–60* and highlights the need to consider the following:

1. The nature and history of the business enterprise.
2. The economic outlook in general and the condition and outlook of the specific industry in particular.
3. The financial condition of the business and the book value of its stock.
4. The earnings capacity of the business.
5. The dividends paid or dividend-paying capacity of the business.
6. The nature and value of the tangible and intangible assets of the business.
7. The market price of companies engaged in the same or similar lines of business having their stock actively traded in a free and open market.
8. The marketability, or lack thereof, of the securities including an assessment of the effect of any "put" rights on the stock's marketability, and the company's ability to meet any obligations under these put rights.

9. Whether or not the seller would be able to obtain a control premium from an unrelated third party with regard to the block of securities being valued, provided that in cases where a control premium is taken into account: (a) actual control (both in form and substance) is passed to the purchaser with the sale, or will be passed within a reasonable time pursuant to a binding agreement, and (b) it is reasonable to assume that the purchaser's control will not be dissipated within a short period of time subsequent to the acquisition.

Determining the value of a business always requires some form of judgment. However, when a valuation analysis is presented to a prospective buyer, lender, or regulatory authority, it is important to support such judgment with quantifiable facts. Sometimes a company's historical financial statements provide an adequate quantitative basis for determining value. However, in most cases historical figures alone are not sufficient; qualitative factors exist that provide key insights into a company's future that are not reflected in accounting measures based on historical costs.

Such qualitative concerns include competitive position, new product development, distribution methods, labor structure, adequacy of facilities, energy dependence, management capabilities, and involvement in politically volatile countries. In the aggregate, such business fundamentals determine a company's future cash-generating ability as well as risk structure. Often the impact that these factors have on value simply cannot be quantified. However, in many cases quantitative analysis can be used to add objectivity to qualitative judgments.

Once it has been demonstrated that a qualitative factor influences value, the problem remains of how to quantify that influence. In some cases, such influences cannot be quantified; in other cases, quantitative techniques can help analyze qualitative factors and lend objectivity to judgment. Modern finance offers the technique of discounting

future net cash flows to a present value using a rate of
return that compensates the investor for risk assumed.
This fairly standard technique is frequently used by corporate managers in evaluating alternative investments and
in making capital allocation decisions.

Another technique is comparative analysis. Generally,
similar types of companies having different specific characteristics—high versus low financial leverage or dominant
versus weak market positions—will exhibit different relative market valuations. It is possible to review a group of
similar companies and attribute a major difference in their
relative valuations to a specific characteristic within each
company.

These techniques can never replace judgment in determining value; they merely provide an objective framework
for translating judgments into a specific value. Assess-
ments of qualitative factors provide the foundation for implementing these techniques. For example, assessment of a
company's growth potential or capital replacement needs
provides the basis for estimating future net cash flow. Assessment of a company's uninsured product liability risk or
potential loss of market share to an aggressive competitor
can be reflected in the choice of a rate to discount future
net cash flow.

In summary, qualitative factors are important to the
valuation process but difficult to quantify. No magic formulas exist to translate subjective concerns into verifiable
facts; however, techniques are available that can add objectivity to qualitative judgments. Discounting future net cash
flow, examining market-based risk measures, and cross-sec-
tional comparative analysis are all potential ways of adding
such objectivity on a sound basis. However, as even these
techniques require qualitative judgments as inputs, valuation analysis remains an art in which judgment will never
be replaced.

EFFECTIVE DATE OF APPRAISAL

It is important to recognize that value is determined "as of" a particular date. As discussed in *Revenue Ruling 59–60*, "Valuation of securities is, in essence, a prophecy as to the future and must be based on facts available at the required date of appraisal . . . . Fair market value of specific shares of stock will vary as economic conditions change from normal to boom or depression, that is, according to the degree of optimism or pessimism with which the investing public regards the future at the required date of appraisal."[5] Changing investor expectations are reflected continuously by fluctuating stock prices, and, as such, any valuation can only be accurate as of a specific date.

From a fiduciary standpoint, it is important that the independent valuation be updated periodically, because a stale valuation can be just as dangerous as an improper valuation. The landmark ESOP case of *Donovan* v. *Cunningham* clearly illustrates the risks of a stale valuation.[6] In this case, the ESOP trustees relied on a June 30, 1975, appraisal for purchasing shares in August 1976 and in February 1977. Although the trustees claimed that they acted in good faith through reliance on an independent appraisal, the Court of Appeals determined that, as of the transaction dates, the appraisal was outdated and relied upon assumptions that were no longer accurate. In the words of the Court of Appeals, "a pure heart and an empty head are not enough" (p. 285).

Fiduciaries must recognize that fair market value can be accurate only as of a specific date, and to assume its accuracy for any other date is to rely on mere chance. ESOP appraisals should be updated at least annually. In the case of a rapidly changing company (either positively through new product growth or a significant acquisition or negatively through rapid financial deterioration), quarterly updates may be appropriate.

ASSUMPTIONS UNDERLYING APPRAISAL

Appraisers are not auditors, and they typically rely on and assume, without independent verification, the accuracy and completeness of all information supplied to them by the subject company and its representatives. Each fiduciary should review the report of the appraiser to make sure that, based on his own personal knowledge of the company and its financial condition, nothing indicated that the appraiser was not given the complete information needed to conduct the appraisal properly. Each fiduciary should be satisfied that there was nothing that suggested that the facts on which the appraisal was based were not accurate. In *Donovan* v. *Cunningham*, the Appellate Court included the following comment in its opinion:

> The appraisal represented a quantitative analysis of specific facts and assumptions. Prudent fiduciaries would have sought to analyze the effect of obvious changes in those facts and assumptions—either through their own efforts or with the help of advisors. An independent appraisal is not a magic wand that fiduciaries may simply wave over a transaction to ensure that their responsibilities are fulfilled. To use an independent appraisal properly, ERISA fiduciaries need not become experts in the field of valuation of closely held stock—they are entitled to rely upon the expertise of others. However, as the source of the information upon which the experts' opinions are based, the fiduciaries are responsible for ensuring that the information is complete and up-to-date. In failing to do so, the fiduciaries breached their duties of prudence under Section 404 (of ERISA) and likewise cannot establish that they paid adequate consideration. Accordingly the ESOP transactions were prohibited under Section 406 (of ERISA) (pp. 292–93).

RELATIVE LEVELS OF VALUE

The size of the block of stock itself is a relevant factor to be considered in valuation. If a specific block allows the purchaser to control a corporation, a higher value (relative to a minority position) is justified. Just as a controlling interest is worth more on a per share basis than a minority interest, a marketable minority interest is worth more than a non-marketable minority interest. Thus, there are three relative levels of value as illustrated by Figure 3.1.

These three levels of value are: enterprise or controlling interest, marketable minority interest, and nonmarketable minority interest. Notice the distinction between the discount for minority interest and the discount for lack of marketability; these two discounts are often considered to be synonymous rather than distinct considerations. When both of these discounts are applied, they are sequential.

The fair market value of a marketable minority interest is that price at which securities trade in a free and active market. Prices quoted in *The Wall Street Journal* for public companies whose shares trade on any of the various exchanges represent the per share value of marketable minority interests.

It is accepted valuation practice to discount the value of minority interests that are not traded in a free and active market. Minority interests in closely-held companies lack the inherent liquidity of traded securities, and thus some discount is justified. While the magnitude of discount for lack of marketability depends on the particular facts and circumstances, it will generally fall within the range of 10-40 percent of the value otherwise determined. The difference in value between a marketable and nonmarketable security could partially be measured by the approximate costs associated with bringing the shares to market at or near the valuation date. Such costs would include all underwriting fees and commissions, as well as company and/or shareholder expenses to prepare the stock for market. Another method of determining a discount for lack of marketability is to analyze the price difference between letter stock (stock restricted from trading on the open market for some period) of a public company and the freely traded stock of the same company at the same point in time.

Figure 3.1
Relative Levels of Value of Stock

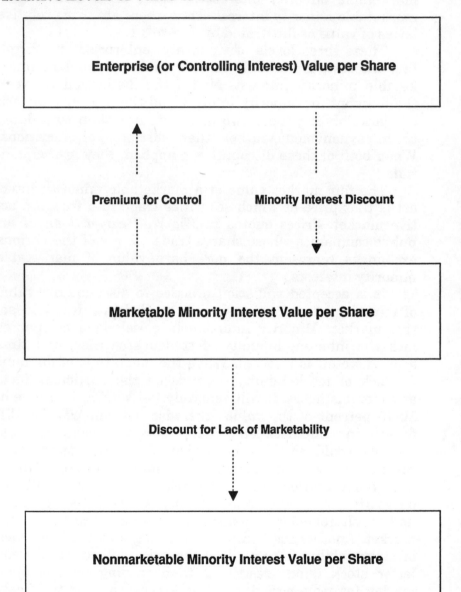

In the case of the closely held company that adopts an ESOP designed to offer participants a put option to redeem their stock at fair market value after distribution, the plan effectively creates liquidity for the ESOP securities. Assuming prudent administration and planning, the ESOP or the company plays the part of an organized securities exchange by providing liquidity for the employer securities. Thus, in ESOPs where such options exist and where sufficient liquidity exists to satisfy the option demands, it is inappropriate to discount the value for lack of marketability.

Controlling, or majority, blocks of stock generally have the power to effect changes in the overall corporate structure and to influence corporate policies. Minority shareholders, of course, do not have this ability. Consequently, a controlling interest is considered to be worth more per share than a minority interest. A measure of the difference in value between a controlling interest in a corporation and a marketable minority interest can be found in public tender offerings where the tender offer, if successful, will give the acquirer a control position. The market price of the stock before the tender offer is related to the higher premium offer price, resulting in the premium paid for the control position.

In recent years, control premiums in major mergers and acquisitions have ranged from less than 25 to more than 100 percent over the unaffected market price (the marketable minority price prior to the price activity relative to takeover) and averaged about 40-50 percent on an industrywide basis (see Figure 3.2). There is no rule of thumb for the size of premium for an adequate control offer. Many factors must be considered; however, the premium is based on the buyer's assessment of opportunities for a control shareholder, which are not available to or which incumbent management is not exploiting for the benefit of the target company's minority shareholders. To the extent the suitor believes that control can be purchased for less than the maximum, a lesser price will be offered.

Figure 3.2
Average Control Premiums Industrywide

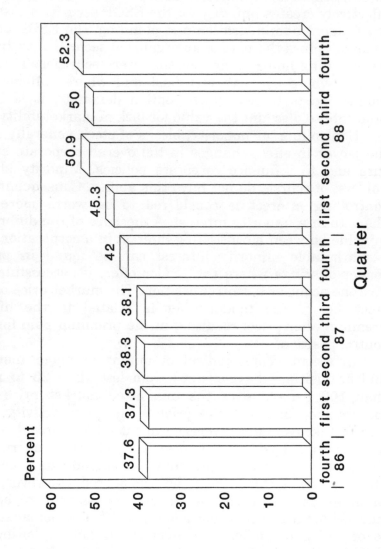

Percent

Source: Prepared by Houlihan, Lokey, Howard & Zukin, Inc.

In transactions in which an ESOP purchases a sizable block of employer stock but less than 50 percent of a company's outstanding shares, the issue of using a control level of value or a minority interest level of value frequently becomes controversial. The proposed DOL regulation attempts to clarify this by stating that a control premium can only be paid if actual control is acquired (or will be acquired within a reasonable period of time) and that control will not be dissipated within a short period of time. Some practitioners and selling shareholders have argued that a minority discount is unnecessary if it is intended that the ESOP will acquire a control block of shares through a series of subsequent minority purchases. This argument usually develops when a majority shareholder wishes to receive a control level price when initially selling only a minority block, since he intends to sell all of his remaining shares to the ESOP sometime in the future. In the meantime, he retains his control position, and if the ESOP originally purchased at least 30 percent of the company, he receives a tax-free rollover.

This have-my-cake and-eat-it-too scenario is naive, at best, and dangerous at worst. If an ESOP were to pay a control price for a minority block, it would be paying more than an independent investor would pay. Paying more than an independent investor (which assumes a transaction at fair market value) creates a prohibited transaction under ERISA.

Under the proposed regulation, an ESOP can only purchase minority blocks of shares at premiums when the transaction price includes some type of lock-up provision on additional shares, which will pass control in form and substance to the ESOP within a reasonable period of time. In an ESOP such lock-up provisions might include:

1. A contractual right by the ESOP to purchase enough additional shares to give it actual control within a reasonable time.
2. An interim voting trust controlling more than 50 percent of the outstanding vote, which is ad-

ministered by an independent (not directed) trustee.

3. A liquidating damage provision providing that if the ESOP ownership of actual control is not accomplished within the specified time frame, then the difference in value between a minority level and control level will be contributed in cash to the ESOP, whether or not such additional contributions are deductible.

An example of an ESOP using a lock-up provision in a multiple-stage transaction is the ESOP leveraged buyout of Lyon Metal Products. In this transaction, the ESOP purchased 100 percent of the company in three stages—a large minority position in May 1985; a small minority block in June 1985, and the balance in September 1985. The ESOP paid a pro rata control price for the initial minority blocks, but that price was premised upon ultimately acquiring control.

In the fairness opinion provided to the ESOP trustee on May 16, 1985, the ESOP's financial advisor included the following caveat:

> The fair market value of the (minority) block of securities to be purchased by the ESOP in the proposed transaction may be significantly lower should the ESOP fail to acquire at least 50 percent of the outstanding common stock of Lyon. Accordingly, Lyon has entered into an agreement with the Trustee, whereby should the Trust fail to acquire, for any reason, at least 50 percent of the outstanding shares of Lyon, Lyon has agreed to contribute to the ESOP an amount equal to the difference between the fair market value of the shares purchased by the ESOP (on a minority basis) and the amount paid for the shares by the ESOP (which includes a control premium). In such an event, we shall determine the fair market value (of the minority block purchased), as financial advisors to the Trustee.[7]

The Lyon case was unique in that it involved a hostile

takeover, which explains the short time between the initial minority purchases in May and June 1985 and the subsequent buyout of all remaining shares in September. Normally, the time might range from 3 to 5 years in a nonhostile transaction involving a privately held company. It is unclear whether or not this constitutes a "reasonable period of time" under the proposed regulation. However, it does illustrate how the trustee effectively protected the ESOP from paying too much (a pro rata control price) for too little (less than a control block). In this case, the 100 percent buyout was consummated, and the liquidated damage provision never came into play. However, without such a lock-up provision, the ESOP could not have purchased the initial minority block of shares at the same pro rata control price.

It is also important to note that under the proposed regulation the participation by an ESOP in an acquisition as part of a buying group appears to be precluded, unless the ESOP ends up with control. In a typical acquisition, investors pool resources to acquire the entire equity of a company. All the investors pay a price that incorporates a control premium, although no one single investor may come away with voting control. The proposed regulation clearly states "The Department's position is that the payment of a control premium is unwarranted unless the plan obtains both voting control and control in fact."[8] Even if an ESOP ends up with a majority of the stock after the transaction, the existence of dilutive securities (such as options or warrants) that could reduce the ESOP's position in the future to a less-than-majority position may preclude a determination that control in fact has passed to the ESOP.

The fact that a strict interpretation of the proposed regulation may eliminate ESOPs from participating in transactions that make economic sense and could provide substantial benefits to employees may result in different language on this issue in the final regulation. As proposed, however, the ESOP cannot pay a control premium unless it acquires and maintains voting control.

FAIRNESS

Many recent ESOP transactions involve investors other than
the ESOP who also purchase employer securities. These may
include members of the company's management or outsiders.
In such a transaction, the outside investors typically invest
cash, the management group invests "sweat equity," and the
ESOP puts up a nonrecourse note. Each has different objectives, and their risk-return preferences can conflict. In such a
situation, the fair market value of the securities purchased by
the ESOP is influenced by the potentially dilutive effect of the
securities purchased by the other investors (which might
include convertibles, options, or warrants). In this cir-
cumstance, fairness to the ESOP becomes an important valuation issue. While fair market value is an absolute concept,
fairness must be determined on a relative basis. Fairness
dictates that the ESOP receive a risk-adjusted return at least
as favorable as the other investors'.

Again, the case of Lyon Metal Products illustrates the
fairness issues that surface in structuring a leveraged
buyout with an ESOP and other investors. Prior to retaining valuation specialists with expertise in ESOP fairness
issues, the leveraged buyout of Lyon was structured so that
the Lyon ESOP would pay $12 million for class A common
stock that would initially represent a 100 percent ownership position in the Company. However, under certain circumstances, the ESOP's ownership could have been diluted
to as little as 68 percent because of convertible securities
that would have been issued to management (class B common stock). Relative to the ESOP's $12 million investment,
management would pay only $300,000 and potentially own
up to 32 percent of the company upon conversion.

The problem stemmed from the fact that the company,
a maker of industrial lockers with an extremely long useful
life, is in a low-growth or slow-growth industry. Under the
originally proposed plan for the management stock, management would be well represented on the board of directors and would own up to almost one-third of the company
after 5 years. Since little growth could be expected, conver-

sion of the class B stock would dilute the ESOP's ownership position so much that its total value would likely grow very little, or even diminish after conversion of management's securities.

Under the most likely scenario, the effective return on investment for the ESOP would have been significantly less than could have been obtained in a good certificate of deposit or Treasury bill. Management would have been granted a major ownership position in the company and significant board control for a relatively small contribution. Moreover, there were no incentives to encourage management performance, because ultimate ownership was not keyed to any levels of company earnings or growth in stock value.

The proposed arrangement was clearly unfair to Lyon's ESOP, which was putting up a significant amount of money to purchase the company. To remedy the situation, the Lyon plan was restructured in several significant ways. First, management's required contribution was increased to $600,000, double the original level, and the members of the management group individually guaranteed repayment of the last $400,000 of Lyon's acquisition debt. Second, the maximum ownership share of the management team was limited to 20 percent of the company, down from the originally contemplated 32 percent. This limitation helped protect the equity position of the ESOP. Third, management representation on the board of directors was decreased to one seat—a more equitable arrangement.

More important, however, the plan was restructured to prevent conversion of any class B management stock into regular class A common stock until the ESOP received a 13 percent cumulative annual return on its $12 million investment over the first 5 years of the plan. This change had a significant impact on the fundamental incentives affecting management and put them at a significant level of risk. Basically, the better the company performed over the next 5 years, the more valuable the management securities would become. To understand how this works, consider two possible cases: If the company's value grows at 13 percent or less over the first 5-year period, all of the increased value will accrue to the ESOP. Management will not receive any common stock, and the management team will lose its entire $600,000 investment and still be obligated for the last $400,000 of the original acquisition debt.

However, if management performs significantly better and generates a growth rate in value higher than 13 percent for the company, the class B stock will convert into an equity position representing exactly half the growth in value over the 13 percent first provided to the ESOP. For example, if the company is valued at $12 million at the time of the leveraged buyout, a 13 percent annual growth rate will yield a value of about $22 million in 5 years. But if management generates a 20 percent rate of growth in value over the same period, the company will be worth nearly $36 million. Under the terms of the management stock plan, this additional $14 million would be divided evenly between the ESOP and the management team—the management class B stock would convert into class A stock worth approximately $7 million. The management team would thus receive for its efforts about 19.4 percent of the company.

Essentially, the revised structure will protect the ESOP but will penalize management for mediocre performance and substantially reward both the ESOP and management for superior performance. Rather than expropriate value from the ESOP, management must maximize the value for everyone in order to receive a substantial reward. Under the revised structure, all the employees have an interest in seeing management receive its full 20 percent allocation, even if the employees are diluted down to 80 percent ownership of the company, because that 80 percent will represent a substantially enhanced value. Such a revised structure was fair to the ESOP from a financial point of view.

SUMMARY

In addition to employing an independent appraiser to value employer securities, ESOP fiduciaries should also be careful to observe the following diligence procedures:

1. Understand what "fair market value" or "fairness" means and how it is being applied to the subject transaction.
2. Make sure the appraiser has complete and accurate information.
3. Make sure the valuation is current.
4. Review the valuation report carefully to understand all assumptions used and ask questions where appropriate.
5. Make sure the appraiser has provided written documentation supporting the valuation.

An ESOP fiduciary need not be a valuation expert or second guess the appraiser's opinion. However, it is important to follow the procedures just mentioned to properly understand the valuation process before acting upon the conclusion of an expert.

NOTES

[1] ERISA §3(18).
[2] *Revenue Ruling 59–60* §2.02.
[3] Prop. DOL Reg. 29CFR 2510 §B.2.
[4] Much, Paul J. and Chester A. Gougis, "Subtitle Considerations, Hard to Quantify, Vital in Determining a Business's Value," *The National Law Journal*, May 26, 1980.
[5] *Revenue Ruling 59–60* §3.

[6] *Donovan* v. *Cunningham*, 541 F.F.upp 27b (S.D.Tex. 1982).

[7] Lyon Metal Products, Inc. Proxy Statement, August 8, 1985. Exhibit IV.

[8] Prop. DOL Reg. 29CFR 2510 §B.5.

FOUR

Lending to ESOPs

Robert F. Schatz

Robert F. Schatz is a partner with Schatz & Schatz, Ribicoff & Kotkin, one of Connecticut's oldest and largest law firms, with offices in Hartford, Stamford and Bridgeport, Connecticut. A graduate of Cornell University (B.A. 1973) and Suffolk University School of Law (J.D. 1977), Mr. Schatz specializes in commercial and corporate finance law and the structuring and financing of ESOP transactions for lenders and companies. Mr. Schatz is the author of several articles, including, "ESOPs: Are they as great as everyone says?" presented at the 1989 New York University Institutes on Federal Taxation and published by Matthew Bender & Co.

Mr. Schatz is a member of the Banking Law Committee and Subcommittees on Savings Institutions and Regulatory Enforcement of the American Bar Association, the Attorneys' Committee of the U.S. League of Savings Institutions and the Financial Institutions and Legislative Committees of the ESOP Association. Mr. Schatz is a frequent speaker/lecturer for the ESOP Association, National Center for Employee Ownership, American Management Association and New York University Institutes on Federal Taxation.

FOUR

ESOPs have gained popularity in recent years in large part because of their potential as an effective tool of corporate finance that provides benefits to both the sponsoring companies and lenders in the form of tax advantages not available in conventionally financed transactions. By using an ESOP, many companies are able to purchase outstanding shares of their own stock, refinance their outstanding debt, or make acquisitions with pre-tax dollars.

This chapter will address certain principal issues arising in connection with the structuring of loans made to fund the acquisition of stock of a company that has established an ESOP. The issues addressed in this chapter are of interest not only to lenders. By understanding the constraints imposed on lenders, the sponsoring companies, the trustees of the trust established under the ESOP (the "ESOT"), and the respective advisors of the principals will be better able to structure the loan transaction to ensure that everyone involved will realize the maximum benefits.

THE STATUTORY FRAMEWORK—THE LENDER'S INTEREST EXCLUSION

The increased attention by lenders to ESOPs has resulted in large part from the tax benefits that lenders can realize from making ESOP loans. These benefits are provided for in Section 133 of the Internal Revenue Code of 1986, which was added to the Code by the Tax Reform Act of 1984. Eligible lenders are allowed to exclude from gross income 50 percent of the

95

interest earned on loans to ESOPs and corporate sponsors, provided that such loans meet certain specific criteria so as to qualify as "security acquisition loans" under the Code. These critieria include (a) which lenders may be eligible for the 50 percent interest exclusion, (b) use of loan proceeds, (c) the status of the ESOP as a qualified plan, (d) the structure of the securities acquisition loan transaction, and (e) the status of the loan as an exempt loan.

Eligible Lenders

Not every institution that lends money to an ESOP is eligible for the 50 percent interest exclusion. Under the Code, only banks, insurance companies, corporations (other than S corporations) actively engaged in the business of lending money, and regulated investment companies and mutual funds are eligible for the interest exclusion. Thus, for example, a selling stockholder who lends money to the ESOP for the purchase of employer securities or who accepts a purchase money note from the ESOP as part consideration for the sale of employer securities to the ESOP is not entitled to the interest exclusion (even though such a loan might be an exempt loan as described later).

Use of Proceeds

In order to qualify for the 50 percent interest exclusion, the proceeds of a loan may only be used to:

1. Purchase common stock of the sponsoring company that is readily tradable on an established securities market or, if not readily tradable, is common stock having a combination of voting power and dividend rights equal to or in excess of that class of common stock having the greatest voting power and dividend rights.
2. Purchase noncallable preferred stock that is convertible at any time into common stock satisfying

the requirement set forth above. (This and the above described stock are referred to as "employer securities.")

3. Refinance a prior loan that met all of the requirements to consititute such prior loan as a securities acquisition loan.

ESOP as a Qualified Plan

Regardless of the structure of the securities acquisition loan, in order to qualify for the interest exclusion, the ESOP must on the date of the loan meet all of the requirements for a qualified plan under the Code and comply with the requirements under ERISA. These requirements include a provision that the price paid for the stock by the ESOP be not more than adequate consideration, which is defined generally to mean fair market value. Methods for determining adequate consideration and the qualification requirements applicable to ESOPs have been dealt with in other chapters.

Securities Acquisition Loans

Once it is determined that the lender is eligible for the 50 percent interest exclusion, and the lender is satisfied that the securities to be purchased are employer securities and the ESOP is a qualified plan, the lender must structure the loan so that it qualifies as a securities acquisition loan. Essentially, three general types of loans can qualify as securities acquisition loans: a *direct loan*, a *back-to-back loan*, and an *immediate allocation loan*.

In a direct loan, as depicted in Figure 4.1, a loan is made to the ESOP directly, and the proceeds are used to purchase employer securities for the ESOP from the sponsoring company. The loan may be structured as a secured or unsecured loan, but if secured, the only collateral that the ESOP is permitted to pledge is the employer securities purchased with the proceeds of the loan. However, the direct loan may be (and usually is) guaranteed by the spon-

Figure 4.1

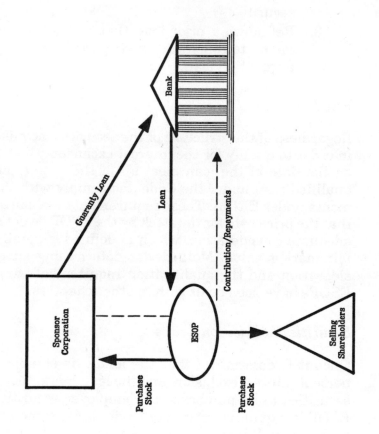

soring company and other persons, and the guaranty can be secured by any or all of the assets of the guarantor.

In a back-to-back loan, as depicted in Figure 4.2, a loan is made by the lender to the sponsoring company (the "front-end loan") and the sponsoring company relends the proceeds (the "mirror loan") to the ESOP on "substantially similar terms." The ESOP uses the proceeds of the mirror loan to purchase employer securities either from the sponsoring company or its stockholders. While the front-end loan can be secured and collateralized by any or all of the assets of the sponsoring company, the only collateral that the ESOP may give to the sponsoring company for the mirror loan (or as collateral for the ESOP's guaranty of the front-end loan, if such guaranty is required) is employer securities acquired with the loan proceeds.

In the immediate allocation loan, a secured or unsecured loan is made by the lender to the sponsoring company (based on the amount of the company's annual contribution to the ESOP). The sponsoring company may use the loan proceeds for any purpose it desires (including the acquisition of employer securities from stockholders), provided that within 30 days after the loan is made, the company contributes employer securities to the ESOP that are equal in value to the loan proceeds. These securities must be allocated to the accounts of participants within 1 year. The immediate allocation loan structure allows a lender to finance the ESOP's purchase of employer securities by making a series of term loans annually rather than making the entire loan at one time. It is especially useful for companies with large payrolls. One advantage of the immediate allocation loan is that, because the ESOP is unleveraged, the risk of a decline in the stock price (which commonly occurs in back-to-back loans and direct loans) and of a decline in the value of the employees' retirement accounts is minimized.

Seven-Year Term Issue. Many lenders unfamiliar with ESOPs labor under the misconception that the 50 percent interest exclusion is only available to a lender for 7 years

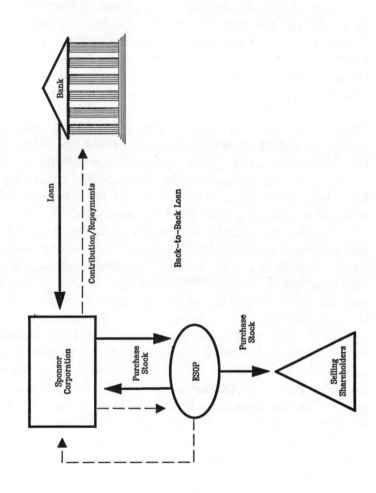

Figure 4.2

and, by extension, have limited the term of ESOP loans to a maximum of 7 years. However, if the securities acquisition loan is (a) a direct loan to the ESOP, or (b) a back-to-back loan in which the repayment terms of the mirror loan are substantially similar to those of the front-end loan, or (c) if the securities acquisition loan is made to refinance a loan described in (a) or (b), the interest exclusion will be available to the lender for the entire original term of the loan, regardless of the length of the loan term. However, if the securities acquisition loan is structured as an immediate allocation loan or if, in a back-to-back loan, the mirror loan does not have substantially similar repayment terms as the front-end loan, the 50 percent interest exclusion will be available to the lender only during the period that the loans had substantially similar terms or for 7 years, whichever is less.

Sometimes a lender is asked to refinance a back-to-back loan that had substantially similar repayment terms when it was originally structured but that is no longer "substantially similar" when the refinancing is sought. Currently pending legislation would provide that when this situation arises, the original back-to-back loan will not be considered substantially similar and the lender's tax exclusion will be limited to a 7-year term from the date of the original back-to-back loan's being refinanced.

Substantially Similar Terms—Back-to-Back Loans.
Special rules apply when the lender structures the securities acquisition loan as a back-to-back loan. Under temporary regulations issued by the IRS, the front-end loan will be eligible for the 50 percent interest exclusion to the extent and for the period that the mirror loan qualifies as an "exempt loan" and (a) has "substantially similar terms" as the front-end loan or (b) has substantially similar repayment terms, except that the mirror loan can be repaid faster than the front-end loans.[1]

To determine whether the loans have substantially similar terms, the timing and rate at which employer securities would be released from encumbrance if the front-end loan were the exempt loan must be compared with the timing and rate at which the employer securities actually will be released from encumbrance. If the two loans are determined in such manner to be substantially similar, there is no limitation on the term of the loans. If the two loans are not substantially similar by such comparison, the interest exclusion will still be available to the lender, but only if the allocation of employer securities attributable to such repayment does not discriminate in favor of highly compensated employees and the original commitment period of the front-end loan does not exceed 7 years.

The Exempt Loan

In addition to complying with the rules under Section 133 of the Code relating to the 50 percent interest exclusion, a loan must also constitute an " exempt loan" within the "safe harbor" exemption from the prohibited transaction rules of ERISA and the Code for loans made to leveraged ESOPs.[2] Among the requirements to qualify a loan as an exempt loan are the following:

1. The loan must be primarily for the benefit of the ESOP participants.
2. The loan must be without recourse to the ESOP.
3. The sole collateral for the loan must be employer securities acquired with the loan proceeds.
4. The source of repayment of the loan must be limited to contributions made pursuant to the ESOP to meet loan obligations, earnings attributable to the collateral, and the investment of contributions and dividends.
5. The interest rate on the loan must be reasonable (although a variable rate is permitted).
6. The loan must be for a specified term.
7. The employer securities pledged to the lender as collateral for the direct loan or to the sponsoring corporation as collateral for the mirror loan by the ESOP must be released as the loan is repaid.

8. In the event of a default, the value of plan assets transferred in satisfaction of the loan may not exceed the amount of the default.

In the event that the lender is a party in interest (or a disqualified person), the only default for which the lender can have recourse to plan assets is a default for failure to meet the payment schedule of the loan, and then only for the amount in default. For this reason, unless circumstances otherwise require, it is preferable for the lender to structure the ESOP loan as a back-to-back loan.

PRACTICAL IMPLICATIONS OF LENDING TO ESOPS

The rules set forth in previous sections of this chapter have a number of implications for lenders structuring the financing of ESOP transactions. These rules affect the amount of the loan, the purchase price for employer securities, the interest rate risk, ESOP shares as collateral, posttransaction solvency, and securities law risks.

Amount of the Loan

As noted earlier, for the loan to qualify for the interest exclusion, the loan proceeds may be used only for the purchase of employer securities. Also, the amount of the loan should not exceed the purchase price paid for the employer securities purchased by the ESOP.

Purchase Price for Employer Securities

The purchase price for the employer securities may not exceed fair market value. While the reasonable expenses incurred by the ESOP for legal, financial, and other advice and assistance may be paid out of the contribution made to the ESOP by the sponsoring company, the loan proceeds may be used only for the purchase of the employer securities. No portion of the loan proceeds may be used to pay for the costs of the transaction.

If the shares being purchased are publicly traded, the market price of the shares is their fair market value. However, if there have been recent market fluctuations that could be viewed as artificially inflating the value of the shares, then the market price may not accurately reflect the fair market value. In such circumstances, it may be prudent for the lender to require that, if the company intends to pay this higher price, it furnish the lender with evidence or a valuation that the higher price being paid for the shares does not exceed their fair market value.

In privately held corporations, ascertaining the fair market value of the shares can be even more difficult. While the law requires that the fair market value of the shares of privatly held companies be determined by an "independent appraiser," the lender should study both the qualifications of the appraiser and the underlying methodology of the appraisal to satisfy itself that the price of the stock being purchased is not more than the fair market value.

Interest Rate Risk

The importance of the valuation of the stock cannot be overstated. A determination as to whether an ESOP is paying more than adequate consideration for shares is seldom made in advance. Instead, the courts and the administrative agencies that conduct such examinations generally do so after the transaction is closed and the money spent, with the benefit of having seen the sponsoring company's performance (or lack thereof) after the transaction. If upon such posttransaction examination it is determined that the ESOP paid more than fair market value for the stock, the ESOP could be found not to be a qualified pension plan. The loan made by the lender would then not be an exempt loan and would not qualify for the interest exclusion since it would not be a securities acquisition loan.

Lenders typically should include clauses in their loan agreements commonly known as "gross-up" provisions. The provisions essentially require the borrower to pay the lender a higher rate of interest if the interest on the loan is determined not to qualify for the lender's interest exclusion for any reason. In addition, lenders (and their counselors), now leery of the ever-changing tax environment, generally include clauses in their gross-up provisions transferring to the borrower the risk that changing laws or administrative regulations or guidelines will adversely affect the yield, or profit, that the lender expects to receive from the transaction. A sample of gross up provisions that are designed to be reasonably fair to all parties can be found in Appendix 4.A at the end of the chapter.

ESOP Shares as Collateral

As noted earlier, the employer securities purchased with the proceeds of the loan must be released annually from encumbrance as the loan is repaid. The formula for such release will generally be set forth in the ESOP and will be based on either the repayment of principal and interest (accruing over the term of the loan) or principal only. If the lender takes a security interest in the employer securities, the lender should pay careful attention to the formula for release set forth in the ESOP. The lender could very quickly find itself having to release from encumbrance more securities than the balance of the principal of the loan if the formula is based upon repayment of principal and interest and the loan is repaid on a mortgage amortization schedule (resulting in an undercollateralization of the loan in the early years since less principal is paid). The following example illustrates this case.

> An ESOP purchases 100,000 shares of employer securities valued at $20.00 per share as of the date of the transaction and finances the purchase with the proceeds of a $2,000,000 ESOP loan. The loan bears interest at a rate of 8.5 percent per year and will be repaid over a 10-year period in equal consecutive monthly installments of $24,797.22. At the end of the second

year, while the ESOP will have made total payments of $595,133.28, payments on account of principal will have totalled only $277,037, and the lender will have released from encumbrance 19,100 shares. As of the end of this second year the employer securities retain their value of $20.00 per share. The remaining 80,100 encumbered employer securities will have a value of $1,602,000, the unpaid principal balance of the loan will be approximately $1,723,000, and the lender's collateral shortfall will be approximately $121,000. At the end of the third year, while the ESOP will have made total payments of approximately $892,700, payments on account of principal will have totalled only $434,180, and the lender will have released from encumbrance 29,512 shares. The value of the employer securities as of the end of this third year increased 10 percent to $22.00 per share, and the remaining 70,488 of the encumbered shares will be worth approximately $1,410,000. The unpaid principal balance of the loan will be approximately $1,580,000, and the lender's collateral shortfall will be approximately $170,000.

In this case, the lender may want to require that the release formula be based on principal repayment only.

One disadvantage of the release of shares based on repayment of principal only is that the shares must be fully released within 10 years. The lender may, therefore, want to limit the term of its loan to 10 years if it desires that the stock collateralize its loan at all times. Alternatively, the lender could (a) require additional collateral for its loan so that it would continue to have the collateral coverage required or (b) not take the employer securities as collateral at all and rely on the sponsoring company's assets as collateral for the loan and/or on the secured (or unsecured) guaranty by the sponsoring company of the direct loan.

Assurance of Posttransaction Solvency

Over the last few years, lenders have become increasingly wary of transactions, commonly known as leveraged buyouts (LBOs), in which the acquiring entity, be it an ESOP or any other purchaser, borrows money to buy the stock of a company using the assets of the company being acquired as security for the loans. In several transactions, the security interests granted by such target companies have been held to be unenforceable based on theories of fraudulent conveyance or other lack of adequate consideration to the target company.[3] Attention must also be given to the applicability of state laws limiting a company's ability to effect a redemption or repurchase of a company's own shares.

As a result of these concerns, a lender should require the sponsoring company to provide it with a pro forma balance sheet reflecting the effect of the transaction on the company (and reflecting tangible assets in excess of liabilities), pro forma cash flow projections (reflecting the company's ability to pay debt service and other obligations as they arise), and a certificate from an independent appraiser certifying to posttransaction solvency. These assurances are especially necessary if the proceeds of the loan are ultimately being used to purchase shareholder's interests rather than being used by the company for its corporate purposes.

Securities Law Risks

A lender must also be concerned that the transaction not violate federal or state securities laws. ESOPs generally will be exempt from the registration and antifraud provisions of the securities laws, since participation in the ESOP generally will be mandatory and the employees will not have contributed or made an investment decision with respect to the ESOP's acquisition of employer securities. However, in several transactions, employees have successfully argued that they contributed to the plan as a result of salary or wage concessions made at the time and in exchange for the establishment of a stock bonus plan, profit-sharing plan, or ESOP and have been able to subject the transaction to review under the securities laws.[4] The 50 percent interest exclusion should not be affected by such actions, but if the claimant were able to show misrepresentation and damage, the company could be found liable for potentially significant monetary damages that could ad versely affect its general ability to repay the loan.

CONCLUSION

While ESOP transactions can be complex, the ESOP loan should not be. The lender's credit analysis in most cases will be the same as in conventional lending situations, and the cash flow benefits to the company resulting from the transaction should serve to enhance that credit. In most cases, the loan will be structured and documented much like conventional loans, with the addition of provisions and documents reflecting the special requirements necessary to ensure that all parties can realize their respective tax benefits and other advantages. If both the company seeking the ESOP loan and the lender making the loan address the issues and particular concerns outlined in this chapter in the early stages of the transaction, the transaction should be able to be structured and successfully completed in a timely and efficient manner.

NOTES

[1]   Treas. Reg. 1.133 1T, Q&A 1.

[2]   Treas. Reg. 54.4975-7 and 11.

[3]   See, for example the following cases: Matter of Ohio Corrugating, Co. 70 Bankr. 920 (N.D. Ohio 1987). In re Anderson Industries, Inc. 55 Bankr. 922 (N.D. Mi. 1985). *United States* v. *Tarbor Court Realty Corp.*, 803 F.2d 1288 (3rd Cir. 1986).

[4]   See, for example, the case of *Harris* v. *Republic Airlines, Inc.*, Sec. Reg. & L. Rep 93, 722 (BNA 1988).

APPENDIX 4.A SAMPLE GROSS-UP PROVISIONS

1.7 Change in Law or Regulations. (a) In the event of a change, as defined below, which is applicable to the Bank and has the effect of (i) changing the basis of taxation to the Bank of the interest on the Term Note, (ii) changing the Bank's marginal composite federal or state tax rate, or (iii) imposing on the Bank any other condition affecting the Term Note, and the Bank shall determine that the future cost to it of carrying the Term Note will be increased or reduced, or that its net after-tax yield on interest earned under the Term Note will be increased or reduced, the Bank shall adjust the interest rate of the Term Note to reflect such increase or reduction as of the effective date of the Change (the "Adjusted Interest Rate"). Such Adjusted Interest Rate shall be payable commencing with the first monthly interest installment date as set forth herein next following the date on which the Change occurs (the "Next Interest Payment Date"). In addition, the Borrower shall promptly pay to the Bank, upon its demand, such additional amount as the Bank would have received had the interest on the Term Note been adjusted to the Adjusted Interest Rate as of the Effective Date of the Change (as defined below).

(b) A Change shall be deemed to have occurred on the effective date set forth in the statute or regulation promulgating such Change (the "Effective Date of Change"), which is applicable to the Bank, on the occurrence of any of the following (each defined as a "Change"):

(i) the enactment of an amendment to or repeal of, Section 133 of the Internal Revenue Code of 1986, as amended (the "Code"), or the issuance of any regulation or proposed or temporary regulation under that Section of the Code unless, with respect to such amendment or repeal, in the opinion of legal counsel chosen by Borrower and satisfactory to Bank, such amendment or repeal does not adversely affect the exemption from tax with respect to the Term Loan evidenced hereby:

(ii) the enactment of new state or federal legislation, or the modification of existing state or federal legislation, or the adoption of any regulations (or proposed or temporary regulations), guidelines, interpretations or rulings dealing with (1) the treatment of interest on loans used directly or indirectly to acquire employer securities ("Securities Acquisition Loans"), (2) the deductibility of interest on debt incurred to finance the making of Securities Acquisition Loans, (3) the treatment of interest on Securities Acquisition Loans or the interest on the debt incurred to carry Securities Acquisition Loans as an item of tax preference, or (4) the method or methods of allocating or calculating any deductions, credits, or items of income in respect of Securities Acquisition Loans.

(iii) a change in the income or franchise tax rates, whether federal, state, or local, imposed on corporations or banks (as defined in Section 581 of the Code), or, with respect to Securities Acquisition Loans, the imposition of a new type of tax on items of income received by such corporations or financial institutions whether such new tax is denominated an excise tax, alternative minimum tax, or otherwise.

(c) The Bank shall give prompt notice to the Borrower of a Change and the Adjusted Interest Rate.

1.8 Determination of Taxability. (a) In the event the Bank receives a notice from the Internal Revenue Service (the "IRS") that for any reason the interest on the Term Note is not subject to the exclusion set forth in Section 133 of the Code (any such Notice being herein referred to as a "Notice of Taxability"), the interest rate shall be adjusted, commencing on the Next Interest Payment Date after the date of the Notice of Taxability, to a variable rate equal to the Prime Rate plus percentage points (the "Taxable Rate"). In addition, Borrower shall pay to the Bank as additional interest on the Term Note for the period beginning on the date set forth in the Notice of Taxability as the date after which interest received by the Bank was not subject to the exclusion set forth in Section 133 of the Code (such date shall be referred to herein as the "Effective Date of Taxability") an additional amount equal to the amount the Bank would have received had the interest on the Term Note been adjusted to the Taxable Rate commencing

on the Effective Date of Taxability. In the event that subsequent to the time the Bank receives a Notice of Taxability
it is determined by the IRS or by any court having competent
jurisdiction over the matter that the interest on the Term Note
is subject to the exclusion set forth in Section 133 of the Code,
then the interest rate shall be adjusted, commencing on the
Next Interest Payment Date after the date of such determination, to the interest rate set forth in this Agreement, and the
Bank shall refund to the Borrower any amounts paid by the
Borrower to the Bank subject to this paragraph (a) as a result
of the receipt by the Bank of the Notice of Taxability.

(b) Upon written demand to Borrower by the Bank,
Borrower shall pay to the Bank an amount (computed
without regard to any deduction in such amount payable by
reason of any set-off, carry-over, carry-back, credit or loss
or gain, or otherwise, which may be available to the Bank)
which (after deduction of all taxes, fees, or other charges
required to be paid by the Bank in respect to the receipt of
such amount under the laws or regulations of the United
States or any taxing authority thereof) will be equal to any
interest (other than additional interest resulting from a
Notice of Taxability as set forth above), penalties, tax
obligations or additional taxes imposed on the Bank with
respect to the loan evidenced hereby under any section of
the Code which are assessed against the Bank with respect
to an Event of Taxability or a "Prohibited Transaction" as
defined under the Code and the Employee Retirement Income Security Act of 1974, as amended ("ERISA").

(c) As used herein, an Event of Taxability shall mean:
(i) a judicial decision by any court, a determination by the
IRS or an amendment of Section 133 of the Code, in any
case which provides that more than 50 percent of the interest payable on the Term Note is includable for federal income tax purposes in the gross income of the Bank; (ii)
Borrower, the Employee Stock Ownership Plan (the
"ESOP"), the plan administrator appointed under the
ESOP or the trustee of the trust established under the
ESOP (the "ESOT") is advised that the ESOP is not a
qualified employee stock ownership plan under ERISA or

the Code or has violated any provision of the Code or
ERISA or any regulation promulgated thereunder which
directly or indirectly regulates or affects employee stock
ownership plans; (iii) a judicial decision by any court which
holds that the ESOP is not a qualified employee stock
ownership plan under ERISA or the Code; or (iv) Section
133 of the Code is repealed and is not replaced by a similar
statute.

FIVE

Financial Aspects of ESOPs*

Robert W. Smiley, Jr.

*The author gratefully wishes to acknowledge the help of Stephen C. Diamond, Senior Vice President, First National Bank of Chicago, and Leonard S. Caronia, Senior Vice President, U.S. Capital Markets, First National Bank of Chicago, whose review and comments were invaluable. Limited parts of this material originally appeared in *Leveraged Buyouts*, edited by Stephen C. Diamond, written by Stephen C. Diamond and Leonard S. Caronia, Copyright © 1985, Dow Jones-Irwin. Reprinted by permission of the publisher.

Robert W. Smiley, Jr., prior to founding Benefit Capital, Inc., founded Benefit Systems, Inc., a Los Angeles-based firm providing ESOP services nationwide. He is also the founder and past president of the ESOP Council of America—a non-profit trade association of ESOP companies now called The ESOP Association. Mr. Smiley is a lifetime honorary director and serves as a member of the Executive Committee. The Association actively promotes cooperation between government, industry, and the professions involved with ESOP financing.

In 1982 Mr. Smiley was the original organizer and principal founder of Brentwood Square Savings and is its immediate past chairman. He was also a co-founder and organizer of Liberty National Bank, which is today the largest bank provider of Small Business Administration loans in California and one of the largest providers of such loans in the nation.

Mr. Smiley received his A.B. in Economics from Stanford University, holds an M.B.A. in Corporate Finance from City University Los Angeles, and an LL.B. from LaSalle University, Chicago. He serves on the faculty of the University of California Los Angeles (UCLA) Extension. He also serves on the boards of several corporations, both public and private. He is a frequent speaker and a nationally published author.

In 1984, in recognition of his contribution to pension policies in the United States, he received the President's Special Achievement Award from the President's Commission on Pension Policy.

FIVE

ESOPs are being financed successfully at an accelerating rate. When an ESOP transaction is properly done, the risks are generally lower than in a conventional non-tax-shielded purchase. This chapter discusses the process of financing or leveraging an ESOP. Aspects of both secured and unsecured financing are considered, including sources of financing, arranging financing, complexity and cost of financing, company and lender expectations, and approaching lenders.

SOURCES OF FINANCING

Financing is usually obtained from one or more institutional investors:

1. Secured lenders.
2. Unsecured lenders.
3. A consortium of lenders, such as banks, savings and loans, insurance companies, leveraged buyout funds, venture capitalists, and other equity and debt sources combining to provide the unsecured financing and equity.

As a user of these sources, a company has two primary alternatives: (1) working through an ESOP investment banker/consultant /loan packager or money finder/ broker to arrange the financing or (2) seeking to package the financing itself.

If the funding is to be 100 percent secured, the company should probably seek the financing itself. A finder can direct the company to the right lending source, but, with a moderate investment of time, the company can find the source itself. Furthermore, the company's accountant can probably provide this service at a cost considerably below a finder's fee. The company simply needs to convince a lender that it can pay the money back, that the transaction is not a fraudulent conveyance, that the money will be used for a good purpose, and that, because it is an ESOP loan, the company should get a lower interest rate, based on the tax savings to the lender through Internal Revenue Code Section 133's exclusion of 50 percent of the gross interest income on an ESOP-related loan. (Not all secured lenders can use the tax benefits currently, although most are optimistic about the future.) If the ESOP will be used to purchase newly issued shares of stock in the company to provide new capital for expansion or for working capital, then the lender only needs to be convinced that this is a good purpose and that the money will be repaid out of the increased earnings and cash flow (and/or currently available cash flow) over the term of the financing.

Structuring the financing on an unsecured basis, however, requires an immense degree of sophistication to determine the appropriate amount of equity capital, subordinated debt, and senior debt that the company rationally can carry. Unless the company is extremely knowledgeable and experienced, it will not possess the skills to propose the optimal financing package. The company instead should work through a professional packager, such as an ESOP investment banker or the corporate finance department of a commercial or investment bank. (However, these bank departments may not have the experience necessary for the company's situation, and they are often hampered by institutional constraints.)

ARRANGING THE FINANCING

In arranging financing, a company and investors are generally seeking to achieve several conflicting goals and must trade off among them:

1. Most important, the parties want to secure the loan. The old story of the miller who has underpriced the market on flour, but is always out of flour, is analogous; the cost of financing is immaterial if the financing sources cannot deliver.

2. Next, the parties normally want to arrange the lowest payment required to service the debt. Since this is a function of the interest rate and principal repayments, the parties should seek the lowest rate and the longest amortization term available (without a prepayment penalty). In a fully leveraged transaction, several of the parties to the transaction are interested in maximizing their upside potential. Logically, each party would want to retain as much of the equity as possible in order to maximize its own return.

3. Finally, the parties must have a financing source that will truly understand their problems and the company's business, will be supportive when appropriate, and will not hit the panic button when inevitable problems arise.

Essentially, the company and other equity parties want to complete the transaction as quickly and inexpensively as possible, with as little dilution of stock and as much of a comfort factor as possible. The financing source, on the other hand, wants to make sure that it has an acceptable risk and an adequate risk/reward payback: the greater the degree of its perceived risk, the more likely will be its insistence on a piece of the action. Understandably, the optimal trade-off between positive and negative aspects of the transaction and the lender's comfort with the credit varies with each transaction.

COMPLEXITY

The less complicated the structure of the transaction, the easier it is to obtain financing. A secured transaction usually involves only three parties: the buyer (generally the ESOP and the company's management), the seller, and the secured lender. An unsecured deal, on the other hand, increases in complexity because different layers of financing are added. Because of its relative simplicity, a secured transaction can be completed more quickly than an unsecured transaction. This type of transaction may be pursued first because it usually leaves the buyer with more equity, and consequently a greater positive potential exists for the buyer. In a secured transaction, the debt service may carry a higher stated interest rate than in an unsecured transaction with equity kickers, but there is some flexibility in the minimum fixed amortization. Also, because the loan is collateralized, the lender may be more ready, able, and willing not to call in the loan or to provide more cash in the event of a temporary downswing in the company's cash flow.

Secured financing has major advantages in smaller transactions, but, as transactions become larger, the likelihood of adequate collateral coverage decreases. This is especially true if the purchase price involves a significant premium over book value. Even lenders who stretch will require some additional payment for their real or perceived incremental risk. The greater the premium over book value and the less tangible the asset base of the transaction, the greater the difficulty in finding a secured lending source.

Finding an unsecured lending source for a small transaction is like searching for the Holy Grail. If the transaction is much below $15 million and secured financing cannot be obtained, it will take a *very* long time to arrange unsecured financing.

COST OF THE FINANCING

Every lender states its charges differently, so it is important to determine the effective interest rate. For example, a prime financing charge on a $5 million facility can be more expensive than a prime-plus-two charge if the prime lender also charges a $50,000 closing fee and a $50,000 per year facility fee and requires compensating balances. Keeping the deal on the books and on the lender's books is also important, and so cost is not the only criterion.

As a rough rule, for most nonESOP transactions, asset-based financing has a target rate of return of a 1 to 4 percent spread over prime plus administration costs and sometimes includes an equity kicker in the form of warrants, cheap common stock, or a percentage of cash flow if the credit requires any relaxation of standards on collateral. Senior bank debt normally requires a commitment fee plus a 1 to 3 percent spread over prime and will rarely include an equity kicker. Fixed-rate senior and subordinated debt, which can be obtained from insurance companies, pension funds, and mezzanine buyout funds, normally aim for at least a 20 to 35 percent compound return on investment, including both the return from rate as well as its negotiated equity. (Mezzanine financing in a leveraged acquisition is special debt or equity participation making up the difference between available financing and the purchase price.) Preferred stock or subordinated debt will usually be available from the institutional variety of venture capitalists, who will look for returns similar to mezzanine buyout funds. However, some mezzanine buyout funds and some insurance companies are looking for at least a 35 to 50 percent compound return on investment from their stated loan rate including equity. Common stock, which can be sold to special leveraged buyout funds and venture capitalists, normally requires a minimum of a 50 percent compound return on investment, entirely from equity. The most expensive money is generally money from venture capitalists.

The relative costs to the company and to the shareholders of an equity investment are quite different, and the ongoing interest expense of debt clearly affects a leveraged company's chance for success more negatively than does an equity investment. If something goes wrong, an equity investment may be the least expensive form of financing, since, unlike a loan, equity does not get called in by nervous lenders.

WHAT SHOULD BE EXPECTED FROM A LENDER?

Lenders are like walking shoes: They may be highly rated and widely acclaimed, but that does not mean that they will fit everyone properly or be appropriate for everyone's pace. A company is entitled to be serviced by a lender that meets its qualifications, since the company is contributing to the lender's salary and revenue stream.

Unfortunately, a number of financing sources promise what they cannot deliver. Sometimes this is through ignorance. At other times, the lender is keeping the buyer on the hook, assuming that, as the time available to complete the transaction evaporates and the company has fewer options, the lender can "bait and switch" by restructuring the initial offer. A company must be certain that the lending institution has a reputation for delivering what it initially says it will and that the individual being dealt with has a similar reputation. This is equally applicable to those nameless faces within the institution who seem to be making the final decision on credit. If the company does not get to work with the people who make the final decision, then caution is advised. A faceless committee cannot be dealt with in a crisis.

In structuring the financing, the lending source must have *both* the ability to get the transaction completed and a willingness to stay with the company afterward. A company should be wary of a quick nod from the lender; the lender may have an even quicker finger on the trigger in the event of problems. No interest rate is low enough to compensate for the additional risk of having loans called. Almost no lender will be 100 percent loyal through extreme problems. The best the company can hope for is a financing source that will have taken the time to understand the company's business and its business plan, can counsel the company after the transaction is complete, understands its concerns, and has loyalty and staying power if events do not materialize according to plans. If any doubts arise about a lender's loyalty, the company should talk to several loan customers as well as the lender's competitors.

A last word on documentation—a company is not protected through documentation but through its working relationship with the lender. Most documentation invariably favors the lender, and unless the company is General Motors, it is difficult to swing the paper pendulum the other way.

If the company finds a lender that can deliver what it promises and has loyalty and staying power, the company has arrived. If that lender charges an effective interest rate that can be supported by cash flow, the company should not look elsewhere to try to save a few extra basis points.

WHAT THE LENDER EXPECTS

Once the lender feels comfortable with the company and its people, meetings should be designed to answer three questions:

1. Does the company know and understand what it is doing in this transaction; that is, do the people know what they are buying?
2. Who is willing to be at risk?
3. Can enough funds be arranged to cover the difference between the payout (plus working capital

needs of the company) and the amount the lender
is willing to lend?

Do the Company's People Know What They Are Doing?

To a lender, risk protection is much more important than
profit potential. In a secured transaction, the lender will be
focusing first on what the company will look like immediately
after the leveraging, on its management team's plans, and on
its contingency plans in case of problems. For example, if the
company is a subsidiary of a major United States corporation,
will any critical strengths of the parent expire after the transaction is complete? If so, the company needs a conservative
business plan and very specific, realistic answers to these
questions: Will the company have the same sales as before?
Will the personal relationships between the company and its
customers continue? And what is the likelihood and effect of
losing particular customers or sets of customers? These vul-
nerabilities must be assessed accurately and carefully.

A company in this situation also needs to consider
some questions about production: What are the company's
relations with labor like? What about strikes? What are
capital expenditures going to be, and over what period of
time, to keep the company in a competitive position? If a
staff reduction has been projected, how detailed is the
projection and how realistic is this new cost structure?

A large interest load is being added in most highly
leveraged situations, and the lender will be interested in
knowing the company's sensitivity to interest rate changes.
(This is a good time for the company to talk to the lender
about insuring interest rate risk by hedging.) Any general
and administrative expense and the corporate overhead
burden levied by the parent company normally does not totally disappear. Services are often rendered by the parent
for this allocated expense, and the company will have to
answer probing questions about the cost of providing those
services in-house or through a third-party vendor.

Through such questions, the company's people explain
to the lender that the business and the risks involved are

understood and that the company is prepared to cope with these risks. If a particular question cannot be answered, the lender would probably prefer to hear that the issue has not been addressed instead of hearing the company bluff. These first meetings are designed to test the company personnel's knowledge base and credibility, and no one is expected to know all the answers.

Who Is Willing to Be at Risk?

In an ESOP transaction, the company stock is probably being purchased at fair market value, not at a deep discount. Therefore, the lender may not feel comfortable with less than adequate collateral. In today's pricing environment, the odds are that the price for the company carries a significant premium over collateral value, and, while there may be sufficient cash flow, there typically is not enough collateral on a fully collateralized basis. Therefore, the lender wants assurances that the buying group, including management and the employees, will not give up and toss in the keys if problems develop. These assurances are usually expressed in the form of one of three guarantees:

1. A full guarantee of payment under which the buyer unequivocally agrees to guarantee the total obligation of the purchase.
2. A full performance guarantee, under which the buyer unequivocally agrees to make good to the lender any shortfall, after a certain time to allow the lender to liquidate the collateral, with the guarantee being limited to the shortfall.
3. A limited performance guarantee, which limits both the maximum dollar exposure of the guarantor and the ability of the lender to call on the guarantee without first having proceeded against the collateral to realize the proceeds from it. Normally this guarantee will be limited to perhaps a 120-day grace period, and the lender will insist on

a waiver stipulating that it need not have exhausted its legal remedies before proceeding against the guarantor.

Whatever the form of the guarantee, the lender's major objective in the event of problems is the cooperation of the borrower in maximizing the value of the collateral. The key element is the significance of the guarantee to the borrower. For example, a $500,000 guarantee on a $20 million loan from an individual who has a net worth of $750,000 is realistically more collectible than a $20 million guarantee from the same individual. On the other hand, a $500,000 guarantee from an individual who has a $10 million net worth may be too insignificant to assure the required cooperation. The more buyers there are, or the more members of a management team involved, the less onerous the guarantees on any one individual; however, if the management group is to end up with a significant part of the equity, the key management employees will be asked, at a minimum, to give limited performance guarantees, either severally or jointly and severally.

Can Enough Funds Be Arranged to Cover the Difference?

To close the gap between the lender's collateral ratios and the total amount of cash required for the transaction, a company can turn to the following sources:

1. A combination of equity and/or subordinated debt supplied by investors.
2. A note or notes taken back by the sellers with repayment consistent with the company's cash servicing ability.
3. A temporary over-advance on collateral by the lenders.

This last alternative can be quite expensive, and the company can expect to pay a premium. Its size will depend on the length of time and degree of uncertainty of the payback as well as the condition of the company after the leveraging is in place. During negotiations, the company should keep in mind that a way must be found to repay lenders for perceived incremental risk.

SECURED FINANCING—WHO ARE THE PLAYERS?

Asset-based lending, commercial finance, and secured financing are all terms used in the marketplace to indicate a lender whose credit decision is based on collateral coverage and the ability to service interest, rather than on the cash flow of the company, to amortize principal. Lenders range across a broad spectrum, from those who look totally to collateral to those who look totally to the borrower's cash flow. Most lenders fit somewhere in between. The difficult part is for the lender and borrower to identify their respective positions and desires. Generally, small commercial banks, finance companies, and insurance companies tend toward the collateral approach, and the larger regional and money-center banks are more interested in cash flow than in collateral. The larger finance companies fall somewhere toward the center of the spectrum.

Asset-based lenders who base their decision on downside collateral coverage analyze collateral from a liquidating perspective. The rates of advance on collateral are based on ratios for accounts receivable that will be netted if the company ceases operations; inventories are figured at auction sale values, with no credit given for converting work in process to salable, finished inventory. Similarly, machinery and equipment will be valued at net realizable values in an auction atmosphere, and real estate values will be based on the most likely quick-sale price. Other intangible assets, including leasehold improvements, normally have little if any value. Over-advances are normally limited to very short periods and are only made if short-term cash flow projections support the repayment. While this very conservative approach has the advantage of enabling the lender to handle a temporary downswing without panicking, it has the disadvantage of limiting the company's chances of finding enough financing for many transactions. If in the worst case the company fails, the odds of any personal guarantee having to be called upon is remote, since the loan is adequately collateralized by business assets. Furthermore, upside equity rate sharing or equity participation normally is not required with such a lender.

On the other hand, the secured lender who relies primarily on projected cash flow can advance high levels on the borrower's assets, including large over-advances, but exacts a high price because of the risk involved in relying on the borrower to bail it out. The lender may even increase its loan during a temporary downswing, although it is more likely to attempt to force the loan down. Living through such a period poses a significant risk to a venture's continued viability, and any borrower's guarantees well may be called upon.

Deciding which secured lender to use is not easy. The ability to structure a transaction is a function both of the institutional strength of the lender and of the individuals who work for the lender. If a company gets involved with an institution that it feels comfortable with and an individual who can get the job done, the company will find that, after the deal is booked and the excitement has subsided, a sound structure has been arranged that will last until the debt is retired.

THE ESOP LEVERAGED BUYOUT— UNSECURED FINANCING

In an unsecured ESOP LBO, the acquisition is financed through the sale of equity securities to the ESOP and the sale of debt and equity securities to a group of lender and investor participants, often including management and in some cases nonmanagement and union employees. These unsecured lenders and investors rely almost exclusively on projected cash flow, and such financing is often called a "cash flow leveraged buyout." In this kind of buyout, the investors and lenders take a longer-term view of the business, sometimes providing financing with 7- to 15-year maturities and even fixed interest rates. Obviously, this has tremendous advantages for any highly leveraged company, since it permits a gradual debt amortization schedule that can be matched against projected cash flow. A fixed interest rate eliminates, and a rate "cap" reduces, the possibly disastrous consequences of increasing interest rates. If available, they should be considered seriously and weighed against the offsetting expense. Lenders and investors recognize that they take a substantial equity risk with such highly leveraged long-term unsecured financing, and they generally participate in the equity ownership of the company through an *equity kicker*. The kicker can be as little as 5 percent of the company's shares or as much as 80 percent, depending on the perceived risk, the desired return on investment, and sometimes upon competition among investors and lenders.

The major advantage of a leveraged cash flow buyout is that it allows the buyer to finance a purchase price in excess of the company's real asset or book value, with the only limit on the available financing being the company's ability to service debt and provide the required return on equity. Such financing is also appropriate when the buyer is one of a group of bidders competing against well-financed corporate buyers, because it allows the buyer to bid competitively regardless of asset values. An ESOP LBO buyer will normally be able to submit the winning bid, unless the corporate buyer is paying the extra premium that "strategic synergy" may be worth to it.

Debt financing in a buyout of this kind usually is left unsecured for two reasons: (1) most cash flow ESOP LBO investors do not have the staff necessary to manage an asset-based loan, and (2) the security is not critical to the investors. This leaves the assets of an otherwise highly leveraged company unencumbered and permits the borrowing firm to maintain favorable supplier, vendor, and trade credit terms. While this approach may seem naive, remember that in a long-term project there is little value in close monitoring of specific assets by the investor group. It is management's job to manage assets carefully to maximize cash flow. Besides, most sophisticated investors and lenders have provisions in their legal documentation to ensure that they become secured at least equally if assets are given to any other creditor.

In short, the unsecured cash flow ESOP leveraged buyout can provide financing well in excess of underlying asset values, offer a fixed interest rate, improve the firm's ability to finance through the trade, and provide a much longer debt repayment schedule. All of these factors significantly reduce the risk of a leveraged transaction.

How to Do a Cash Flow ESOP Leveraged Buyout

An ESOP investment banker or a sophisticated investor can help determine the feasibility of a cash flow leveraged buyout. To secure the money, the company needs good management, properly projected cash flow, and a good presentation of what it hopes to accomplish.

Management is probably the most important ingredient. Investors know that, no matter how closely they analyze a transaction, unanticipated events will occur, making the investors' success totally dependent on the skill, judgment, and action of management. That's why investors and lenders are eager to accept substantial ownership by management for what is generally a very small percentage of the purchase price. A commitment by employees through salary reductions or other means is also a significant plus.

The ability of management to project cash flow confidently and adequately is essential. Internally generated cash flow must be able to service the increased working capital and capital expenditures of increased revenue, research and development costs, and other considerations. Management must consider the influence of any downswings in cash flow. Other factors to consider are: (1) dependency on loyal customers and suppliers, (2) proper diversification of product lines, (3) production costs compared to competitors, (4) market share needed to minimize the impact of economic declines and price wars, and of course, (5) ability to increase prices incrementally as necessary.

What the company believes it can accomplish through the transaction is probably the most difficult concept to present to the lender. The company should consider these questions in presenting its hopes and dreams: How will this acquisition make the company different and enable it to reach projected goals? Can inefficient operations be improved? Can the firm enter new markets? Will it be free of parent company restrictions, resulting in increased earnings? Can low-earning assets be sold to raise cash for debt reduction? Has the parent company been charging excessive management fees or paying the owners excessive salaries or benefits?

In general, the more tangible the presentation and the more credible the company's story, the easier it will be to convince lenders and investors to finance the acquisition. The presentation and story are best constructed in a comprehensive, well-documented business plan and lending memorandum that build a recognizable, concrete case for significant cash flow increases. The business plan and lending memorandum will be discussed in more detail later in this chapter.

In an unsecured ESOP leveraged buyout, the capital structure can be created and tailored to match the projected cash flows and the equity investors' required rate of return as well as the lenders' tolerance for financial risk. The trade-offs and competing interests give rise to almost endless permutations, and professional advice in this critical area is essential. A poor capital structure can destroy an otherwise outstanding leveraged acquisition. Variables include how fast debt is paid, how cash builds up, what liquidity cushions are built into the structure, and when and how short- or intermediate-term bank debt is repaid. All of these variables must be traded off among several competing factors, including (1) the cost of financing, (2) the predictability of cash flow, (3) management's ability to manage a highly leveraged company, and (4) management's tolerance for risk and for the risk associated with floating rates. Going forward with a leveraged buyout on the assumption that it will be refinanced in the future is a very poor decision.

A general rule of all acquisitions: *Do not structure a long-term financing project with short-term debt.* The savings and loans that in recent years financed long-term mortgages with short-term certificates of deposit created their own crises and demises.

The most difficult trade-off is between the amount of equity and the amount of debt. Attaining that appropriate balance between risk and cost is a necessity, although the best solution is anything but obvious. Much work is involved in preparing extensive sensitivity analyses, "what ifs" designed to measure the impact of changes in revenue, margins, interest rates, economic factors, and the like. While this is detailed, time-consuming work if properly done, the result can be a long-term workable capitalization at the lowest possible cost.

PRICING THE ESOP LOAN

How does the lender price the ESOP loan? The business-risk factor, the single biggest element in a loan decision, is generally seen as the same for either a conventional transaction or an ESOP transaction. The same is true of collateral factors. Each lender has established certain criteria that are consistent with its concept of an appropriate risk/reward ratio. The lender's pricing analysis of an ESOP loan compared to a conventional loan, however, should differ considerably.

The lender must have the assurance that the company will pay sufficient funds into the ESOP to tax shelter the principal and interest debt service requirements. Generally, the loan is made to the company, which then "on loans" it to the ESOP. The ESOP's debt is repayable in pretax dollars, giving the company additional ability to repay the loan to the extent of the company's tax bracket. This reduces the risk of the loan, since the corporation is required to earn much less pretax profit to service the principal of the loan compared to after-tax requirements of principal on a conventional loan.

This reduction of risk can be illustrated by a comparison of debt coverage ratios. One ratio that measures the ability of a borrower to service both interest and principal of a conventional loan is the total coverage ratio, expressed as:

$$\frac{Net\ Profit\ before\ Interest\ \text{and}\ Taxes}{Interest\ +\ \dfrac{Principal\ Payments}{(1-Tax\ Rate)}}$$

Because principal payments are made with after-tax dollars, they are adjusted to correspond to the interest payments before taxes.

With the ESOP, the total coverage ratio is expressed as:

$$\frac{Net\ Profit\ before\ Interest,\ ESOP\ Contribution\ \text{and}\ Taxes}{Interest\ +\ ESOP\ Contribution\ +\ \dfrac{Principal\ Payments}{(1-Tax\ Rate)}}$$

The ESOP loan total coverage ratios are generally substantially higher over the amortization period than in conventional debt financing. In fact, comparison of the ratios in a large number of situations indicates that the lender will be able to increase the level of safety on the loans by more than 30 percent over the amortization period.

Obviously, ESOP financing results in lower net profit during the amortization period, since the sum of interest expense and the ESOP contribution exceeds the interest expense incurred in the conventional debt case. Despite the fact that net earnings are substantially less, cash flow coverage on total debt outstanding is significantly greater. Thus, in an ESOP scenario, net earnings are not always a true indicator of ability to service debt.

Because the principal of the company's loan to the ESOP is repaid with pretax corporate dollars, the cash flow coverage of the ESOP loan is substantially greater than with conventional debt. This increased coverage reduces a lender's risks and may enable the lender to make the loan.

The key point to stress in the use of leveraged ESOPs in a buyout transaction is the *tax shield*. The company is going to have to demonstrate to the lender a lower cash flow risk to get a better rate. Sometimes a relatively minor ESOP participation can make the difference in achieving financial viability for a buyout. Another point to stress in the case of divestitures involving unprofitable or marginally profitable companies is that additional advantages can be secured through labor concessions, which are sometimes easier to obtain when employees participate in the future ownership benefits of a healthier company. Also, ESOP financing techniques materially enhance the prospect of the success of a leveraged buyout while extending the excitement of capital acquisition to all employees. In fact, ESOPs make possible acquisitions otherwise impracticable because of inadequate cash flow and motivation only for key executives. An ESOP has the potential for improving employee stability, dedication, earning power, and capital well-being. All of these points can affect the rate and terms of a loan.

How ESOP Loans Are Priced under Internal Revenue Code Section 133

The Tax Reform Acts of 1984 and 1986 added and amended new IRC Section 133, which permits banks, insurance companies, mutual funds, and other qualified corporate commercial lenders to exclude from gross income 50 percent of the interest received with respect to a "securities acquisition loan." A securities acquisition loan is any loan to a corporate employer or ESOP, the proceeds of which are used to acquire certain employer securities for the ESOP.[1] This provision applies to loans used to acquire employer securities after May 23, 1984 or loans used to refinance such ESOP loans.

The 1986 Tax Reform Act extended the interest exclusion to "immediate allocation loans," which made the exclusion available in connection with nonleveraged ESOPs. A loan to an employer will qualify for the interest exclusion if the employer contributes stock to the ESOP equal in value to the amount of the loan within 30 days of the date interest begins to accrue on the loan, the stock is allocated to employees within 1 year, and the loan does not exceed a period of 7 years.

Certain loans do not qualify for the exclusion. These include: (1) any loan made between corporations that are members of the same controlled group of corporations and (2) any loan made between an ESOP and any person that is (a) the employer of any employees who are covered by the plan or (b) a member of a controlled group of corporations that includes such an employer.

In addition, if the loan is made to the employer rather than the ESOP, the legislative history indicates that the employer must, in turn, lend the proceeds to the ESOP on similar repayment terms. Alternatively, the loan to the ESOP may be repaid more rapidly than the company loan, provided the lender's loan is for 7 years or less. Regardless of whether the loan to the ESOP is direct or made via the employer, the ESOP must use the loan proceeds to purchase employer securities.

As with any analysis intended to benefit many different parties, it is sometimes difficult to provide one all-encompassing formula. The following analysis, however, will provide a general idea of the effect of the new provisions.

The primary effect of the interest exclusion for the lender will be a lower corporate tax. The current tax structure and rates for lenders are as follows and are effective July 1, 1987:

Taxable Income	*Tax Rate*
0 – $50,000	15%
$50,001 – $75,000	25%
over $75,000	34%

(There is an additional tax of the lesser of 5 percent or $11,750 on amounts over $100,000.)

As a result of the incremental tax structure, any benefit to be received from the 50 percent interest exclusion will be realized only to the extent of the commercial lender's incremental rate. Table 5.1 provides four examples. As they illustrate, it is not feasible to determine a lender's appetite for the partially tax-exempt interest based on general variables. Each such determination must be made in light of the lender's respective tax situation.

To be competitive, a lender might wish to surrender some or all of the tax benefits from the 50 percent exclusion to the borrower by way of reduced interest rates. This, of course, depends on other considerations in addition to tax, such as competitors' rates, available funds, cost of funds, market integration strategy, and others.

The following formula will enable a lender to determine the rate to charge on the borrowed funds, depending

Table 5.1
Examples of the Effect of Interest Exclusion on Lenders

	Lender A	Lender B	Lender C	Lender D
ESOP loans	$300,000	$1,000,000	$2,000,000	$4,000,000
Interest rate	10%	10%	10%	10%
Interest income	30,000	100,000	200,000	400,000
Exclusion rate @ 50%	50%	50%	50%	50%
Taxable interest	15,000	50,000	100,000	200,000
Other normally taxable income	10,000	35,000	100,000	500,000
Total taxable income	$25,000	$85,000	$200,000	$700,000
Federal tax	$ 3,750	$17,150	$ 61,250	$238,000
Normal federal tax	− 6,000	− 35,900	−100,250	−306,000
Reduction in tax	$ 2,250	$18,750	$ 39,000	$ 68,000

on the amount of benefit it wishes to surrender to the borrower. (This formula assumes an incremental tax rate of 34 percent.)

$$\text{Reduced Interest Rate} = \frac{\left(\begin{array}{c}\textit{Loan Amount}\\ \times \textit{Current}\\ \textit{Interest}\\ \textit{Rate}\end{array}\right) - \begin{array}{c}\% \textit{of Benefit}\\ \textit{be}\\ \textit{Foregone}\end{array}\left[\begin{array}{c}34\% \times 50\%\\ \textit{Exclusion}\end{array}\left(\begin{array}{c}\textit{Loan Amt.}\\ \times \textit{Current}\\ \textit{Interest}\\ \textit{Rate}\end{array}\right)\right]}{\text{Total Loan Amount}}$$

Assuming a loan of $3,000,000, current interest rate of 10 percent, and the desire to surrender 75 percent of the benefit to the borrower, the reduced rate is computed as follows:

$$\text{Reduced Interest Rate} = \frac{\left(\begin{array}{c}\$3,000,000\\ \times 10\%\end{array}\right) - 75\%\left[34\% \times 50\% \times \left(\begin{array}{c}\$3,000,000\\ \times 10\%\end{array}\right)\right]}{\$3,000,000}$$

The reduced rate would be 8.725 percent in the example. This rate would generate $38,250 less interest income but would be offset by tax savings of $51,041 of which $12,791, or approximately 25 percent, would be retained by the lender as additional income.

Table 5.2 highlights the increases in after-tax yields for ESOP loans under different marginal tax-rate assumptions. (The table is computed at a 10.5 percent prime rate, and the results will be different at different prime rates.)

Table 5.2
Increase in After-Tax Yield for ESOP Loans
at 10.5 Percent Prime Interest Rate (in basis points)

Interest rate discount (basis points offered by lender)	*Lender's marginal tax rate*				
	10%	*20%*	*30%*	*40%*	*50%*
0	53	105	158	210	263
50	5	60	115	170	225
100		15	73	130	188
150			30	90	150
200				50	113
250				10	75

Example: A lender with a 40 percent marginal tax rate, including state income tax, would ordinarily lend to a company at the prime rate of 10.5 percent. Instead, the lender lends to the company through an ESOP-related loan, allowing the lender to exclude 50 percent of its interest income. The loan is at 9.5 percent—a 100 basis point discount. As a result, the lender receives an after-tax yield of 7.6 percent, 130 basis points above a nonESOP loan.

APPROACHING THE LENDERS

A well-prepared business package and a well-prepared lending memorandum, detailing post-acquisition operations, are a definite plus in securing a loan. They can significantly improve response time, which may give a funding request a competitive edge. Also, a favorable impression reduces the perceived risk and may result in a lower interest rate. An elaborate strategic planning study is not needed, but all important points should be covered. All relevant ratios should be calculated, and interest coverage should be included.

Table 5.3 illustrates a table of contents of a well-prepared lending memorandum and Table 5.4 shows the essentials of a business plan. While it is true that certain

Table 5.3
Sample Table of Contents of a Lending Memorandum for a Manufacturing Company

Section

1.0 Introduction

2.0 History of the Company

3.0 Industry Overview

4.0 Products, Marketing and Distribution

    4.1 Company Products

    4.2 Customers

    4.3 Marketing Strategies

    4.4 Competition

    4.5 Marketing and Sales Organization

    4.6 Pricing

    4.7 Distribution

5.0 Operations

    5.1 Specific Operations

        (a) Physical facilities

        (b) Equipment

        (c) Production Control

        (d) Quality Assurance

        (e) Production

    5.2 Subsidiaries

    5.3 Employees

6.0 Profiles of Management and Organizational Structure

7.0 Historical Financial Performance

8.0 Financial Projections

9.0   Structure of the Transaction

    9.1   Structure of the Debt

        (a)   Term Loans

        (b)   Revolving Line of Credit

        (c)   Operating Line

    9.2   Capital Expenditures

    9.3   Current Credit Facilities

10.0   An Overview of the Company ESOP Plan

    10.1   Retirement Plans

        (a)   Current Retirement Plan

        (b)   Profit-Sharing Plan

        (c)   Supplemental Benefit Plan

    10.2   Brief Description of the ESOP as a Technique of Corporate Finance

    10.3   Pricing of ESOP Loans

    10.4   Accounting Aspects of ESOP Buyouts

    10.5   ESOP Repurchase Liability

11.0   Professional Advisors and Other Information

    11.1   Company Advisors

        (a)   Auditors

        (b)   Counsel

        (c)   ESOP Investment Bankers

    11.2   ESOP Professional Advisors

        (a)   ESOP Counsel

        (b)   ESOP Valuation Firm

        (c)   Independent Fiduciary

12.0   Litigation

lenders focus on certain sections of these documents, all lenders agree that evidence of a capable and dedicated management must be incorporated in any viable document.

A well-conceived business plan and lending memorandum should be supplemented by information about the company prepared by disinterested third parties, such as outside studies, independent appraisals, and articles about the company and industry in which it competes. A summary page or pages of the loan request go a long way toward making the company's case quickly and clearly. This information helps the lender understand the business and substantiates and proves statements and assumptions in the package. When projections are more promising than a concern's past performance, the package should specify what will be done, when, and the resulting cash flows to achieve these unproven levels of performance. Lenders want to believe in the company. Overly optimistic projections, however, will result in an instant loss of credibility. Projections should not be too conservative either, because

---

Table 5.4
Sample Table of Contents for a Thorough Business Plan

Executive Summary

Business Description

Market Analysis

Product/Services Description

Marketing Strategy

Operations Description

Management and Organization

Timing of Key Events

Financial Information

Financial Requirements

---

the additional automatic discount the lenders apply will tell them the company can't afford the loan. Project these three scenarios: Optimistic (not best case), most likely, and pessimistic (but not worst case).

Lenders also are concerned about any possible fraudulent conveyance. The net effect of certain leveraged acquisitions is to benefit the shareholders of the leveraging company while encumbering its cash flow and assets with an obligation that was incurred without the leveraging company's receiving a direct benefit. The lender wants to be certain that the business is solvent before and after the transaction and financially viable going forward.

Timing is another important factor. Most lenders prefer to be approached when a thorough package has been prepared. Analyzing a credit is a complex, time-consuming task and can't be done properly without all the information—so the company should be prepared. Preliminary meetings don't hurt, however, especially if the buying group lacks financial knowledge and professional assistance.

Lenders expect buyers to contact several institutions, and most acknowledge that a competitive situation on a good deal works to the buyer's advantage. However, the company should not shop extensively. The key, of course, is knowing which institutions to contact, what to expect, and how to present the company's case positively and effectively.

NOTE

[1]   IRC §409(a)(1).

SIX

Accounting for ESOP Transactions by the Plan Sponsor

Rebecca J. Miller, CPA

Rebecca J. Miller, CPA, is the partner in charge of the Employee Benefits Consulting Services sector of McGladrey & Pullen. McGladrey & Pullen is a national accounting firm with over 70 offices from New York to San Diego. Their practice focuses on providing audit, tax and consulting services to the closely-held business community.

Mrs. Miller has a B.A. in Economics and an M.B.A. is accounting, both from the University of Minnesota. She is a member of the AICPA, the Minnesota State Society of CPAs, the American Society of Pension Actuaries, the ESOP Association of America and the National Center for Employee Ownership. For four years, she chaired the administrative advisory committee of the ESOP Association. She is the author of the AICPA's training guide on ESOPs and an adjunct professor on deferred compensation for the University of Minnesota's Masters of Taxation program. In addition, Mrs. Miller is a popular speaker and has regularly appeared on forums sponsored by Prentice Hall Law & Business, the Bureau of National Affairs and various state CPA societies.

SIX

The long-standing accounting guideline for ESOP sponsors has been *AICPA Statement of Position 76–3 (SOP 76–3)*. That position was published more than 12 years ago, during a period in which ESOPs were not nearly as prevalent. The SOP covered the majority of the issues until the 1984 and 1986 Tax Acts were passed.

These recent legislative changes have required the accounting community to rethink the reporting rules of the SOP. *SOP 76–3* was intended for the classic application in which the ESOP borrows the funds, obtains a corporate guarantee, and then either invests the funds in newly issued stock of the corporation or acquires already outstanding stock. Recent developments—the use of ESOPs in leveraged buyouts, the rollover of defined benefit plan reversions to ESOPs, and the two-step or mirror ESOP loan—were not contemplated when *SOP 76–3* was drafted. Therefore, new rules are being developed to handle these transactions.

Some of these rules can be developed immediately by analogy to current authority. In this work, the Emerging Issues Task Force (EITF) is one of the main players. The EITF was organized in 1984 by the Financial Accounting Standards Board (FASB). Its purpose is to address and resolve many of the new problems that confront practitioners every day in dealing with the dynamic financial environment. The task force consists of 17 members—11 practicing CPAs, 4 representatives from major industrial companies, an observer from the Securities and Exchange Commission, and a representative from the FASB. The

EITF meets monthly to cover issues presented by its members or other accounting professionals. If it can reach a consensus opinion based on current accounting authority, that opinion becomes the Generally Accepted Accounting Principle (GAAP) on that matter. It takes a vote of 15 to reach a consensus opinion.

The EITF has reached a consensus of the accounting for the transfer of a defined benefit plan reversion to an ESOP. Other areas, notably the leveraged buyout, may ultimately require the development of new accounting pronouncements. This process could take years, and the current accounting treatment for the more complex LBOs is somewhat in disarray. The EITF has been grappling with the issues associated with LBOs since 1986. Although they have reached consensus on certain LBO structures, there is no uniform principle. Particularly problematic is the accounting for LBOs that involve ESOPs. Parties considering an LBO should bring their accounting firm to the table early to attempt to structure the deal in a manner that will present the most favorable accounting treatment without sacrificing any other goals. This chapter looks at the current state of ESOP reporting for LBOs as well as less controversial ESOP issues.

TRADITIONAL LEVERAGED ESOP RULES

The ESOP application considered when *Statement of Position 76–3* was drafted is typified by the following facts:

- The Employer establishes an ESOP.
- The ESOP borrows $1,000,000 from a lender.
- The Employer guarantees to make contributions sufficient to fund the debt.
- The ESOP purchases $1,000,000 in newly issued stock from the employer.
- The first year's contribution consists of $100,000 interest expense and $100,000 principal amortization.

The impact on the employer's balance sheet is illustrated in Table 6.1.

Assets. The ESOP's assets, including any stock of the employer, are not included in the assets of the corporate sponsor.[1]

Liabilities. ESOP debt is recorded as a liability on the books of the corporate sponsor, if the sponsor company either *guarantees* the debt or *commits* to make future contributions to the ESOP sufficient to meet the debt service requirements. This accounting is based on the assumption that, in substance, the sponsor has assumed the ESOP's debt and the related obligation to service that debt.[2]

This has to be one of the most controversial issues in ESOP accounting. However, if viewed from the perspective of the lender, it does make some sense. The lender's primary criterion in evaluating a loan is the ability of the borrower to service the debt. The underlying value of the collateral is very important, but the lender hopes never to need to recover from that value. In the case of an ESOP, the ability to service the debt is based on the plan sponsor's financial position, not the ESOP's.

Recently, a plan sponsor attempted to circumvent these restrictions by providing that the ESOP could sell its shares to make payments on the loan. Although this language may have been sufficient to circumvent the application of *SOP 76–3* and avoid the recording of the debt on the balance sheet, the accounting community was not required to deal with the matter. The IRS issued a private letter ruling that held such an arrangement violated the terms of the ESOP regulations and would result in the plan not being considered an ESOP and, therefore, not eligible for all the related tax incentives.[3]

Equity. The impact of a leveraged ESOP on the equity section of the corporate sponsor's balance sheet is the mirror image of its impact on the liabilities section. A contra

Table 6.1
Balance Sheet Using Traditional Leveraged ESOP Rules

Balance Sheet—PreESOP

		Accounts Payable	$ 30,000
		Bank Debt	10,000
		Total Liabilities	$ 40,000
		Stockholders' Equity	$ 70,000
		Total Liabilities and	
Total Assets	$110,000	Stockholders' Equity	$110,000

Balance Sheet—PostESOP

		Accounts Payable	$ 30,000
		Bank Debt	10,000
		ESOP Debt	*1,000*
		Total Liabilities	$ 41,000
		Stockholders' Equity	$ 71,000
		ESOP Contra Account	*(1,000)*
		Total	
		Stockholders' Equity	$ 70,000
		Total Liabilities and	
Total Assets	$111,000	Stockholders' Equity	$111,000

Balance Sheet—PostESOP Year Two
No changes except payment of principal on ESOP note.
Assume no profit or loss before contribution of principal
(compensation expense) and interest.

		Accounts Payable	$ 30,000
		Bank Debt	10,000
		ESOP Debt	*900*
		Total Liabilities	$ 40,900
		Stockholders' Equity	$ 71,000
		ESOP Contra Account	*(900)*
		Current Year's Loss	*(200)*
		Total	
		Stockholders' Equity	$ 69,900
		Total Liabilities and	
Total Assets	$110,800	Stockholders Equity	$110,800

equity account is established to reflect the obligation recorded in the liabilities section. As the debt is retired by the ESOP, the contra account is reduced symmetrically.[4]

In cases in which the ESOP acquires newly issued shares, this is not a severe consequence. The equity section is increased by the amount of the newly issued stock. This effect is offset by the creation of the ESOP contra equity account.

The journal entry to record the above transaction would be as follows:

Cash	$1,000,000	
ESOP Contra Equity Account		
Unearned Compensation	$1,000,000	
Guaranteed ESOP Indebtedness		$1,000,000
Paid in Capital		$1,000,000

As the loan is retired the equity section increases.

However, if the ESOP acquires stock that is already outstanding, more dramatic consequences may arise. In many cases, the ESOP contra equity account can result in a negative equity section for the plan sponsor. This occurs because the equity section on any balance sheet is based on historical costs. It does not reflect the current market value of the stockholders' interests. Therefore, when the ESOP acquires a significant interest in the corporation at current market prices, the amount of debt used frequently exceeds the total historical equity.

To the sophisticated lender, this alone does not present a problem. It is similar to the situation experienced when the company repurchases shares into treasury stock. However, this consequence must be recognized when the transaction is structured. It may require that other loan agreements be amended to revise certain ratio tests. Also, any contracts that refer to the company's "book value" must be reviewed. For example, it is not uncommon in controlled corporations that a buy-sell agreement exists between shareholders. Commonly, that agreement reflects a purchase price based upon the company's book value. Alternatively, there may be some kind of executive compensation package based upon the book value of the business. These types of contracts usually need to be modified after a leveraged ESOP is installed. Frequently, the changes can be minor, that is, simply basing such tests on the company's ratios without regard to the booking of the ESOP debt.

Occasionally, the recording of the ESOP debt and the offsetting contra equity account are simply not acceptable. Unfortunately, there is no easy, surefire method of avoiding this effect. Accountants are trained to be conservative in their approach to the recording of financial transactions. Therefore, when the ultimate source of the debt service is going to be the corporate plan sponsor, it is likely that the debt will be recorded on its books. It will not matter how artfully the loan papers are drawn or what kind of legal language is used rather than the terms "guarantee" or "commit." This is not to say that it is impossible to keep the debt off the books of the corporate plan sponsor. Any such result, however, will be factually very specific and rare.

Once the debt is recorded on the balance sheet, it becomes necessary to classify it between current and long-term indebtedness. In most cases the current portion is reflected in the accrued contribution to the plan, but not always. It is not unusual for there to be monthly payments on the ESOP loan. This will mean that the current portion of the debt includes a portion of the following year's plan contribution. This does not present any problem.

Frequently the entire current year's contribution to the plan is made after the end of the fiscal year. When this occurs, concern is raised over the possibility of having to book the liability twice—once as an assumption of the ESOP's debt and once as an accrued contribution. This does not occur. The entries can be illustrated as follows:

Facts: Current ESOP contribution is $100,000 principal and $100,000 interest.

To record the accrual:

Compensation Expense	$100,000	
Interest Expense	$100,000	
Accrued Contribution to ESOP		$100,000
Accrued Interest		$100,000

Once the contribution is made, the following entry is made to eliminate the accruals and to reflect the adjustments in the ESOP debt and the contra account.

Accrued Contribution to ESOP	$100,000	
Accrued Interest	$100,000	
ESOP Debt	$100,000	
Cash		$200,000
Contra Equity Account		$100,000

Because this entry is not recorded until the payment is actually made, the debt is recorded twice. However, only one element is reflected in current liabilities. Few plan sponsors consider that to be satisfactory. This is another area in which advance planning might be helpful to control the timing of debt service requirements.

Dividends. Dividends paid on ESOP shares are not compensation expenses. They are charged to retained earnings, just as dividends paid to any other stockholder.[5] Under this general rule, it does not matter whether the dividends are paid on allocated or unallocated shares or if they are used to make debt service commitments or distributed to plan participants. At the time *SOP 76–3* was drafted, some practitioners believed that the dividends paid on any unallocated shares should be an element of compensation expense. This belief has recently won recognition on certain other ESOP applications (such as on excess contributions to a plan, *EITF Issue 86–27*). However, any effort to report dividends as compensation expense on a transaction that is recorded following the SOP would be a divergence from GAAP.

The 1984 and 1986 tax acts provided for tax deductible dividends to the extent that such dividends are paid into an ESOP and distributed to participants or used to amortize an ESOP loan. Under *SOP 76-3*, these dividends are still dividends—chargeable to retained earnings, not compensation expense. However, a tax benefit may be realized on these payments (because of the potential impact of the alternative minimum tax). Under the new accounting rules covering the reporting of income taxes, the tax benefit from these dividends is to be recorded as an adjustment to the income tax expense of the period.[6] Prior to the effective date of these new rules, the tax benefit from these dividends did not reduce the current income tax provision. Rather, it was credited to retained earnings.[7]

Profit or Loss. A significant disagreement arose in the accounting profession over the reporting of the contribution to a leveraged ESOP. The GAAP position is that the interest element must be reported as interest expense and the principal portion is to be reported as compensation expense. This segregation reflects the view of the ESOP loan as an obligation of the plan sponsor. The nonGAAP, minority view was to report the entire contribution as compensation expense. This treatment is not appropriate if the plan sponsor intends a clean opinion on the financial statements.[8]

In the event a contribution is made to the plan in excess of what is currently deductible for income tax reporting, the full amount is considered a deduction for financial statement purposes. The difference must be taken into account as a timing difference in measuring the current and deferred income tax liabilities.

Earnings per Share. The SOP's conclusion is that all shares contributed to an ESOP must be shown as outstanding shares.[9] In this case, the minority opinion, although not

representing the GAAP position, does have some significance.
The minority view was that only the unencumbered, that is,
allocated shares should be treated as outstanding. This
minority view has won approval for other types of ESOP
transactions. (See the reporting for the transfer of excess
assets from a defined benefit plan to an ESOP.) Perhaps the
minority perspective from the SOP may also become GAAP in
other areas as the uses of ESOPs become more complex.[10]

Footnote Disclosure. A general consensus of accounting
authority recommends disclosure of the following information:

- Plan description, including the purpose,
  qualified status, vesting provisions, contribution formula, and description of the
  employer's securities held by the plan.
- ESOP loan description, including the terms,
  interest rate and payment commitments,
  guarantee terms, covenants, and so on.
- Disclosure of the determination method, the
  amount of compensation expense, and the
  amount of interest expense.
- The shares purchased by the plan at the
  balance sheet date and during the reporting
  period, including their origin.
- Disclosure of the repurchase commitment on
  nontraded, distributed shares. To the extent
  that shares have been put to the employer
  before the end of the fiscal year, the liability
  would have to be booked, not just footnoted.
  Under current accounting authority, there is
  no requirement to record the projected repurchase liability, even if the amount is significant.

MIRROR LOAN TRANSACTION

The special terms applicable to ESOP loans and the special incentives available to ESOP lenders make the mirror or *back-to-back* ESOP loan one of the most common lending structures. In this type of loan, the lender advances the funds to the plan sponsor. The plan sponsor then makes a loan to the ESOP under virtually identical terms. Initially, the staff of the Financial Accounting Standards Board did not believe that *SOP 76-3* should apply to this situation. However, they have come to agree that the substance of a mirror loan is the same as a direct loan to the ESOP accompanied by a corporate guaranty. Therefore, the same accounting rules discussed previously will also apply to this situation. However, there is no published position on this scenario. Therefore, opinions of various accounting firms on this matter may vary.

The one item that must be noted in this case is the treatment of the note receivable from the ESOP to the corporate plan sponsor. Consistent with the reporting under *SOP 76-3*, the note receivable is treated as a contra equity account, not an asset. (No entry is needed to reflect the ESOP debt, since that is already recorded due to the direct loan to the plan sponsor.)

The problem arises in recording the entries for the plan contributions and interest. Normally, a note receivable would generate interest income. If that were recorded in this case, there would be a doubling of interest expense— the actual bank debt and the SOP treatment of the ESOP debt. In coming to net income, the interest income element from the ESOP note receivable would offset this overstatement. However, because of special capitalization rules for interest expense (inventory accounting, self-constructed capital assets, etc.), there could be a material difference under this approach in contrast to a direct loan. Therefore, the rules of *SOP 76-3* should be specifically applied, with the result being the recording of no interest income. The interest income on the note receivable is not to be recorded as interest income, rather it is a reduction in the interest expense. Therefore, the net effect will be identical to a direct loan to the ESOP. Table 6.2 illustrates this situation under the same circumstances as shown in Table 6.1, except that the employer borrows $1,000,000 from a bank and loans it to the ESOP under identical terms.

When the first year's debt service payments are made, the following entries should be recorded:

To record contribution from plan sponsor to ESOP.

Compensation Expense	$100,000	
Interest Expense	$100,000	
Cash		$200,000

To record the receipt of the ESOP's payment on its note.

Cash	$200,000	
Contra Account—ESOP Receivable		$100,000
Interest Expense		$100,000

To record the payment to the lender.

Note Payable	$100,000	
Interest Expense	$100,000	
Cash		$200,000

The net effect is an entry of $100,000 compensation expense and $100,000 interest expense in the same manner as a direct loan to the ESOP.

TWO-STEP ESOP LOAN TRANSACTION

The two-step loan is the same as the mirror loan transaction, except that the loan terms are not the same. (Please note, this does not necessarily mean that the ESOP loan will not be at tax-advantaged interest rates. The rules under IRC Section 133 leave some room for dissimilar loan terms if the loan to the corporation is for a period of no more than 7 years.) In this area, the FASB staff has apparently not reached a firm conclusion. Also, the EITF has not specifically addressed this issue. Therefore, again, this discussion covers the interpreta-

Table 6.2
Balance Sheet for Two-Step ESOP Loan

Balance Sheet—PreESOP

		Accounts Payable	$ 30,000
		Bank Debt	10,000
		Total Liabilities	$ 40,000
		Stockholders' Equity	$ 70,000
		Total Liabilities and	
Total Assets	$110,000	Stockholders' Equity	$110,000

Balance Sheet—PostESOP

		Accounts Payable	$ 30,000
		Bank Debt	11,000
		Total Liabilities	$ 41,000
		Stockholders' Equity	$ 71,000
		ESOP Receivable	*(1,000)*
		Total	
		Stockholders' Equity	$ 70,000
		Total Liabilities and	
Total Assets	$111,000	Stockholders' Equity	$111,000

Year two will be comparable to Table 6.1 unless compensation expense is charged for the fair market value of the shares allocated, not the principal payment. In that case the effect will be similar to Table 6.3.

tion of these rules by the author. Other accountants may come to a different interpretation.

It appears that the accounting for these transactions will depend on the degree of difference in the loan features. If the employer retains significant controls over the allocation of the shares to participants, the accounting will most likely vary from the rules discussed earlier. In this case, the transaction will be reported using the rules discussed in the following section, "Excess Contributions to Defined Contribution Plans." For example, if the loan from the plan sponsor to the ESOP was for 40 years, the employer has total discretion on potential prepayments of the note, the employer appoints the trustee, and the plan administrative committee directs the voting of the ESOP shares, the SOP would likely not apply. Instead, the loan would be recorded using the treasury stock method as covered in the discussion of excess contributions to defined contribution plans.

This difference in reporting approaches does not affect the recording of any assets or liabilities or the initial entry into the equity section. It will affect the measurement of the amount of compensation expense into any period and also the calculation of earnings per share. It addition, in limited circumstances, it may result in the reporting of dividends as compensation expense. If the treasury stock method is employed, the compensation expense will be measured by the fair market value of the securities actually allocated to plan participants during the year. This can lead to substantial differences from the SOP method in certain cases. For example, assume this is the first year of a 15-year loan. Under the loan amortization table, the current year's contribution would be $35,000 of principal and $115,000 interest. However, because it is a 15-year loan, the plan administrator must use the principal and interest method in releasing shares from collateral. This results in the release of one-fifteenth of the shares in this period. These shares are currently worth $70,000. If the transaction was accounted for under *SOP 76–3*, the compensation expense would be $35,000. Using the treasury stock method, the compensation expense is $70,000, instead. In later years, this effect might reverse, as principal becomes a disproportionate part of the total debt service. On the other hand, if the stock appreciates in value, the compensation amount may always be greater than the principal reduction.

The potentially negative impact on earnings is the bad news of this treatment. The good news is the impact on the measurement of earnings per share. Under the treasury stock method, only the allocated shares are treated as outstanding. Therefore, in the initial periods, when earnings might be lower due to the higher interest expense and so on, the number of shares outstanding is less.

EXCESS CONTRIBUTIONS TO A DEFINED CONTRIBUTION PLAN

Certain changes made by the Tax Reform Act of 1986 have made it very attractive to transfer all or part of the reversion from a defined benefit plan to an ESOP. For transfers attributable to plan terminations that were effective no later than December 31, 1988, IRC Section 4980(c)(3) exempts from penalty and tax a reversion that is transferred to an ESOP and allocated to plan participants within an 8-year period. The accounting community considers this fact pattern to constitute an excess contribution to the ESOP. That is, simply, a contribution that cannot or will not be allocated within a single plan year. Although the tax incentives for this transaction are scheduled to expire, the accounting treatment that was developed to handle this situation will have continuing impact on other transactions that possess similar attributes.

The reporting of this series of events is discussed in *EITF Issue No. 86–27, Measurement of Excess Contributions to a Defined Contribution Plan.* In general, the accounting for this transaction follows the treasury stock method.[11]

The application of the conclusion reached by the EITF is illustrated in Table 6.3A and 6.3B under the following facts:

- A reversion of $2,000,000 is received upon termination of a defined benefit plan.
- The full amount is transferred to an ESOP.
- One-fifth of the shares, or $400,000, is allocated in the first year.
- The stock has appreciated in value 5 percent by the time of the allocation.

Table 6.3A
Defined Benefit Plan Reversion Transferred to ESOP

Balance Sheet—PostESOP Gain on Reversion Is Included in Equity

		Accounts Payable	$ 30,000
		Bank Debt	10,000
		Total Liabilities	$ 40,000
		Stockholders' Equity	$ 72,000
		ESOP Contra Account	*(2,000)*
		Total Stockholders' Equity	$ 70,000
Total Assets	$110,000	Total Liabilities and Stockholders' Equity	$110,000

Table 6.3B
Defined Benefit Plan Reversion Transferred to ESOP (Assumes Operations Were at Break-even prior to Effect of ESOP on Profit or Loss Statement.)

Balance Sheet—PostESOP Year Two

		Accounts Payable	$ 30,000
		Bank Debt	10,000
		Total Liabilities	$ 40,000
		Stockholders' Equity	$ 72,020
		ESOP Contra Account	*(1,600)*
		Current Year's loss	*(420)*
		Total Stockholders' Equity	$ 70,000
Total Assets	$110,000	Total Liabilities and Stockholders' Equity	$110,000

Assets. The EITF initially considered showing the unallocated stock as an asset, prepaid compensation. This position was dropped in the final consensus for a transfer to an ESOP.

Therefore, there is no effect on assets. The exception might be in cases where the funds are temporarily invested by the ESOP in assets other than company stock and this temporary period spans a report date. If this is the case, an asset of the employer would be recorded. It would be accounted for at the lower of cost or market. This situation can occur because the tax provision grants the plan 90 days in which to invest the reversion funds into stock or to make a payment on a securities acquisition loan. When the stock is acquired, the asset is eliminated and the equity section adjusted.

Liabilities. In the set of facts presented to the EITF in developing their position there was no debt. The tax law, however, authorizes the ESOP to use the excess to make a payment on a securities acquisition loan. The EITF did not address this situation. Given that there is specific accounting authority covering each type of transaction, it is likely that the two transactions would be accounted for separately under the authority applicable to each.

Equity. To the extent that new shares were acquired by the ESOP with the reversion it received, equity would increase. However, this effect would be offset by the creation of a contra equity account for the unallocated portion of the shares acquired with the reversion funds. This contra equity account is recorded in the same way as treasury stock. If the reversion were used to pay off part of a securities acquisition loan, the equity section might be left with two distinct ESOP contra equity accounts: one for the remaining shares held as collateral on the securities acquisition loan and one for the unallocated shares attributable to the excess contribution reversion. As shares are allocated, this excess contribution contra account is reduced by the cost of the shares allocated.

The paid-in capital or capital stock accounts will be adjusted annually for any market value adjustments applicable to the shares allocated during the year for which the transaction is accounted, following the treasury stock method. If the shares have increased in value at the time they are allocated, paid-in capital will increase by the amount of that market value increase. Likewise, in the event the shares decline in value, paid-in capital will be reduced by the amount of the decline in value of the shares allocated during that accounting period. However, when looking at net equity, the effect of these market value adjustments is reduced because the compensation expense for the period undergoes the same market value adjustments. Thus, paid-in capital will increase with a market gain on allocated shares, but the compensation expense will be greater by the same amount, resulting in less net income. The bottom-line net equity, including earnings, is affected only by the tax consequences of the transaction.

If the dividends paid on the unallocated shares are to be invested in additional unallocated shares, they will increase treasury stock, that is, the contra account, rather than reduce retained earnings. If the dividends are allocated to participants as trust income, they should not be distinguished from other dividends, that is, charged to retained earnings. If dividends on allocated shares are distributed to participants, they are treated as normal dividends reducing retained earnings. If dividends are used to make scheduled debt service, they are accounted for as normal dividends. As discussed next, in certain limited cases, the dividends may be considered to be compensation expense.

Profit or Loss. This is the area in which the financial reporting may vary significantly from the SOP's rules. Under *SOP 76-3*, the compensation expense is measured by the principal payment on the ESOP debt. No adjustment is made for any change in market value of the shares actually released from collateral and allocated to the accounts of the participants.

In *Issue 86–27*, the EITF agreed that compensation expense should be measured by the fair market value of the shares allocated during the accounting period. For example, under the facts listed above, if shares with a current fair market value of $420,000 (historical cost $400,000) are allocated, the journal entry to reflect this would be as follows:

Compensation Expense	$420,000	
Contra Account (treasury stock)		$400,000
Paid-in Capital		$ 20,000

The use of the treasury stock method is based on the EITF's assumption that the plan sponsor retains significant attributes of ownership over the shares held by the ESOP. Thus, different elements of control by the plan sponsor may affect the accounting of this transaction. Frequently, the employer has control over how the shares are allocated due to its ability to limit the amount of the IRC Section 415 benefit available for use by the ESOP, that is, the required contributions to other plans. Also, under IRC Section 4980, the shares could return to the employer if the plan were terminated with an unallocated IRC Section 415 suspense account remaining. Finally, other incidents of ownership retained by the employer could be created by the plan and trust design.

However, in many cases, the employer may have little unilateral control over plan assets. For example, the transfer may have come from a plan that prohibited the excess returning to the employer. In this case, in the event of an early termination, the excess would still go to participants. Which accounting approach would apply to this scenario has not been resolved. This hypothetical situation illustrates how the accounting position expressed in *Issue No. 86–27* must be handled on a case-by-case basis.

In its April 1987 meeting, the EITF again referred to this concept of control. They justified the treasury stock reporting approach on the basis that the risks and rewards of ownership of the unallocated shares, ultimately reflected in compensation expense, are retained by the plan sponsor.

This is clearly the basis for this accounting approach. Therefore, where that fact is diminished or nonexistent, the financial presentation should be thoroughly researched. (*NOTE*: Under *Statement of Financial Accounting Standards No. 88*, the full amount of the reversion will already have been booked into income. Therefore, this transaction will have a net effect of a significant increase in book income.)

Dividends. In its August 20, 1987, meeting, the EITF added some new language to the discussion on dividends. It recognized that dividends paid to an ESOP might be deductible by the plan sponsor if the dividends are distributed to participants within the appropriate time frame or are used to repay an ESOP loan. The revised language provides that:

> Compensation expense should be charged for dividends paid to participants applicable to unallocated shares and retained earnings charged for dividends on the allocated shares. Any *prepayments* on ESOP debt using dividends on *unallocated shares accounted for as treasury stock pursuant to this consensus should be treated as compensation expense*. [Emphasis added.]

Thus, this provision is also applicable to dividends paid into a leveraged ESOP that are used to *prepay* the ESOP loan. This is only where the transaction is accounted for under the treasury stock method, rather than following *SOP 76–3*. This becomes relevant in structuring the loan transaction. A true mirror loan will be recorded following *SOP 76–3*. However, a two-step loan may be accounted for under the treasury stock method. Depending on whether deductible or nondeductible dividends are preferred, the structure will affect the accounting. In making this decision, the planners must look carefully at the language of the EITF; this treatment is limited to prepayments of debt.

Earnings per Share.   Again, there is a major difference in the accounting treatment in contrast to the reporting under *SOP 76-3*. The unallocated shares of the employer's common stock are treated as not outstanding for purposes of the computation of earnings per common share if the transaction is accounted for under the treasury stock method, as set in *Issue 86-27*. This consensus was determined not to conflict with the SOP, because the two cases are sufficiently different in facts to justify different accounting results.

The conclusions reached in *Issue 86-27* may have a broader application than simply the reversion case. For example, in the two-step ESOP loan, if the plan sponsor retains significant controls over the rate of release of the shares to the ESOP participants, it may become appropriate to consider only the allocated shares in the calculation of earnings per share. The same argument regarding the risks and rewards of ownership can be made. Thus, once again, the structure of the loan transaction can have significant impact on the accounting treatment.

LEVERAGED BUYOUTS

The accounting community has not yet reached a consensus on the proper accounting treatment of certain leveraged buyout transactions (LBOs). The focus of attention seems to be on determining the basis in corporate assets following the buyout. This chapter is not a forum for the discussion of basis adjustments in leveraged buyout transactions. Suffice it to say that controversy exists in this area, elements of which can be managed through properly structuring the transaction. The accounting for the ESOP transaction will follow either the rules of *SOP 76-3* or of *EITF 86-27*. Of course, new rules may apply once the controversy is settled. The following discussion simply highlights some of the considerations when an ESOP participates in an LBO.

Assets.   When the ESOP's involvement in the LBO has no direct impact on assets, the rules for leveraged ESOPs would be followed, whether it is a direct ESOP loan, a mirror loan, or a two-step loan. LBOs frequently do have an impact on asset values, however. When there is an 80 percent change in ownership or the corporation is acquired through the use of a new corporation, there may be basis adjustments in the carrying value of assets to reflect the actual market value of the stock. This effect is not unique to the ESOP LBO.

Liabilities. The presentation of the ESOP's debt would follow the rules just discussed.

Equity. There is dispute in the area of equity over the use of *SOP 76–3* and *APB–25* to cover ESOP participation in LBOs. This matter is discussed in *EITF Issue No. 85–11.* The basis of the controversy can be illustrated with the following example:

- A new corporation is formed by management and an ESOP.
- Shares of Newco. go one-third to management and two-thirds to the ESOP.
- Management contributes $5,000,000 in cash.
- The ESOP puts up $100,000,000, all borrowed.
- Newco. uses these funds to acquire all of the stock of Oldco.
- Oldco. becomes Newco.

The reporting for this transaction is illustrated in Table 6.4.

Current accounting authority would record this transaction following *SOP 76–3.* Shareholders' equity would show $105,000,000 of capital with a contra equity account of $105,000,000. However, there is a fair amount of support in the accounting community to rely upon *Accounting Principles Board Opinion 25* and record the ESOP's equity at the value of what it is apparently acquiring, not at the price paid. If we can assume that a one-third interest paid in cash is worth $5,000,000, then the ESOP's interest would be recorded at $10,000,000, not $100,000,000. This gives recognition to the fact that the ESOP shares are actually being paid for by the corporation, not the ESOP.

This example is probably unrealistic as the difference between the assumed value of $10,000,000 and the purchase price of $100,000,000 is extreme. However, it was chosen to illustrate the point. This is an aspect of the same problem that the Department of Labor is wrestling with in reviewing multiple investor LBOs in which ESOPs participate. There is a difficulty in reconciling what the ESOP pays with what it apparently receives. The accounting community is not outside of this dispute. However, for the cur-

---

Table 6.4
Balance Sheets for ESOP LBO Applying SOP 76-3

Balance Sheet—PostESOP

	Accounts Payable	$ 30,000
	Bank Debt	10,000
	Total Liabilities	$ 40,000
	Stockholders' Equity	$ 70,000
	Total Liabilities and	
Total Assets $110,000	Stockholders' Equity	$110,000

Balance Sheet—Postacquisition

	Accounts Payable	$ 30,000
	Bank Debt	10,000
	ESOP Debt	*100,000*
	Total Liabilities	$140,000
	Stockholders' Equity	$105,000
	ESOP Contra Account	*(100,000)*
	Total	
	Stockholders' Equity	$ 5,000
	Total Liabilities and	
Total Assets $145,000	Stockholders' Equity	$145,000

rent period, the GAAP approach is to follow the SOP or other applicable authority.

Profit or Loss.   The impact of the transaction on the profit or loss is a reflection of which method just discussed will ultimately be sustained. Under the current GAAP approach, the principal payments would be reflected as compensation expense because of the use of a direct loan to the ESOP. The interest element would be interest expense.

Under the alternate nonGAAP view, the interest remains interest. The compensation expense would be measured by the fair market value of the shares released from collateral and allocated during the year. Once more we see the treasury stock approach appearing.

Earnings per Share.   Again there is a contrast between the SOP, all shares outstanding, and the treasury stock method, only allocated shares are outstanding. The current GAAP method is to show all shares as outstanding.

ACCOUNTING FOR THE NONLEVERAGED ESOP

The accounting rules covering the sponsor of a qualified plan that invests significant assets in corporate securities are not too surprising. The plan is treated like any other shareholder with respect to purchases and sales of securities between the plan sponsor and the plan. Dividends are also reported in the same manner as another shareholder.

The major reporting issues arise with respect to contributions to the plan. If the contribution is to be paid in cash, any accrued contribution at year-end is to be reflected in the current liabilities. If the contribution is to be paid in stock after the balance sheet date, the contribution would be reflected by a disclosure in the equity section of the amount of new shares to be issued as part of the plan contribution. If the plan sponsor has not decided by the date the statements are issued whether the contribution is to be made in cash or stock, the liability would be booked with accompanying footnote disclosure of the possibility of the liability being satisfied with stock. In the event stock is contributed to the plan, the dollar value of the compensation element is measured by the fair market value of the stock on the earlier of the statement date or the transfer date.

CONCLUSION

It is clear that the accounting for ESOP transactions is undergoing a process of review, modification, and clarification. This is happening now because of the extreme popularity of ESOPs. The attention given to these transactions is good and has resulted in a refining of the accounting treatment, which, in turn, results in more realistic financial presentation. The accounting community is attempting to make the financial statements communicate to users the actual economics of the transaction. Like all technical areas, change leads to opportunity.

NOTES

[1] *Statement of Position 76–3*, paragraph 6. The reader should be aware that 76–3 was acknowledged as GAAP after the establishment of the Financial Accounting Standards Board in *SFAS 32*.

[2] *Statement of Position 76–3*, paragraph 5.

[3] *Private Letter Ruling 8828009*.

[4] *Statement of Position 76–3*, paragraphs 7 and 8.

[5] *Statement of Position 76–3*, paragraph 12.

[6] Paragraphs 75 and 141 of *SFAS 96*.

[7] *EITF Issue No. 86–4*.

[8] *Statement of Position 76–3*, paragraph 10.

[9] *Statement of Position 76–3*, paragraph 11.

[10] *Statement of Position 76–3*, paragraph 13.

[11] *APB. Opinion 25*.

SEVEN

ESOP Administration: A Practical Guide

Karen Bonn

Karen Bonn is Vice President of National Benefit Services, Inc. and has ten years experience as a consultant in the benefit and compensation area for publicly traded companies, closely-held companies, and not-for-profit organizations.

She joined National Benefit Services, Inc. in October 1980. Prior to becoming a member of the firm, she worked as an ERISA Legal Assistant at a major Chicago law firm. She was one of the first individuals to complete the Lawyer's Assistant Program at Roosevelt University in 1974.

Ms. Bonn has completed continuing professional education courses conducted by the American Society of Pension Actuaries and the Certified Employee Benefit Specialist Program of the Wharton School.

She has direct responsibility for major clients' employee benefit programs with respect to administration, consulting and employee communication services.

SEVEN

An employee stock ownership plan is arguably one of the most flexible and effective of all corporate finance and tax planning techniques. But after the dust settles and the deal closes, the ESOP becomes an employee benefit plan with all the attendant legal, accounting, tax investment, and human resource ramifications.

The administration of an ESOP is similar in most ways to the administration of any employee benefit plan; ESOPs must follow the general requirements for all benefit plans. But, in addition, there are some special requirements for ESOPs. This chapter serves as a guide for ESOP administrators to both the general and special regulations for ESOPs.

GENERAL QUALIFICATION REQUIREMENTS

Congress provided the first specific statutory authority for ESOPs as part of the Employee Retirement Income Security Act (ERISA) of 1974. In the Act, an ESOP is defined as an individual account plan (a) which is a stock bonus plan and money purchase plan both of which are qualified under Section 401 of the Internal Revenue Code of 1954 and which is designed to invest primarily in qualifying employer securities and (b) which meets other requirements as the Secretary of the Treasury may prescribe by regulation.

Therefore, like all employer-sponsored retirement plans, an ESOP must meet the requirements of the Internal Revenue Code for qualification with respect to par-

ticipation, vesting, benefit limitations, reporting requirements, and fiduciary standards.

Participation

Individual participation may be limited based on the satisfaction of certain age and service requirements. Generally, however, an employee who has attained age 21 must be eligible to
participate if he has met the other requirements. A plan is free
to provide for a lower age requirement or for no age requirement. Up to 1 year of service can be required before an
employee may participate in a plan. Two years of service
before participation can also be required if the employee
enters the plan fully vested after that time.

The Internal Revenue Code also requires the satisfaction of certain minimum standards involving the group of
employees covered by the ESOP. A comparison of the group
of individuals covered by the plan must be made with those
not covered to determine whether the plan has dis-
criminated in favor of the officers, shareholders, and "highly compensated" employees.

For purposes of this and other tests, the Tax Reform
Act of 1986, unlike prior laws, objectively defined "highly
compensated employee." The term *highly compensated*
refers to any employee who during the plan year or the
preceding plan year:

1. Was at any time a 5 percent owner of the company.
2. Received compensation in excess of $75,000, as
   originally enacted. (This number is subject to indexing to reflect inflation and in 1989 was
   $81,720.)
3. Was an officer of the employer and received compensation greater than 50 percent of the maximum
   annual benefit (in 1989, $49,032) applicable to
   defined benefit plans under Section 415 of the
   Code. (This situation is defined further under the
   section on "top-heavy" regulations.)

4. Was an employee who earned more than $50,000 (indexed to $54,480 in 1989) in compensation and was among the top 20 percent of all employees in terms of compensation.

The following categories of employees can be excluded in determining how many employees are in the top 20 percent:

1. Employees who have not completed 6 months of service.
2. Employees who normally work less than 17½ hours per week.
3. Employees who are included in a unit of employees covered by a collective bargaining agreement.
4. Employees who have not attained age 21.
5. Employees who are nonresident aliens and receive no U.S. earned income.

The Internal Revenue Code mandates that a qualified plan must meet one of three mathematical tests requiring broad coverage of employees. These are the precentage test, the ratio test, and the average benefit percentage test. These minimum coverage rules became effective for plan years beginning after December 31, 1988.

The Percentage Test. The plan must benefit at least 70 percent of all employees who are not highly compensated.

The Ratio Test. The percentage of nonhighly compensated employees covered by the plan must be at least 70 percent of the percentage of the highly compensated employees covered by the plan. If 100 percent of the highly compensated employees benefit under the plan, the percentage test and the ratio test are equivalent. Under both tests, 70 percent of the nonhighly compensated employees must be covered. However, if, for example, only 50 percent of the highly compensated employees benefit under the plan, the ratio test will be satisfied if at least 35 percent (50 percent × 70 percent) of the nonhighly compensated employees benefit under the plan.

The Average Benefit Percentage Test. The average benefit percentage test requires that (a) a plan must satisfy the prior law's nondiscriminatory cross-section test, using the new definition of highly compensated employees, and (b) that the average benefit provided for nonhighly compensated employees must be at least 70 percent of the average benefit provided to highly compensated employees.

If a plan is found not to be in compliance with the new minimum coverage rules, it will not be disqualified, unlike under prior law. Instead, the highly compensated employees under the plan will be taxed on the value of their vested benefits and the income on those vested benefits.

In addition to meeting the new minimum coverage rules, a plan must also meet minimum participation requirements. The Tax Reform Act of 1986 amends Section 401(a) of the Internal Revenue Code by adding Section 401(a)(26). This section requires that a plan, in order to be qualified, must on each day of the plan year benefit at least the lesser of 50 employees or 40 percent or more of all employees of the employer. This requirement must be satisfied by all plans on an individual basis. Employees who do not meet the minimum age and service requirements of a plan and those who are subject to collective bargaining can be excluded for purposes of this test. Plans that do not satisfy these minimum participation requirements must either be terminated or merged into another plan of the employer that meets the requirements. This new IRC section became effective the first day of the first plan year beginning after December 31, 1988.

Vesting

Once an employee becomes eligible to participate in the plan, benefits on termination of employment are determined by multiplying the participant's account balance by the appropriate vesting percentage. A plan must meet one of two alternative minimum vesting schedules. Rate of employee turnover is a major factor in chosing which vesting schedule to use. The benefits must either be (a) 100 percent vested upon completion of 5 years of service, but up until that time do not need to be vested at all, or (b) 20 percent vested after 3 years of service, with an additional 20 percent for each additional year of service and 100 percent vested after 7 years of service. An employee's years of service before age 18 and prior to the effective date of the plan can be excluded from the vesting schedules. Special vesting requirements apply to the plan in any year in which it is top heavy.

Benefit Limitations

Contributions made by the employer must be allocated to the participants using a formula in the plan document. Most plans use compensation as the basis for allocation, but some use a combination of compensation and service. Once the contributions are made, a plan's individual allocation provision must meet certain statutory limitations. These limitations are called the "annual addition" to a participant's account, which is the sum of employer contributions, employee contributions, and forfeitures. Generally, these limitations affect only the highly compensated employees. The annual addition to a participant's account is limited to the lesser of $30,000 or 25 percent of the participant's compensation. Under the Tax Reform Act of 1986, the $30,000 limitation was retained. This limitation applies in the aggregate to all individual account plans of the employer.

Indexing of the $30,000 limitation will not begin until the defined benefit plan limitation of $90,000 reaches $120,000 through indexing. In 1989, the defined benefit limitation of $90,000 increased to $98,064, a 8.96 percent increase since the effective date of this provision.

Top-Heavy Status

A defined contribution plan is *top heavy* if, as of the determination date, the total of the accounts of all key employees exceeds 60 percent of the total of the accounts of all employees. Two or more retirement plans may be required to be aggregated before the top-heavy definition is applied.

The determination date for a new plan is the last day of the first plan year. For an existing plan, it is the last day of the preceding plan year. For example, a calendar year ESOP established on January 1, 1989, would first be tested on December 31, 1989.

A top-heavy plan can only qualify for tax-favored status if it meets several special requirements in addition to the regular qualification requirements for benefit plans. Provisions to automatically meet these requirements if a plan becomes top heavy must be included in almost all types of plans, including ESOPs.

A *key employee*, for the purposes of top-heavy plans, is one who at any time during the plan year or during the four preceding plan years is one of the following:

1. An officer of the company having compensation greater than 50 percent of the maximum annual benefit applicable to defined benefit plans (in 1989, $49,032) for the plan year in question
2. One of the 10 largest owners of the employer having annual compensation in excess of the annual addition limitation in effect for such plan year
3. A 5 percent owner of the employer
4. A 1 percent owner of the employer with an annual compensation of more than $150,000

The determination of whether or not an employee is an officer is made on the basis of the facts and circumstances of the employee's position. For example, the source of the employee's authority and the extent of the employee's duties are both considered. The number of employees that can be called officers is equal to 10 percent of all employees or three employees, whichever is greater. In no event can the number of officers counted exceed 50.

The special qualification requirements that top-heavy plans must satisfy include minimum vesting, minimum benefits or contributions, and a limitation on compensation.

Minimum Vesting Restrictions.   In any year that a plan is top heavy, it must meet special vesting requirements. Participants must be either fully vested after 3 years of service, or a graded vesting system must be followed that fully vests participants after 6 years. The 6-year schedule is as follows:

Years of service	Percentage vested
2	20
3	40
4	60
5	80
6 or more	100

Minimum Contributions.   A top-heavy defined contribution plan must provide minimum contributions to non-key employees. The minimum contribution must not be less than 3 percent of compensation. However, if the highest contribution percentage rate for a key employee is less than 3 percent, the contribution rate is reduced to the rate that applies to the key employees. Under these rules, reallocated forfeitures are considered as employer contributions. If no contribution is made but forfeitures are allocated to key employees, the same rules apply. If a non-key employee participates in more than one plan, minimum contributions are provided for in only one plan.

Limit on Compensation.   Only the first $200,000 in compensation of each key employee can be taken into account in any year in which a plan is top heavy. For plan years beginning after 1988, this limitation, subject to cost of living adjustments, will be extended to all plans, not just top-heavy ones.

Reporting Requirements

Part of the administration of qualified plans includes the filing of various reports with the Internal Revenue Service and, to the extent necessary, with the Department of Labor. These reports are required to protect the rights of participating employees and their beneficiaries in the areas of funding, investment, fiduciary responsibility, and plan administration. Failure to file certain of these forms may result in civil penalties. The various due dates of the forms, schedules, and statements generally are measured from the last day of the plan year. Exhibit 7.1 illustrates some of the various required reports and their corresponding due dates for filing with the appropriate governmental agencies or participants.

Exhibit 7.1
Required Reports and Their Due Dates

Summary plan description—Summary of the plan written to be understood by the average participant. Must be given to each new participant 90 days after entry into an established plan or 120 days after the later of the effective date of the plan or the adoption date of a new plan. Must be sent to the Department of Labor within 120 days after the applicable date for a new plan.

Updated summary plan description—Same as above report, but incorporates changes. Due to each participant and the DOL every 5 years or due every 10 years if no changes are made.

Summary description of material modification of plan—Explains the changes that have taken place in the plan. Given to participants within 210 days after the close of the plan year in which the change is adopted. Filed with the DOL within 60 days after the modification is adopted.

Employee benefit statement—Statement indicates the total benefits accrued and the vested benefits in a participant's account or the date benefits become vested. Distributed upon request at least once in each 12-month period.

Annual return report of employee benefit plan, Form 5500—Financial statement of changes in net assets available for plan benefits. Includes details of revenue and expenses incurred during the plan year as well as information concerning employees for that year. Form 5500 (C) is used for companies with fewer than 100 employees. Form 5500–R is a simplified form, generally filed instead of Form 5500(C) for 2 out of every 3 consecutive years. Either report generally must be filed with the IRS within 7 months after the close of the company's fiscal year with extensions automatically applying if the employer's federal income tax due date is extended or granted on a discretionary basis. Schedule SSA, identification of separated participants with deferred vested benefits, is filed with the Form 5500 series for each terminated participant with deferred vested benefit rights due and not paid as of the filing date.

Summary annual report—Statement of assets and liabilities aggregated at fair market value. Includes information relevant to the value of assets, such as a statement of receipts and disbursements. Generally due to each participant by the end of the ninth month after close of the plan year or 2 months after the extended due date for the Form 5500 series.

Form 1099, W2P—Describes the amount and method of payment from the plan to terminated participants. Given to employee on January 31 following the year of payment. Filed with the IRS by February 28 of that year.

Fiduciary Standards

Every plan provides for one or more individuals who alone or jointly have authority to control and manage the operation and administration of the plan. These individuals are fiduciaries of the plan. ERISA imposes on all fiduciaries a general requirement that they discharge their duties solely in the interest of the participants and beneficiaries of the plan. The assets of the plan must never be used for the benefit of the company. Although the same person or group of people may serve as both plan administrators and trustees, often in an ESOP different individuals will be named.

The trustees of the plan hold title to the assets, generally shares of employer stock in the case of an ESOP, and are responsible for managing these assets. The trustees are appointed by the board of directors. For most small plans, the trustees are usually the officers, while in larger companies, an independent bank or trust company is used.

The administrator of the ESOP is responsible for running the day-to-day operation of the plan and has duties such as determining eligibility, allocating shares, making distributions, and complying with reporting requirements. The administrator for most small companies is usually the company itself, while in larger companies there is usually an administrative committee. In most cases, the administrator is assisted by outside service providers.

ESOP ADMINISTRATION

The administration of ESOPs is unlike the administration of other qualified employee retirement plans. Before any company takes on such an involved task, it must realize the complexities inherent in ESOP administration. In addition to the general qualification requirements, ESOPs have special administrative considerations. These include the calculation of the contribution/deduction limits, the release of collateral, the determination of increased benefit limitations if certain conditions are met, investment diversification, distribution options, voting of ESOP stock, and cost basis of shares of stock.

Contribution / Deduction Limits

Special limits are afforded ESOPs with respect to deductible contributions by the employer. The maximum deduction that an employer can take in any year in the case of a leveraged ESOP, whether or not combined with other plans, is up to 25 percent of participants' compensation—if this amount is used to make principal payments on an ESOP loan used to acquire employer securities. All employer contributions used to repay ESOP loan interest are fully deductible. In addition, the employer may also claim a deduction for a taxable year with respect to dividends paid on employer stock held by an ESOP if the dividends are paid directly to plan participants by the last day of that year or are paid first to the trust and then to participants by the last day of that year. The Tax Reform Act of 1986 expanded this deduction to permit employers to deduct dividends that are paid on employer stock held by an ESOP to the extent the dividends are used to repay exempt loans.

Release of Collateral

All shares of stock in the company that the ESOP acquires with a loan are held in a suspense account. They are withdrawn from the suspense account as the loan is paid. At the end of each year, the withdrawn stock is allocated according to a formula specified in the plan document. Stock held in the suspense account must be released from that account pursuant to one of two methods. Either the *fractional method* or the *principal only method* may be specified.

Under the fractional method, the number of shares of stock to be released is determined by multiplying the number of shares encumbered immediately prior to the release by a fraction. The numerator of that fraction is equal to the sum of the principal and interest of the loan to be paid for the year. The denominator is the sum of (a) the numerator plus (b) the principal and interest to be paid for all future years without taking into account any possible renewal or extension periods. The example given in the Internal Revenue Code regulations regarding ESOPs shows the release calculation based on an amortized loan schedule with level annual payments inclusive of principal and interest. This would result in the release of the same number of shares each year. However, recent practice has been to compute the loan schedule and subsequent share release based on level annual principal payments with interest computed on the unpaid balance. The following example presents this latter method.

> Company A establishes an ESOP that borrows $2,500,000 from a bank to acquire 2,500 shares of Company A stock. The loan is for 7 years at 8.5 percent interest and is payable in level annual principal payments of $357,142.86. Interest is computed on the unpaid balance. Interest for the first year is $212,500, and total principal and interest payments are $3,350,000. The number of shares of stock to be released for the first year is 425.1066 shares, that is, 2,500 shares × ($357,142.86 + $212,500) ÷ $3,350,000.

Although the amount of interest paid each year is not constant, it is determined at the onset of the loan. Accordingly, the number of shares to be released in each succeeding year of the loan can be easily determined.

> The number of shares remaining in the suspense account at the end of the second year is 2,074.8934 (2,500 − 425.1066), the principal payment is the level amount fixed in the first year of $357,142.86 and the interest for the year is $182,142.86. The number of shares to be released is 402.4520, that is, 2,074.8934 × ($357,142.86 + $182,142.86) ÷ $2,780,357.13.

If a variable interest rate is charged, the interest rate applicable as of the end of each plan year is used to determine the amount of interest to be paid for all future years in the denominator of the release fraction. If the rate being charged during the second year was increased to 8.75 percent, a new schedule would be computed at that time. Since the rate will vary from plan year to plan year, the number of shares that would be released each year cannot be determined at the plan's inception. Based on a variable interest rate and the preceding facts, the release for the second year would be based on a different fraction, as shown in the following example.

> The principal payment remains at $357,142.86; however, interest paid for the year was $187,500, and total principal and interest payments at 8.75% are $2,798,214.28. The number of shares to be released is 403.8561, that is, 2,074.8934 × ($357,142.86 + $187,500.00) ÷ $2,798,214.28.

Alternatively, an ESOP could release shares of stock under the principal only method. Under this method, shares of stock are released strictly on the basis of the amount of principal paid each year. The number of shares released through this method the first year will be less than through the fractional method, as shown in the following example.

> The principal payment remains at $357,142.86 and the total of all principal payments equals the initial purchase price of $2,500,000. The number of shares of stock to be released for the first year is 357.1429, that is, 2,500 × $357,142.86 ÷ $2,500,000.

Use of the principal only method requires that three additional rules apply. The term of the loan, including extensions and renewal periods, cannot exceed 10 years; annual payments of principal and interest under the loan may not be cumulatively less rapid than level annual payments of principal and interest for 10 years; and in computing the payments of principal, interest is disregarded only to the extent that it would be disregarded under standard loan amortization tables.

The choice of method of release of shares of stock from the ESOP suspense account is a matter of negotiation between the ESOP, the sponsoring employer, and the lender. The stock would be released from the suspense account of the ESOP each year in the same manner.

Benefit Limitations

As previously mentioned, the limitation on annual additions to a participant's account is the lesser of $30,000 or 25 percent of the participant's compensation. Since the employer contribution generally includes the loan interest paid, which is often greater than the value of the shares of stock allocated, special rules regarding these limits are afforded ESOPs. If no more than one-third of the employer contributions used to repay ESOP acquisition debt, both principal and interest, are allocated to highly compensated employees, then the portion of the employer contribution applied to pay interest and the forfeitures of stock originally acquired by the leveraging can be disregarded when computing participant limitations.

In addition, if the above rule is met, the annual addition limit is increased to the lesser of 25 percent of compensation or $60,000. However, for limitation years beginning in 1989, the $200,000 limit on participant compensation used for allocation purposes will limit the dollar limitation to $50,000, which equals 25 percent of $200,000. The total amount added to an employees' ESOP account can be substantial.

Investment Diversification

ERISA's requirement that trustees diversify a plan's investments does not apply to an ESOP since, by definition, ESOPs are designed primarily to invest in employer securities. However, under the Tax Reform Act of 1986, a diversification option is required to be given to participants who are nearing retirement age.

Any participant who has attained age 55 and completed at least 10 years of participation in the ESOP must be offered a diversification election with respect to stock acquired by the ESOP after December 31, 1986. This election must be made in the first 90 days of each plan year following the plan year in which the participant attains age 55. This election must then be offered during the first 90 days of the next 5 succeeding plan years.

During the 90-day election period, the participant may elect to diversify up to 25 percent of his account balance in other than employer securities. The election is cumulative. If an election is made in the first year to diversify only 10 percent of the assets, the participant may elect to diversify an additional 15 percent in the second year. Any participant who has attained the age of 60 and completed the 10 years of participation requirement may elect to diversify up to 50 percent of the account balance less any prior elections.

Compliance with the diversification elections may be met in either of two ways: the plan may distribute the percentage of employer securities that the participant elected to diversify, or the plan may offer three investment alternatives other than employer securities. If the participant receives a distribution, the distribution may be rolled over to an IRA. This offers the participant the ability to sell the stock if it is readily tradable or to exercise his *put option* (described in the next section) if it is not. Investment alternatives might be offered to the participant by permitting him to direct the investment of his account in a fixed income fund or a common stock fund. Exhibit 7.2 presents a sample investment diversification.

Distribution Options

Unless the participant elects otherwise, distributions from ESOPs will begin within one year after the end of the plan year which is the fifth plan year following the plan year in which the participant separates from service, provided the participant does not return to work, or upon repayment of the

Exhibit 7.2
Sample Investment Diversification

Shares Distributed

First Election:

Account Balance at December 31, 1986: 1150 shares
Account Balance at December 31, 1988: 1675 shares

Required to Diversify—25% of Account Balance on
December 31, 1988.

$$\begin{array}{r} 1675 \text{ shares on December 31, 1988} \\ \underline{-1150} \text{ shares on December 31, 1986} \\ 525 \text{ shares aquired after December 31, 1986} \end{array}$$

525 shares × 25% = 131.25 shares

Participant receives 131 shares and cash for the .25 share if shares are distributed. If shares are not distributed, the market value of 131.25 shares is transferred to alternative investment funds.

Second Election:

Account Balance at December 31, 1986: 1150 shares
Account Balance at December 31, 1988: 1675 shares
Account Balance at December 31, 1991: 1950 shares
First Diversification: 131.25 shares

Required to Diversify—25% of Account Balance on December 31, 1991.

$$\begin{array}{r} 1950 \text{ shares on December 31, 1990} \\ \underline{-1150} \text{ shares on December 31, 1986} \\ 800 \text{ shares acquired after December 31, 1986} \end{array}$$

$$\begin{array}{r} 800.00 \text{ shares acquired after December 31, 1986} \\ \underline{+131.25} \text{ shares diversified} \\ 931.25 \text{ shares in account had there been no diversification} \end{array}$$

931.25 shares × 25% = 232.8125 shares
$$\underline{-131.2500} \text{ shares already diversified}$$
101.5625 additional shares to
diversify

Participant receives 101 shares and cash for the .5625 share if shares are distributed. If shares are not distributed, the market value of 101.5625 shares is transferred to alternative investment funds.

Cash Transferred

First Election:

525 shares × 25% = 131.25 shares to diversify

131.25 × $100 per share = $13,125.00

Participant would elect how to invest $13,125.00 in the three alternative investment funds.

Second Election:

The value of the $13,125.00 which was transferred is now $15,000.00.
Current market value of stock is $150 per share.

800 shares acquired after December 31,	$120,000.00
Add back of cash payment already made	+15,000.00
Value of account	$135,000.00

$135,000.00 ÷ $150 per share = 900 shares acquired
after December 31, 1986

900 × 25% = 225 shares to diversify × $150 =	$33,750.00
Cash already diversified	−15,000.00
Additional cash to diversify	$18,750.00

Participant would now elect how to invest the additional $18,750.00 among the three alternative investment funds. The trust would have liquidated 125 shares.

ESOP loan, if the loan has not been repaid. Distributions will begin no later than 1 year after the close of the plan year in which the participant terminates employment due to normal retirement, disability, or death. Benefits may be distributed to participants in either cash or shares of stock; however, shares must be distributed if the participant so requests.

Unless the participant elects a longer distribution, an ESOP is required to distribute a participant's account balance over a period not longer than 5 years. If the account balance exceeds $500,000, the 5-year distribution period is extended by 1 year for each additional $100,000, or a fraction thereof, by which the account balance exceeds $500,000. These dollar amounts are indexed in the same manner as the dollar limitations for defined benefit plans under Internal Revenue Code Section 415.

If the participant receives stock that cannot be readily sold, then he shall be able to *put options* to the employer or the ESOP if he so wishes. In other words, the participant would require either the employer or the ESOP to purchase the stock at a price equal to its fair market value. The participant may exercise the put option during any of two periods: the first 60-day period beginning on the date the stock is distributed or the second 60-day period beginning after a new determination of fair market value of stock is made and is given to the participant in the following plan year.

Put options granted to participants of an ESOP can provide for payment of the purchase price in an immediate lump-sum payment or in installments. For stock acquired prior to 1986, payment of the purchase price under the put option could be in installments over 5 years from the date of exercise. The payment period could extend up to 10 years if the ESOP loan is still outstanding. However, for stock acquired after 1986, payment for all stock in the participant's account must be paid in full within 5 years from the date of distribution. In addition, in the case of a put option as part of an installment distribution, the employer is required to pay the put option price in cash within 30 days of exercise.

Employer stock distributed by an ESOP to a participant is generally subject to a *right of first refusal* in favor of the employer or the ESOP itself. In other words, if the participant wishes to sell the stock at any time the employer or, if refused by the employer, the trustees on behalf of the ESOP must be given the first opportunity to purchase the shares of stock, on the same terms offered by the other prospective buyer, before any of the stock is sold.

Voting of ESOP Stock

Voting of ESOP shares is based on whether the company is privately or publicly held. In a privately held corporation that does not have a class of securities required to be registered under Section 12 of the Securities Exchange Act (known as a *registration-type class of securities*), the ESOP would not be required to pass through voting rights to participants and beneficiaries except in certain specific instances. These circumstances include only those corporate matters relating to the voting of shares to approve or disapprove a corporate merger, consolidation, recapitalization, reclassification, liquidation, dissolution, or sale of all, or substantially all, of the assets. However, while participants would be entitled to instruct the ESOP trustee on the sale of corporate assets or merger with another company through an exchange of stock, they would not be entitled to vote on the sale of ESOP stock in the event of an offer from another corporation. In all other cases, the stock owned by the ESOP would be voted by the trustee, who is generally appointed by the board of directors of the company.

If the company is a publicly held corporation with registration-type class of securities, the ESOP participants would be entitled to direct the trustee as to the manner in which company stock owned by the ESOP should be voted. If the company has a registration-type of security other than common stock, such as preferred stock or debentures or another class of common stock publicly traded, then the ESOP must pass through the vote even though stock held by the ESOP itself is privately held and not registration type. The pass-through requirement applies to stock allocated to participants' accounts, whether or not vested.

There is, however, one major exception to the pass-through requirement: unallocated stock. Such stock would consist of leveraged stock purchased by a loan—the stock being held in a suspense account and withdrawn and allocated to participants' accounts as the loan is repaid. At the inception of a leveraged ESOP, 100 percent of the stock would be in the suspense account and allocated over the life of the loan.

There are at least four ways that the suspense account can be voted: (1) the trustee can vote in its own discretion; (2) the trustee can vote in the same proportions as the participants vote allocated stock; (3) the trustee can vote according to the majority of allocated stock for which it has received instructions; or (4) the trustee can vote as directed by a committee, usually consisting of management. Unlike privately held corporations, ESOP companies with registration-type securities may have an independent bank or trust company.

Multiple classes of stock or possible tender or exchange offers are best dealt with on an arm's-length basis by an independent trustee—independent from the ESOP in terms of ownership, employment, or lending. This independence helps fulfill the ERISA fiduciary requirements that the ESOP must be managed for the exclusive benefit of the participants and their beneficiaries.

Cost Basis of Stock

In determining a participant's tax liability upon distribution of benefits, the plan administrator must first determine whether the distribution is a lump-sum distribution. To qualify as a lump sum distribution, payment must be made within one calendar year of the entire vested balance of a participant's account and be made by reason of the participant's death or after the employee attains of age 59½.

If the distribution qualifies as a lump-sum distribution

except for a 5-year participation rule, all net unrealized appreciation in employer stock is excluded from income upon distribution to the employee or beneficiary. When the participant subsequently sells the employer stock after the distribution, the gain on the sale will be taxed as ordinary income. However, the participant may elect to pay tax currently on net unrealized appreciation instead of deferring the tax until the stock is sold.

Net unrealized appreciation is defined as the difference between the plan's cost basis in any employer securities distributed and the fair market value of those securities on the date delivered to the transfer agent.

The Internal Revenue Code provides for four methods of determining the basis of employer stock held by the ESOP. (Cost is the price paid by the ESOP for the shares acquired by the purchase.)

1. The cost of shares earmarked for the account of a particular employee as tracked within the account of that employee.
2. The average cost of shares acquired during the plan year when annual allocations are made.
3. If neither of the above apply and there is very little activity, the actual cost by class of securities can be used.
4. Average cost of all securities by type at the time of distribution.

OTHER ADMINISTRATIVE ISSUES

In addition to both the general and special administrative considerations in adopting an ESOP, other issues must be addressed. Among these are existing retirement plans, repayment terms of the loan, employee contributions, and repurchase liability.

Existing Retirement Plans

What should be done with an existing retirement plan after a decision is made to adopt an ESOP? An existing retirement plan can be maintained, terminated, or converted into an ESOP. Its fate should depend on resolving such issues as whether both the ESOP and the existing plan are affordable; whether the ESOP should be the sole source of retirement benefits for the employees; and, in the case of a closely held company, what the impact would be on the company's principals.

There are employee relation issues to consider with respect to whether or not the ESOP should be the sole source of retirement benefits for employees. The employees' retirement benefits would depend totally on the performance of company stock. Older employees could receive less retirement benefits, for example, from the combination of a terminated defined benefit pension plan and an ESOP than they would if they received a benefit at normal retirement age from the defined benefit pension plan alone.

Under certain circumstances, a combination of plans could provide a maximum payment under another plan to a principal who has elected for a tax-free rollover and is, therefore, not eligible for participation in the ESOP. The law permits a selling shareholder to defer taxes from the proceeds of the sale of his stock to an ESOP if the ESOP owns at least 30 percent of the company after the sale and he reinvests his proceeds in "qualified replacement property." This is known as a *tax-free rollover*. However, no portion of the employer securities acquired in the tax-free transaction can be allocated to him, a member of his family with a *de minimis* exception for lineal descendants, or any person who owns more than 25 percent of the value of employer securities. The question becomes: is the tax-free rollover worth the loss of the ESOP allocation? The answer could be as simple as realizing that a selling shareholder could receive maximum benefits under another company retirement plan and would otherwise be precluded under the individual benefit limits from receiving an ESOP allocation.

The relationship between other qualified plans maintained by the employer and the ESOP must be kept in mind. The company must determine the impact of Section 404 of the Internal Revenue Code, which regulates the amount the company can contribute and deduct to two retirement plans. The maximum deduction for two plans is 25 percent of participants' compensation. The required contribution to a leveraged ESOP to repay loan principal plus the required contribution under, for example, a defined benefit pension plan subject to the Internal Revenue Code minimum funding requirements could exceed the 25 percent limitation. This could result in nondeductible required contributions and therefore an excise tax.

The company should also determine the impact of Section 415 of the Internal Revenue Code with respect to individual annual additions. A participant in one or more defined contribution plans cannot receive an annual allocation, greater than the lesser of 25 percent of compensation or $30,000. Even with the increased limits afforded ESOPs under certain circumstances, a company that maintains both an ESOP and a profit-sharing plan could be forced to reduce the benefits under one of the plans. Generally, the reduction is provided for under the profit-sharing plan to ensure deductible loan principal repayments for the ESOP. Contributions in excess of the permitted limits are both nondeductible and subject to a 10 percent excise tax applicable to excess contributions.

Repayment Terms of the Loan

The repayment terms of the exempt loan have to be drafted with the employer's compensation base in mind, since deductible contributions to the ESOP to repay the loan and the maximum annual additions under Code Section 415 are measured by reference to compensation. If this is done properly, the employer should have no trouble making contributions to meet the loan payments and stay within the Code Section

415 limitations. If the employer's compensation base shrinks for some reason, it might be possible that certain loan payments in excess of the permitted limits would have to be made on a nondeductible basis.

Employee Contributions

Can employee contributions be part of the ESOP? Many companies allow employees to contribute to the ESOP either to purchase employer stock or other investments. However, if employee contributions are used to purchase employer stock, there may be a sale for security law purposes that would require a registration with the SEC. Because of the expense involved, most ESOPs do not allow employees to purchase stock.

Many companies do permit employees to make employee contributions on a pretax basis as a 401(k) contribution. This enables employees to increase their retirement benefits and to replace their individual retirement accounts, to which they may no longer be able to make tax-deductible contributions because of provisions of the Tax Reform Act of 1986. There are special administrative concerns with a 401(k) option. Care must be taken so that neither the employer deductibility limits nor the individual allocation limits are exceeded when a 401(k) option is part of an ESOP. Adding a 401(k) feature to an ESOP also requires the plan to meet the required antidiscrimination requirements with respect to 401(k) contributions made by highly compensated employees. Again, if employee contributions are used to purchase employer stock, there may be a sale for security law purposes that would require a registration with the SEC.

Repurchase Liability

The term *repurchase liability* refers to the legal obligation of the company, not the ESOP, to repurchase shares of stock distributed to any plan participant who leaves the company. The repurchase liability is important since the need for cash will continue to increase as the ESOP matures. Stock must be repurchased when an employee terminates as a participant of the ESOP. This will result from death, disability, retirement, or other termination of service. The need for cash will also increase as the vesting of ESOP shares must be complete no less rapidly than one of two schedules provided by the Tax Reform Act of 1986—100 percent vesting after 5 years or 20 percent vesting each year, beginning after 3 years and continuing through year 7. The new diversification requirements, noted earlier, will force companies to give greater consideration to repurchase liabilities.

These repurchase liabilities will continue to accumulate over the years and will cause a severe fiscal crisis if not funded for over time. One of the first considerations is to prepare a forecast of the expected extent of future repurchase obligations. A repurchase liability study should be conducted when the ESOP is adopted and periodically thereafter. Valuation and actuarial firms can assist a company in preparing for these liabilities. Employee turnover, retirement, contribution levels, and the market value of the company are some of the variables affecting these studies.

CONCLUSION

With the changes in the Tax Reform Act of 1986, the administration of an ESOP has become more complex. It requires more diligence than the normal administration of a benefit plan, but it is possible to administer an ESOP effectively and to shape a rewarding employee-benefit program.

EIGHT

The Use of
an ESOP for
Corporate Finance

R. W. Pricer

Robert W. Pricer is a Professor of Management at the University of Wisconsin-Madison. He is a past Assistant Dean and Director of the University of Wisconsin Small Business Development Center and Business Outreach. The SBDC mobilizes the statewide resources of the University of Wisconsin System to provide management education and one-to-one counseling to small business owner/managers and prospective entrepreneurs. A former small business owner himself, Dr. Pricer has extensive teaching, research, publication and consulting experience in the area of entrepreneurship and small business management. Recently, Dr. Pricer completed a venture development and management Fulbright scholarship.

EIGHT

ESOPs are typically used as benefit plans for employees or as part of leveraged acquisitions. Little attention is usually given to their numerous advantages as vehicles for corporate finance. This chapter provides an overview of the use of an ESOP to increase liquidity or to provide debt and equity financing and covers the role of an ESOP in mergers and acquisitions.

TAX ADVANTAGES OF ESOPS

The advantages of ESOPs as financing vehicles revolve around the tax incentives designed by Congress to encourage the transfer of ownership of firms to employees. Therefore, to effectively use an ESOP for financing purposes, most companies need to have projected major federal income tax expenses as well as have a cost structure that includes a significant payroll component.

Up to 25 percent of employee wages can be contributed to an ESOP by a company on a tax deductible basis.[1] If the ESOP has borrowed money to purchase company stock, the interest on the loan is also deductible from the taxable income of the company.

Dividends on shares held by the ESOP are tax deductible by the company if they are distributed to the ESOP shareholders or if they are used to repay an ESOP loan.[2] This deductibility from taxable income is in addition to the limitation of 25 percent of employee wages.

A tax incentive for banks also works to the advantage of a company with an ESOP. Banks that make loans to an

ESOP can deduct 50 percent of the income from an ESOP loan from their taxable income. This provides an attractive lending situation and results in below market interest rates for ESOP loans used to purchase company stock. A 10 percent discount from the prime rate is very common, and interest expense charges may be as much as 20 percent below the prime rate.

The final tax incentives involving an ESOP allow an owner to defer taxes on the capital gains on stock sold to an ESOP if certain requirements are met.[3] Also, estate taxes can be reduced or, in some situations, eliminated through estate contributions of company stock to an ESOP.[4] These advantages to stock owners are important because they provide an incentive for owners to transfer shares of company stock to an ESOP, which facilitates the use of various financing options.

IMPROVING LIQUIDITY

For many businesses, improving cash flow and liquidity is necessary for growth or even survival. This section gives examples of the ways in which a business can use an ESOP to improve liquidity and cash flow.

A company that holds stock and has income that is exposed to significant federal income tax can improve liquidity through establishing an ESOP and making contributions of company-held stock to it. The fair market value of the contributed stock is deductible from taxable income, and the savings will increase cash flow.

If a business already has a qualified pension plan, all or part of the plan can be converted to an ESOP. In lieu of cash contributions to the prior plan, company stock can be contributed to the ESOP. This will increase cash flow through tax deductions for the stock contributions and reduced or eliminated pension plan payments.

A business with existing debt can reduce the cost of servicing it through the use of a leveraged ESOP. This is accomplished by securing a loan that is used by the ESOP to purchase stock held by the company. The money from the sale of the stock is used by the company to retire existing debt, and the new loan is serviced through company contributions to the ESOP. Both the interest and principal payments are deductible with this technique. Also the fact that lenders can deduct 50 percent of income on an ESOP loan results in a lower interest rate. Thus, the deductibility of interest payments and the low interest rates will improve liquidity and the cash flow of a firm.

Dividends that are distributed to ESOP shares can be deducted from taxable income if they are used to repay an ESOP loan used to purchase company stock or if they are remitted to members of the ESOP. The fact that dividends are deductible means that less tax will be paid and cash flow and liquidity improved. To use this strategy, a company should be making regular dividend allocations and have significant taxable income with a large number of shares held by the ESOP.

If a company is considering a public offering, an alternative sale to an ESOP, usually on a leveraged basis, will save all or some of the cost of making a new issue. Even for smaller firms, a public offering can cost $250,000 or more and the sale of a large block of stock to an ESOP can save these fees and improve liquidity.

DEBT FINANCING

An ESOP can be a useful mechanism for generating debt financing given the tax incentives available. The financing can be either of new debt or of existing debt. However, ESOP debt financing will probably use the existing debt capacity of a firm, since the company usually must guarantee the repayment of an ESOP loan, and the debt amount is then shown as a liability of the business.

To secure new debt financing, a loan is secured for the ESOP and the proceeds are used by it to purchase company stock held by the business. The company services the loan by making contributions for this purpose to the ESOP. The money received by the company for the sale of the shares to the ESOP can be used by the business just as if it were debt capital.

As discussed previously, existing debt can be consolidated and refinanced through the use of an ESOP. To refinance debt, the company obtains a guaranteed loan for an ESOP. The loan proceeds are used by the ESOP to purchase company stock and, in turn, the business uses the proceeds of the sale of stock to retire existing debt. The ESOP loan is serviced through company deductible principal and interest contributions to the ESOP.

When considering the use of debt financing through an ESOP transaction, a company can structure the transaction either as a direct business loan or as the more typical leveraged ESOP. Figure 8.1 illustrates a direct company loan.

With the direct company loan, a business secures debt financing from a lender and makes repayment on the loan. The company contributes tax-deductible stock to the ESOP in an amount equal to the loan repayment. The advantage of this technique is that the value of contributed shares is not fixed at the time of the loan. Stock contributions to the ESOP are made as loan repayments are made. If the value of stock increases, the resulting dilution of ownership will be less than with a leveraged ESOP.

For example, if the shares of a company are valued at $10 each, a leveraged ESOP transaction of $10,000 will result in a block of 1000 shares of stock being transferred to suspense for allocation to the ESOP as the loan is repaid over a period of years. If the value of the stock increases beyond $10 per share during the term of the loan, the shares will still be allocated at the value established at the time the loan was initiated, $10 per share. However, if the company secures the debt directly and donates stock to the ESOP in an amount sufficient to generate increased tax flow equal to the loan payment each year, the amount of the deduction per share will be established each year when the company is valued.

The leveraged ESOP transaction is illustrated in Figure 8.2.

Figure 8.1

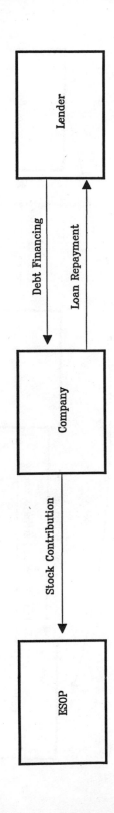

Figure 8.2

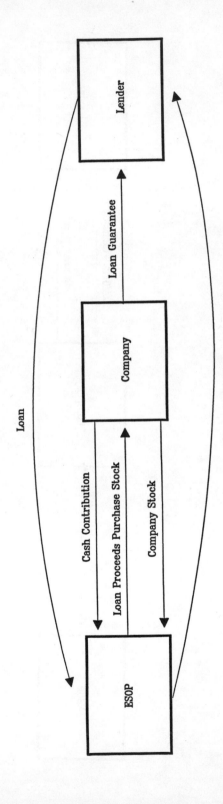

With the common leveraged ESOP transaction, a lender makes a loan to an ESOP with repayment guaranteed by the company. The ESOP uses the loan proceeds to purchase company stock and the business makes deductible contributions to the ESOP for loan repayment.

In a variation of the typical transaction, a *mirror loan* is made to the company and the proceeds transferred on by the business to the ESOP to be used for the purchase of stock. A mirror loan operates exactly like a direct ESOP loan guaranteed by the company. The only difference is that the company itself borrows the funds that are used by the ESOP to purchase company stock. The disadvantage of these transactions is that the liability for loan repayment rests with the company and is shown on the balance sheet as a company liability just as any other debt. This will result in a reduction in the available debt capacity for the company and may limit the availability of future needed financing.

The leveraged ESOP transaction has the disadvantage of fixing the price of the shares at the market value at the time of the loan. If a company's value is increasing, this will result in greater ownership dilution than may be necessary or desirable.

In 1988, The ESOP Association published an excellent reference titled "Structuring Leveraged ESOP Transactions." Among the topics covered therein is the following section on immediate allocation loans:

> The 1986 Tax Reform Act provided ESOP companies with a new financing alternative, which technically does not involve lending to an ESOP, but still qualifies for the 50% lender interest exclusion. TRA '86 amended the definition of a securities acquisition loan to include loans made directly to a company that contributes employer stock to an ESOP of value to the proceeds of the loan within thirty days. Those shares contributed to an ESOP as a result of an immediate allocation loan must be allocated to employees' individual ESOP accounts within one year. Because the loan is made to the corporation which in turn contributes an equivalent amount of shares to the ESOP, this type of ESOP is in theory unleveraged. How-

ever, it must meet all the requirements of a leveraged ESOP.
Furthermore, the term must not exceed seven years.

ESOPs financed through an immediate allocation loan provide an alternative to normal leveraged ESOPs for public
companies. Due to the accounting treatment recommended by
AICPA Statement of Position 76–3 for leveraged ESOP shares
held in a suspense account, a contra-equity account must be
maintained, with the net effect that shares are not treated as
equity in the employer company until they are allocated; but,
like all other outstanding shares, they must be included in
calculating the earnings per share of the company. Under the
immediate allocation provision, however, this problem is
eliminated because all shares contributed to the ESOP are
allocated to employee accounts within one year, enabling them
to be included as equity on the company's balance sheet. the
loan is accounted for like any standard loan, avoiding the
requirements of SOP 76–3 for leveraged ESOPs.

Because an ESOP transaction financed with an immediate
allocation loan is not technically a "leveraged" ESOP, these
loans tend to be smaller and are generally limited to an amount
equal to 15% of covered payroll (up to 25% for certain ESOPs).
However, because the stock is allocated to ESOP participants
within one year, a company is able to receive tax deductions for
dividends passed through to employees for all the ESOP shares
of stock. An immediate allocation loan is therefore very attractive for companies that traditionally pay dividends by allowing
companies to contribute stock to employees' ESOP accounts
and receive a tax deduction for future dividends paid on that
stock, while employees' receive a second income from dividends.

As a result, with an immediate allocation loan a corporation
may finance its annual contributions to an ESOP. The proceeds
of the loan can be used for any purpose, and the employer is not
under any obligation to make future contributions of a specified
level.

Because of the tax incentives an ESOP provides, it will
often be significantly less expensive to use a company's
debt capacity for ESOP loan purchase of stock. This
mechanism allows for the low cost addition of debt to the
capital structure of the firm.

EQUITY FINANCING

The use of an ESOP for equity financing has many benefits including the combination of equity financing with debt tax deductibility. Since use of an ESOP for equity financing often involves a change of ownership as individuals retire or look for new investments, the tax advantages to existing owners of shares provide an incentive for these transactions. IRC 1042 allows a major owner of company shares to defer federal income tax on the capital gain on the value of stock sold to an ESOP if the ESOP owns at least 30 percent of the company's stock after the sale has been completed. The owner who sells the stock must reinvest the proceeds in qualified securities within 15 months of the sale. In addition, the capital gain tax on the company stock sold is waived if the selling owner dies while the proceeds from the sale of shares is invested in qualified replacement securities.

If an estate sells company shares to an ESOP, up to 50 percent of the proceeds from the transaction can be excluded from the taxable value of the estate.[5] In some cases, an estate that holds a large block of company stock can make contributions of shares to an ESOP, and the value of the stock will reduce the federal tax obligation of the estate.

Equity financing is accomplished by having the ESOP purchase company stock with a savings in the costs that would be associated with an equivalent public offering. This money can instead be used directly for equity if an equivalent amount of stock is contributed to the ESOP or if the money is donated to the ESOP that purchases company held shares. In addition, the ESOP can borrow the money to purchase shares held by the company and the loan can be repaid with the savings generated from not making a public offering and through dividend payments on shares held by the ESOP.

The cash contributions are deductible up to the payroll limit, and the dividend payments on ESOP shares are fully deductible. In essence, the company will have equity financing while making tax-deductible distributions to the ESOP to service it.

Usually, it is necessary for a company to guarantee repayment of the loan, because most lenders will not make a loan directly to an ESOP. This results in a disadvantage to the company, since the lender would have full recourse to the company if there were default on the ESOP loan, just as if the loan had been made directly to the business.

One technique to avoid this disadvantage is to have a specially created subsidiary guarantee the ESOP loan, with recourse limited to the subsidiary in the event of default. The subsidiary can hold assets as collateral in a form and amount negotiated with the lender.

Another way to avoid the disadvantage of direct company liability for the ESOP loan is for the firm to contribute additional stock to the ESOP, beyond the amount purchased but not beyond the payroll limit, to provide collateral for the ESOP loan and make a company guarantee unnecessary. This has the added advantage of the tax deductibility benefit of the shares donated to the ESOP, and this will improve cash flow if the company has taxable income.

The use of a subsidiary to accomplish equity financing is illustrated in Figure 8.3.

With a subsidiary ESOP transaction, a special or existing subsidiary of the company secures a loan, and the proceeds are transferred to the ESOP for the purchase of company stock. The company makes deductible cash contributions to the ESOP that are used for loan repayment, and the debt is guaranteed by the subsidiary without recourse to the company in the event of default. This arrangement allows the company to have the benefit of equity financing along with the tax advantage of debt.

Many options are possible when considering the best strategy for structuring equity financing. For example, the company could buy from another corporation bonds that pay an interest rate at, or above, the market. The purchase of the bonds would be financed through the sale of company stock, with a loan using the recently purchased bonds

Figure 8.3

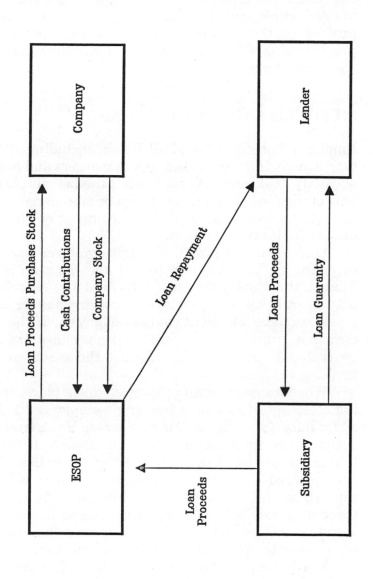

as collateral. The company would collect market interest on the bonds and repay the ESOP below-prime-rate loan with tax-deductible contributions. If the net present value of the interest on the bond's tax savings is greater than the net present value of the ESOP contribution, this can be an effective financing technique.

MERGERS AND ACQUISITIONS

Employee benefit plans of all kinds, including ESOPs, are increasingly important elements in mergers and acquisitions of closely held corporations. Even if the benefit plan is not a part of the formal financing structure of a merger or acquisition, its presence will have a direct impact on the operation and profitability of the firm.

Under current law, if a single-employer pension plan, including an ESOP, is terminated and the plan is not fully funded, the employer is liable to fund the shortfall. If the plan is an ESOP, the employer must arrange for the potential repurchase of ESOP shares obligation. If the employer does not provide funds for the repurchase liability, the government can file a lien against the assets of the company.

When an acquisition or merger takes place, the emerging company will assume the single-employer ESOP repurchase liability of the presale companies if the transaction is a general reorganization or a consolidation. If the acquisition is accomplished through a straight purchase of shares, the acquired company will retain the entire obligation to repurchase ESOP shares. If the acquisition is accomplished through a purchase of assets not covered by bulk transfer statutes, the purchaser will not assume the obligation to repurchase the stock of the acquired company.

The important fact for a buyer to understand is that if an ESOP of an acquired company is continued, the purchaser will incur the obligation to repurchase ESOP shares. From the seller's point of view, if the purchaser continues an existing ESOP, the seller will generally incur no repurchase obligation, even if the plan is eventually terminated by the acquirer. However, if the seller has made no effort to fund the repurchase obligation, it is possible that the seller could be held liable for the fund shortfall.

Acquisition Techniques

Innumerable techniques exist for using an ESOP for the acquisition of a business. The following section provides a brief overview of the methods available for an acquisition.

An individual can acquire a company through the purchase of the firm's stock, and an ESOP can be a significant part of the financial package. In this situation, the buyer combines personal financing with an ESOP loan to purchase the stock of a company and uses salary and dividends to recover individual funds and tax-deductible contributions to service the ESOP loan. The individual purchase of company stock is illustrated in Figure 8.4

Even though this acquisition is very simple and straightforward, there are still several potential problems. To begin with, the proceeds from the sale of the company will usually be taxed as a long-term capital gain to the seller. Also, the transaction will probably result in double taxation on the buyer. This happens because income from the acquired company will be taxed at the appropriate rate for corporations before distribution as income to the buyer, and the buyer will, in turn, pay individual income tax on the earnings prior to recovery of the personal funds used to purchase stock or to repay a personal loan used for the purchase of company stock.

A company can also be acquired by an existing corporation or by one created to acquire the company. An existing or new leveraged ESOP is a part of the acquiring corporation and provides all or part of the purchase capital.

After the sale has been completed, the acquired corporation can remain a subsidiary of the purchasing corporation, or the acquired company can be liquidated into the acquirer. If the purchased company remains a subsidiary, the ESOP loan can be paid from the earnings of

Figure 8.4

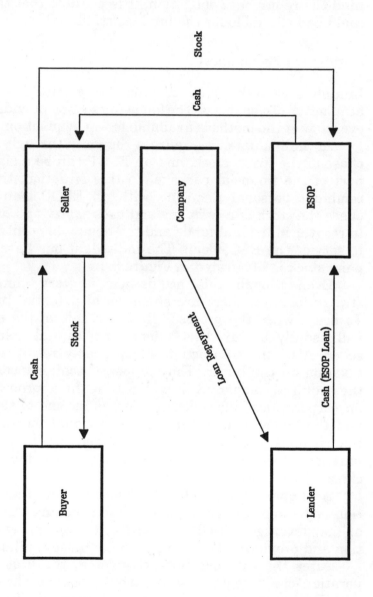

the subsidiary that are distributed to the purchasing company as tax-exempt dividends.[6] If the acquired company is liquidated on a tax-exempt basis into the purchasing corporation, the earnings can be directly used to service the ESOP loan.[7]

Structuring the acquisition in this manner avoids the double taxation associated with individual purchases of stock in acquisitions and also shields the individual buyer from the transaction.

Potential problems exist with the purchase of stock for the acquisition of a company, regardless of the method used. For example, under most circumstances, the book value of the purchased company's assets will carry over to the new books of the acquired corporation. However, the book value of the assets is usually well below their market value, and the purchaser normally will want to gain the advantage of the higher depreciation charges available from the market value of assets.

After completing the acquisition, the purchaser will have three potential courses of action. First, the acquisition can remain a subsidiary and book value can be used for the purchased assets. The second course of action would be to liquidate the acquired company into a new or existing corporation and accept the book value of the acquired assets.[8] The third option is for the purchaser to increase or "step up" the value of the acquired assets of the purchased "subsidiary" to the value (basis) of the acquired stock.[9] However, the increase in value of assets will probably result in the IRS collecting or recapturing the lost tax from depreciation from the seller.[10]

Another potential problem with the purchase of stock for an acquisition is the issue of minority shareholder rights, including the employees with allocated shares in an ESOP that is a part of a purchased corporation. In almost all cases, the minority shareholders must be given the opportunity to vote their shares for approval of the purchase to take place.

Another problem is that when a buyer purchases the stock of a corporation, the liabilities of the acquired company transfer with it. These obligations might include pending litigation awards, tax liabilities, or other known and unknown responsibilites of the purchased company. To avoid some of the problems associated with the purchase of stock to acquire a company, buyers may want to consider buying some or all of the assets of the acquisition candidate. Either of the two methods described for the purchase of stock can be used for the purchase of assets. Generally, 70 percent of net assets or 90 percent of gross assets must be purchased for an acquisition to have taken place. The assets are transferred to the buyer at their purchase price, and this usually results in higher levels of depreciation. In some states, it is necessary that a majority of stockholders, including employee members of an ESOP, approve the transfer of assets before a sale can take place.

In addition to the transfer of assets, mergers that meet specific requirements are not taxed by the IRS. Basically, the acquisition is not taxed if the merged business continues to function as a continuation of the old business.

Under the terms of almost all mergers, the acquired company is liquidated and consolidated into the buying corporation with a complete transfer of all assets and liabilities. The remaining shareholders, if any, of the acquired company become shareholders of the purchasing corporation, and the creditors of the acquired company become creditors of the acquiring firm. This type of merger can use a leveraged ESOP as a part of the acquisition financing and is generally not a taxable transaction.[11]

These acquisitions are referred to as *A mergers*. In A mergers, the seller exchanges stock for securities or cash, including the possibility of funds generated from a leveraged ESOP. This type of transaction is illustrated in Figure 8.5.

The seller will normally be taxed on any cash or property gain from the transaction other than stock of the buyer that is received from the sale. To qualify for tax-exempt treatment, the seller must continue to have an interest in the merged corporation similar to that which predated the acquisition. Therefore, the leveraged ESOP can be used to generate funds to be used to purchase the

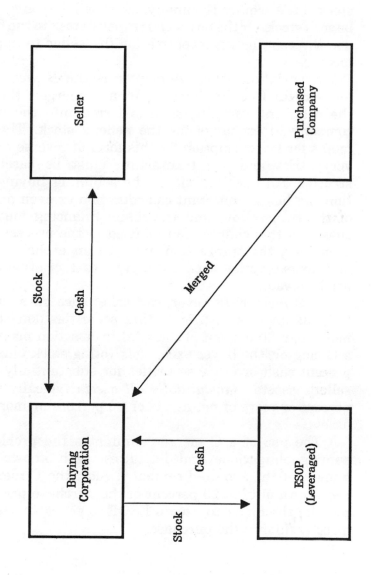

Figure 8.5

stock of the acquired company, which will be converted to the buyer's stock. Or the buyer can transfer stock to the ESOP and use the cash as an incentive for the seller to approve the merger.

A variation of the A merger is the *B merger* that is allowed tax-free treatment.[12] In a B merger, the stock of the acquiring company is transferred into the purchased company in exchange for the seller's stock. The requirements for tax exemption for this form of reverse merger are very strict and the transaction must be carefully constructed. An ESOP in either the selling or buying corporation can be an important consideration or even an initiator of the transaction, and the many financing methods discussed in this chapter can be used in the process. Under a B merger, the transaction must be an exchange of stock, and tax exemption does not apply if cash or other securities are involved.

A *C merger*, however, can take place on a tax-exempt basis as long as cash and other securities don't constitute more than 20 percent of the total transaction price.[13] Under a C merger, the buyer exchanges voting stock plus up to 20 percent cash or other securities for substantially all of the seller's assets. *Substantially all assets* typically means 70 percent or more of net assets or 90 percent or more of gross assets.

The use of a C merger eliminates the problem of assuming obligations and liabilities, both known and unknown, of the acquired company. Also, the C merger, with the allowability of 20 percent of the purchase price in cash, permits the buyer to use an ESOP to generate cash to help directly finance the purchase.

CONCLUSION

The use of an ESOP as a financing vehicle, either for operating cash or merger or acquisition, is not right for every company, even though attractive tax incentives are available. The company with an ESOP is obligated to repurchase ESOP shares as employees retire, and there will usually be dilution of ownership. However, when developing financing plans, every company with realistic earnings potential and a significant number of employees should consider carefully the use of an ESOP to improve debt and equity capitalization, to increase cash flow and liquidity, or to help finance an acquisition or merger.

NOTES

1   IRC §404 (a)(9).
2   IRC §404.
3   IRC §1042.
4   IRC §6166.
5   Ibid.
6   IRC §243.
7   IRC §332.
8   Ibid.
9   IRC §338.
10   IRC §337.
11   IRC §368(a)(1)(A).
12   IRC §368(a)(1)(B).
13   IRC §368(a)(1)(C).

Unions and Employee Ownership

Deborah Groban Olson

Deborah Groban Olson is the General Counsel of the Midwest Employee Ownership Center and a partner in the Detroit law firm of Groban Olson & Bachmann which specializes in creation and representation of employee ownership plans, especially in unionized companies.

NINE

Employee ownership is not something that the labor movement has sought as a benefit for its members, nor has it been on the agenda as a political goal, such as improvements in labor laws, trade laws, minimum wage, unemployment compensation, or civil rights have been. Rather, employee ownership has been thrust upon labor, and labor has reacted.

In recent years, the AFL-CIO and some of the larger unions, particularly the United Steel Workers of America (USWA), have begun developing policies to deal with this new phenomenon in the workplace, and in some instances, they have found their own uses for it. However, labor unions have had very mixed experiences with employee ownership, just as they have had with profit sharing, gainsharing, and quality of worklife. Labor's reaction to ESOPs has most often depended on whether or not the plan was, in reality, a good deal for the union members.

This chapter acquaints the reader with the current employee ownership thought and practice of the trade union movement in the United States. Provided here are examples of projects viewed unfavorably and favorably by labor. Also provided are the basic policy statements currently available and the results of a Governement Accounting Office study showing that only with employee participation does employee ownership provide significant increases in productivity. It is wise to consider these labor views in developing an ESOP, because participation of the type desired by labor in ESOP companies is also directly correlated to productivity.

219

ESOPS THAT LABOR VIEWS UNFAVORABLY

ESOPs are very flexible financing mechanisms that can be, and have been, used to benefit all employees (some more than others), outside investors to the detriment of the employees, or outside investors and management to the detriment of employees. In general, labor is satisfied with those ESOPs that have provided job security and fair stock value to their members. Labor is unhappy with those plans that have unfairly enriched others at the expense of their members, that have been used to keep unions out of companies, or that have been used to replace a diversified defined benefit pension plan, leaving all the employees' eggs in one basket. Some examples of ESOPs that labor has found objectionable are discussed in the following sections.

ESOPs that Are Not Good for Employees Financially or in Terms of Job Security

Scott & Fetzer.[1]   In 1985 the management of Scott & Fetzer Company, with the assistance of a lender and an investment banker, proposed to take the then public company private by borrowing $400 million. The proposed ESOP was to borrow $182 million to purchase 41 percent of the company stock at $44.39 per share. Management and its investment banker, Kelso and Company, were to pay $15 million for 29 percent of the company at the (average) rate of $3.85 to $7.06 per share. The company's lender, General Electric Credit, was to be given the right to purchase 30 percent of the company for $4.5 million, or $1.50 per share.

While this proposal was being advanced, the Amalgamated Clothing and Textile Workers Union (ACTWU) was engaged in an organizing campaign at one of Scott & Fetzer's subsidiaries, Carefree of Colorado. Two days before a National Labor Relations Board (NLRB) election, Carefree's management circulated a letter among the employees explaining that the ESOP was a new benefit available only for nonunion employees and describing it as a "superior" retirement plan. ACTWU won the union election. Promptly thereafter, ACTWU analyzed the proposed ESOP transaction and found it to be extremely unfair to the employees. ACTWU raised its concerns with the Department of Labor, at a Scott & Fetzer stockholders meeting, and in the press.

The Labor Department intervened before the transaction was completed, objecting that the ESOP was receiving less than "fair market value" for the price it was paying. The DOL argued that the ESOP should receive 67 percent of the company for the price it was paying and that management and the Kelso group should get only 3.3 percent. Scott & Fetzer and their investment bankers negotiated with the DOL, but ultimately the transaction was not completed.

The DOL's intervention led to a lot of concern in the investment community about the future of multi-investor deals in which investments of cash equity investors were assigned a value greater than that given to the stock in the ESOP.[2] This ultimately led to the promulgation of a regulation on "adequate consideration" by the Department of Labor in May of 1988.[3] The regulation defined the term "fair market value" (which is the maximum price an ESOP is allowed to pay for stock pursuant to the Internal Revenue Code and the Employee Retirement Income Security Act [ERISA]).[4] The regulation also determined that an ESOP may pay a control premium only in circumstances in which another investor would pay a control premium, and only where "the Plan obtains both voting control and control in fact."[5]

Congress and the DOL have thus attempted to protect the rights of ESOP participants to get a fair price and normal control rights for their participation in an ESOP. However, without active efforts by the ACTWU to protect these rights, it is quite possible that the Scott & Fetzer deal might have been concluded, as were similar transactions at that time, such as Blue Bell, Raymond, and Dan River.[6]

South Bend Lathe. At South Bend Lathe (SBL), a management designed ESOP was installed, and a defined benefit pension plan was removed with very late and inadequate notice to the International Union. There is a long vesting and allocation schedule so that, even though the company is 100 percent owned by the ESOP and has been since 1975, the hourly employees still do not control the voting power of the ESOP stock. The United Steelworkers of America (USWA) struck in 1980 and sued the ESOP fiduciaries for breach of fiduciary duty in 1988.[7] The USWA and most other trade unionists use SBL as the example of what not to allow in an ESOP.

ESOPs that Do Not Provide Ownership to All Employees on a Reasonably Equitable Basis

Labor unions believe that their members' work provides significant value in a business and that it must be given proper respect when a transaction is designed. The specific policy positions of the AFL-CIO and the USWA on this matter reflect both a strongly held belief that employees should get voting rights in their stock and that they should not pay more than fair market value for their stock.

Labor unions take different positions on the subject of voting rights based on the case-by-case facts. In some instances, one vote per person is desired. In other cases, unions prefer voting rights on the basis of seniority, on a share basis, or on some combination of these.

ESOPs Intended to Get Rid of Unions

In some instances employee ownership has been used in attempts to get rid of unions, thus obtaining an unfavorable reputation for ESOPs among some unions. One such attempt at Scott & Fetzer has already been described.

Fort Vancouver Plywood. Fort Vancouver Plywood provides another example. The company was a cooperatively owned plywood mill in which employee owners hired non-owner employees. These nonowner employees formed a union and were all fired for it. This action and the ensuing NLRB fight did not endear the idea of employee ownership to the International Woodworkers of America (IWA).[8]

It is common for managers to ask whether there will be any need for a union in an employee owned company and to promote the idea that employee ownership obviates the need for a union. In reality, employee ownership usually does not significantly change labor–management relations or daily shop floor practices. Thus the role of the union often does not change after employee ownership, particularly as to labor contract enforcement, although labor relations often do improve. But the fact that some managers view employee ownership as a replacement for the labor union and promote that concept reinforces labor's suspicions that employee ownership efforts are primarily aimed at ridding the workplace of the union.

ESOPs that Orphan One Facility and Expose it to Likely Failure while Undercutting its Sister Plants

Many labor organizations have master national collective bargaining agreements or at least try to maintain a national wage and/or benefit level. This is particularly true in the auto industry, in which the United Auto Workers (UAW) have been able to maintain a high degree of parity across the country in the wage and benefit packages of workers in the major organized auto manufacturing companies.

Employee ownership presents two problems for a facility that has been a single plant within a major conglomerate system. First, it is likely that employees will have to make concessions to make the deal work, which will have a negative impact on the bargaining position of sister plant local unions and the international union. Second, if a conglomerate is spinning off a plant, experience has shown that often the product or facility is obsolete or the seller is getting out of that product line. The proposed new employee-owned company thus would need to develop a new product line and market. To date, the UAW's experience, on a case-by-case basis, has been that most of the employee buyout proposals in situations where new products and markets must be found have not worked.[9]

Hyatt Clark. In the case of Hyatt Clark, the oldest of several General Motors New Departure Hyatt Division plants, both of these problems occurred. The local union at Hyatt Clark accepted a concession package that was lower than the UAW-GM package in order to help finance the employee buyout. The company ultimately went into bankruptcy and closed because it produced bearings for rear-wheel-drive cars at world prices as the product became obsolete.[10]

The UAW reviews prospective employee ownership projects on a case-by-case basis. To date, few have seemed feasible due to structural changes in the relevant industries. Franklin Forge, is an exception. It became employee owned in 1982 and has remained competitive in the steel forging industry without generating any complaints from within the union that it is undercutting labor rates. Franklin is competing with other independent parts suppliers, making some of the same products it made before the buyout. Franklin Forge is discussed at length later in the chapter.[11]

ESOPS THAT LABOR VIEWS FAVORABLY

Labor has begun to use employee ownership as a means to save jobs and, less frequently, to gain control over profitable companies to keep them out of the hands of speculators. Some of the ESOPs that labor views as successful involve corporate divestitures of profitable firms, profit- or gain-sharing, and preserving jobs in troubled, but not hopeless, industries.

ESOPs Involving Corporate Divestitures of Profitable Firms

Some of the most successful employee ownership projects have been companies sold by their parent corporation due to the parent's need for cash. Two of these success stories include the subsidiaries of Republic Steel—Republic Container and Republic Storage Systems—sold by LTV corporation in 1985 before LTV went into bankruptcy. In both cases, the hourly employees received stock in profitable companies as part of their compensation, and they were able to keep the companies from being sold to competitors who might have closed them or moved their production to other facilities.

Republic Container.[12] LTV Steel Corporation's divestiture of its profitable subsidiary, Republic Container, presented Republic Container's employees with an ideal opportunity to buy the company and prevent job loss. Mike Cable, president of the United Steelworkers of America Local 5712, recognized this opportunity and aggressively led a worker buyout effort. As a result, the employees outbid and outmaneuvered competitors who sought to buy the business.

In 1985, LTV Steel decided to sell all the companies in its manufacturing division. Many of these companies, including Republic Container, were profitable and had been captive markets for LTV's steel. Unlike many companies acquired by their employees, Republic Container was not threatened with bankruptcy.[13] During its 27 years of operation, Republic Container, located in Nitro, West Virginia, turned a regular profit making steel barrels for Union Carbide, DuPont, Monsanto, and other customers.

After learning that LTV Steel was seeking a buyer for Republic Container, Mike Cable sought information on the sale and competing offers, made the union's interest in the sale known, and organized the employees to form a buyout association. All Republic Container employees, including non-union workers and the plant's general manager, became members of the buyout association.[14] The State of West Virginia granted $30,000 to the buyout association for consultants to study the feasibility of the employee buyout plan. When the consultants advised that the buyout could succeed, the association then obtained a $61,000 grant from Kanawha County to pay the lawyers, business consultants, and appraisers needed to implement the buyout.

In September 1985, 66 Republic Container employees purchased the company from LTV Steel. The purchase was accomplished through the use of an employee stock ownership plan that holds all the stock of the company in a trust for the employees. Stock gives the employees two benefits: voting rights and financial rights. Employees are entitled to vote in the election of the company's board of directors and on other matters resolved through voting. When employees retire, they are paid the value of their shares.

Republic Container's ESOP gives each employee one vote. By creating two classes of stock, voting and nonvoting, only one share of voting stock, with a value set at $1 per share, is allocated to each employee. Three thousand shares of nonvoting stock, with an initial 1985 appraised value of about $475 per share, are gradually being allocated to the employees' ESOP accounts over 7 years. The value of the shares increased to $575 in 1986, to $626 in 1987, and is expected to exceed $700 per share in 1988. The amount of nonvoting stock an employee receives is based on annual wages not exceeding $22,500 per year.

The value of an employee's ESOP stock, however, depends on the fortunes of the company. If Republic Container prospers, the value of the stock is likely to increase. If the company falters, retiring employees may find that the shares in their account are worth less than they had anticipated. At the end of 1988, the typical employee's vested ESOP account is estimated to be worth approximately $16,000.

Republic Container employees did not have to make any out-of-pocket payments as part of the purchase or put up personal property as collateral for the loans used to purchase the company. Republic Container was sold for $1,424,000, an amount raised by two loans: $924,000 from the National Bank of Commerce and $500,000 from the West Virginia Economic Development Authority. The Bank of Nitro lent the new company an additional $600,000 for working capital. The loans are being repaid out of company profits over 7 years.

As part of the buyout, employees agreed to take a 1-year wage adjustment of $1.25 per hour. Union wages after the cut ranged from $9.20 to $11.60 per hour. Wages will rise, under the union contract, an average of 42.5 cents per hour each year over 4 years after the buyout.

In January 1986, Republic Container employees elected their first board of directors. The board has final authority to operate Republic Container and to hire and fire management employees. Due to a compromise reached prior to closing the buyout sale, voting and nonvoting directorships were alloted to certain groups. Among the five voting directors, one represents the lenders, one represents management, and one is a member of the USWA. The only restriction on the other two voting directors is that they cannot be employees of Republic Container. The one nonvoting director must be a member of the USWA.

During its first 4 months of operation after the buyout, Republic Container cleared a $78,000 profit, higher than that originally projected, and it has been quite profitable ever since. The purchase of Republic Container by its own employees demonstrates that an organized and knowledgeable union can successfully purchase a profitable company and increase its profitability while giving employees a strong voice concerning its future direction.

ESOPs as Profit- or Gain-sharing

Many unionized firms instituted ESOPs as a type of employee benefit, especially when tax credits based first on investment and later on payroll were available for certain ESOPS called TRASOPs. General Motors, Ford, and many other companies

instituted such plans, but they were for such small percent-
ages of stock that they did not give the employees any real
sense of ownership. The most notable firms that have used
ESOPs as a part of their profit- or gain-sharing programs are
nonunion firms such as the Herman Miller Company, which
also uses a very well-developed employee participation system.

ESOPs that Preserve Jobs in Troubled but Not Hopeless Industries

Saving jobs has been the primary use of employee ownership
in the unionized sector.[16] Many of the early union employee
ownership projects began as strike shops or as cooperatives
organized by the Knights of Labor.[17] Since the advent of tax
qualification for ESOPs, many of the ESOPs in unionized
firms have been created in distressed companies where
employee ownership seemed the only reasonable alternative
to closing the operation. The following are typical examples.

Franklin Forge.[18] Unprofitable subsidiaries are often offered for sale to employees. Employees should approach
such opportunities with care and predicate their actions on
feasibility studies conducted by skilled consultants who
know when to say no to a bad deal. The feasibility and
success of the Franklin Forge worker buyout depended on a
number of factors, including the strength and skill of both
the workers and management, the community's need for
the plant, the fact that the workers initiated the buyout,
and the parent corporation's motivation to sell at a low
price and make the deal work.

Located in West Branch, Michigan, Franklin Forge was
a subsidiary of Capitol Manufacturing, a company in the oil
field equipment business. Franklin was and continues to be
one of Capitol's suppliers. During most of the years it was
owned by Capitol, Franklin lost money. These losses
resulted mainly from Capitol's cost structure and lack of
experience in the forging business. Yet, because Capital

was quite profitable prior to 1982, Franklin's losses did not become important to Capitol until 1983 and 1984.

In early 1984, Franklin Forge employees sensed that the company's continuing losses threatened their future. The union, International Automobile, Aerospace, and Agricultural Implement Workers of America (UAW) Local 1874, organized a jobs committee to explore how they could save their jobs. After investigating Franklin's financial condition, the employees determined that purchasing the company was the best way to protect themselves.

At the same time, Harsco Corporation, which owned Capitol manufacturing, decided to sell Franklin due to the increasing significance of Franklin's losses. Harsco could not close Franklin without a buyer because it had a take-or-pay contract with the gas utility that ran a gas line to Franklin. Since the contract was in effect for at least another year, and no other buyer seemed interested in the less than desirable West Branch manufacturing location, Harsco knew that the employees' offer was the best it would get.

The employee effort to buy Franklin began in earnest when UAW International Representative Jack Laskowski sought assistance from the Michigan Employee Ownership Center (MEOC) and its general counsel. The employees subsequently formed a buyout association, retained counsel, and commissioned a feasibility study. The employees recognized that they needed strong management to make Franklin profitable and asked the company's former manager, Bob Stoner, to be the plant's new manager and chief executive officer. He had managed the plant for several years, was well acquainted with the forging business, and was well respected by local businesses and lenders.

Franklin's recent losses made it difficult to raise the money to finance the buyout. Union members made numerous calls to lenders and worked hard to raise funds from employees and various governmental bodies. The perseverance and positive attitude of the buyout association impressed the lenders. The National Bank of Detroit

(NBD), for example, became involved in finding other lenders to join it in financing the deal.

In addition to raising money, the buyout association worked hard to educate themselves and the community on the concept of employee ownership. Aided by the MEOC, the association developed its own employee ownership education program. As a part of this program, the Industrial Cooperative Association (ICA), the MEOC, the NBD, and the Michigan Department of Labor led education sessions attended by those involved in the buyout and interested community members.

As a result of the buyout association's efforts, Franklin Forge is now a worker cooperative. Each worker owns one voting membership share and a proportionate share of capital in the company's internal equity accounts. The workers were able to purchase their membership shares, which initially cost $5,000, with loans primarily from the Industrial Cooperative Association Revolving Loan fund and the Farmers and Merchants Bank of Hale. These loans required down payments of $250 and payments of $1 per working hour for 3 years to settle the $4,750 balance. Other lenders whose help was essential to finance the buyout included the State of Michigan, Ogemaw County, the National Bank of Detroit, the seller, and Franklin's chief executive officer. In the fall of 1986, employees invested an additional $2,000 each to cover working capital costs caused by a rapid increase in business.

Although Franklin Forge sustained heavy losses in its first year of operation as a cooperative, it was profitable in 1986 and 1987 and expects to be more profitable in 1988. As of the end of 1988, Bob Stoner reports that "Survival is no longer a paramount issue."[19]

Even more impressive than Franklin's move toward profitability is the number of jobs the buyout has created. In 1984, when the employees first contemplated a buyout, Franklin employed 20 people and had 82 on a seniority list. At the time of the buyout, management projected that Franklin would employ 38 workers by the end of the first full year of operation. After 6 months of operation,

Franklin already had 38 employees and by the end of 12 months, it employed 54 people. By December of 1986, Franklin employed 68 people. The 1988 employment figure averaged 82. For the year of October 1988 through September 1989, the average employment is expected to be approximately 100.[20]

McLouth Steel.[21] McLouth Steel has been resurrected by employee ownership several times. In December 1981, Mc-Louth Steel Corporation, located in Trenton and Gibraltar, Michigan (an area downriver from Detroit), filed for protection from its creditors under Chapter 11 of the Bankruptcy Code. McLouth, a steel manufacturer with over 2,000 employees, soon faced a situation that threatened even its short-term survival. A bankruptcy court ruling had given McLouth's secured creditors the right to close the company at virtually any time.[22]

In response, the union representing McLouth's employees, the USWA, took extraordinary actions to keep McLouth open. The USWA enlisted the support of the local political leaders of the downriver communities as well as the area's state and congressional representatives. The union also organized a march in Washington, D.C., using local high school bands, as part of its campaign to obtain federal assistance.[23]

At the same time, however, the secured creditors were unable to find a buyer for the company, despite a worldwide search conducted by Lazard Freres. Confronted with the impending closing of the plant, the International Union's District 29 Director, Harry Lester, became interested in the idea of employee ownership as a vehicle to save the facility and the employees' jobs. With funds voluntarily donated by McLouth's employees and major suppliers, consultants studied the feasibility of an employee buyout. Although the consultants determined that an employee buyout was feasible, the sellers decided not to pursue this alternative after Chicago industrialist Cyrus Tang expressed interest in purchasing the plant.[24]

Tang reached an agreement with the company and its secured creditors to purchase McLouth's steelmaking assets for $60 million, using primarily notes and income debentures. Tang also agreed to make a capital infusion of $15 million, $10 million of which was a subordinated loan from Tang. In addition, after over 3 months of intense negotiations, Tang and the USWA agreed to a labor contract under which USWA members obtained a 15 percent ownership interest and a 15 percent profit-sharing plan.[25]

While the new company, McLouth Steel Products Corporation, was profitable in its first year of operation, worsening conditions in the United States' steel industry jeopardized the company's future. In February 1987, the State of Michigan, McLouth, and the USWA engaged Touche Ross & Company to study whether the company's operations could be successfully restructured.[26]

According to USWA District 29 Newsletter, McLouth, which became majority employee owned in 1988, is turning around financially. The newsletter described the employee takeover and the company's future prospects in this manner:

On May 26, the collective efforts of thousands of Steelworkers paid off when the empoyees of McLouth Steel Products Corporation became the majority owners of the Downriver steel mill. The event was the end result of over 18 months of planning and negotiation coordinated by UWSA District 29 Director Harry E. Lester, with the support of International President Lynn Williams and other top UWSA Officers.

McLouth Steel Products Corporation was purchased by the employees through an Employee Stock Ownership Plan (ESOP). In return for an 87 percent share of the common stock of the company, the empoyees voted to invest 10 percent of their wages for the next five years. The alternative was bankruptcy leading to liquidation of the company established in 1982 when Chicago industrialist Cyrus Tang bought the steel making assets of McLouth Steel Corporation.

The ESOP agreement is part of a comprehensive five-year plan, the terms of which are virtually unprecedented in the industry. The agreement provides for the establishment of a Cooperative Partnership, a system in which the union plays an equal role in decision making concerning the company's operations. In addition, an Equality of Sacrifice agreement limits the number of non-union personnel that can be employed, and also requires that the ratio of non-union to union salaries and benefits not change during the life of the agreement.

Also an important part of the package is an agreement by the Pension Benefit Guaranty Corporation (PBCG) to withdraw its lawsuit filed in November, 1986, seeking the involuntary termination of the McLouth Union Pension Plan.

"This is another truly historic moment for the Steelworkers," stated Director Lester. "This effort could never have been accomplished without the cooperation of the workers, McLouth management, the State of Michigan, local communities, McLouth's creditors and customers, and the company's lenders."

Representing the UWSA on McLouth's Board of Directors are Director Lester; Doug Fraser, former President of the International Union, UAW; and Stephen Hester of the Washington, D.C. law firm of Arnold & Porter.

In early 1987, responding to the struggle to save the company from bankruptcy, a group of union and non-union McLouth employees established the "USWA/McLouth Survival Committee" (with Lester as Chairman), and rallied support for the ESOP concept, adopting the slogan: "The Future Is In Our Hands."

McLouth's future prospects, while considerably brighter than they were prior to the buyout, are not guaranteed. The employees must pay off $130 million of preferred stock over the next 15 years, and tens of millions of dollars must be raised in the next 5 years for blast furnace relines and other capital projects.

*ESOPs that Could Provide Better Management or Make
Firms More Profitable or Stable*

In some cases a company with a history of marginal
profitability that has recently become unprofitable is offered
for sale. It may be sold, or it may be closed if it is not sold.
Under these circumstances, union leaderships often feel that
employee ownership provides a better means of job security
than the other alternatives. Without employee ownership, it
is likely that the employees will be forced to take concessions
by a new owner or that a new owner will liquidate some or all
of the equipment or consolidate the work of the target company at some other facility of the new owner. Employee
ownership is particularly attractive as an alternative where
the union leadership feels that there is still an adequate
market for their product, that the state of technology at their
facility is adequate, that a lack of strong management has
caused the current distressed situation, and that better
management may cause the company to return to its former
profitability. The purchase of the Chase Brass Sheet Division
of Sohio by its employees and the creation of North Coast
Brass is a good example of this type of situation.

North Coast Brass and Copper Company.[28] On   January
29, 1988, 535 employees of Chase Brass Sheet Division, in
Cleveland, who were about to lose their jobs to a plant closing, bought the Sheet Division assets and became the
owners of North Coast Brass and Copper Company. Four
hundred and fifty of them were members of the International Association of Machinists (IAM) Local 1108, 45 were
members of OPEIU Local 17. North Coast Brass probably
has more immediate employee and union control in its
governance structure than any other employee buyout yet
of this size. The purchase price was significantly lower
than liquidation value. The total authorized borrowing for
asset purchase and working capital was $30 million.

Clarence Davis, International Association of Machinists District 54 Representative, said of the employee
buyout:[29]

When Sohio offered us the Sheet Division, our first reaction was, why should we be able to make a go of it if Sohio can't? If it's such a good deal why don't you keep it? We had also heard that ESOPs could be good or bad for our members, depending on how they were organized. Negotiating an ESOP buyout is a lot like negotiating anything else. You have to know what you want, what it is really worth, what the real alternatives are, and get good advice about the technicalities.

We then hired specialists to look at the proposal from our point of view....We concluded that Sohio had decided to stick with a decision it made years ago to invest in narrow strip technology rather than reinvesting in the Sheet Division. We weren't so sure about that decision and thought that we could make a success of the Sheet Division if we bought the assets at a more reasonable price than was being offered to us. We knew the plant would need substantial capital investment to make it competitive in the long run. Sohio's sale price, however, was based solely on its analysis of what it would cost Sohio to shut the plant down.

From the beginning our position was that if we had to make concessions to finance the deal (and it was clear from the beginning that we had to), every employee in the company would have to share in the sacrifice, and that since our members' share in the pain was the largest, we must be treated as the chief investor.

We feel that so far we have carried out that role, by our involvement in choosing a chief executive officer, by jointly choosing the outside directors, and by obtaining a strong voice for our members and their unions on the corporation's board of directors and the ESOP administrative committee. We believe strongly that the management must manage the company on a day to day basis, and must manage with a firm and fair hand. But where the future of the company is at stake or where major policy decisions about the company's future are being made we will have a strong voice.

Chase Brass was originally a family-owned company that established its Euclid facility in May 1929. It was purchased in the 1950s by Kennicott, which was subsequently bought by Sohio, which was acquired by British Petroleum (BP). The sheet division makes copper and brass sheet used largely for auto, electrical, and original equipment manufacturing purposes and also to make musical instruments.

Early in the 1980s Sohio made a decision not to reinvest in modernization of the sheet division, but rather to invest in a new continuous strip plant in Shelby, North Carolina. Then in the spring of 1987, when the Sheet Division began to lose money, Sohio offered the Sheet Division to the employees as an ESOP.

In the Spring of 1987, Standard Oil (commonly called Sohio) contacted the general manager of the Chase Brass Sheet Division and the Union representatives and offered the employees an opportunity to purchase the plant.[30] Sohio made it clear that they planned to close the plant if they could not find another buyer and that they had not succeeded in their efforts to sell "into strong hands," according to Alex Goldstein of Sohio.

Once the Unions concluded, based on their independent feasibility study, that employee ownership at the right price and with proper controls was a viable option, they began to work with local management as an ad hoc employee buyout committee to negotiate with Sohio regarding the price, terms, and conditions of the proposed sale.

The buyout committee's feasibility study concluded that if the employees were able to buy the company at a reasonable enough price and could cut costs through both operating efficiencies and labor cost reductions enough to make approximately $16 million in capital improvements over the first 4 years of the new ownership, the business would survive, remain competitive in the long run, and provide some recoupment of the employee sacrifices over a period of years.

The unions and the buyout committee, aided by their consultants, succeeded in:

1. Negotiating a low enough price with Sohio.

2. Leaving pension liability and much environmental liability with the seller.
3. Recruiting a CEO and several other highly qualified individuals to top management and board of director positions, while retaining much of the existing management.
4. Bringing back as an active consultant Paul Totten, a former general manager of the sheet division and former vice president of Chase Brass Corporation.
5. Ultimately obtaining an $8 million term loan and a $22 million revolving credit line from AmeriTrust to finance the transaction, using an Employee Stock Ownership Plan (ESOP) acceptable to all parties.

The financing was based on the understanding that $10 million of it would be lent to North Coast Brass through its ESOP. This ESOP provides tax savings for the lender and the corporation. These savings provide North Coast Brass with the essential operating cash it will need to grow, capitalize, and handle the large inventory of raw and finished goods required in a commodity business.

In exchange for the union employees making the necessary substantial financial sacrifices, the unions insisted on having in both the ESOP and the corporate structure provisions giving the employees one vote per person on all stockholder issues. Most ESOPs allow employees to vote their shares only on major corporate issues, such as mergers and acquisitions, not on such matters as the membership of the board of directors. They also insisted on provisions giving their elected representatives to the corporate board of directors and the ESOP administrative committee a strong voice over the future direction of the company.

In most ESOP companies, employee rights exist solely in the ESOP documents and not in the basic corporate structure itself. Similarly, in most corporations, the board of directors has the authority to terminate the ESOP, sub-

ject to some legal restrictions. The Chase Brass Buyout
Committee intends to keep the company substantially
employee owned for a long time, so it put the employee
ownership in the corporate structure itself. Although this
effort initially caused the lender some concern, North Coast
and Ameritrust were able to agree on mechanisms that
protected the short-term security interests of the lender
and the long-term interests of the employee owners.

To make the buyout possible, all employees took a substantial cut in pay and benefits. In exchange, each
employee got:

1. Stock allocated based on pay.
2. One vote per person, not per share.
3. Thirty days notice of all nonbudgeted expenditures
   in excess of $1 million.
4. Four union representatives on a board of nine—two
   elected by local union members, one appointed by
   the IAM District and one appointed by the IAM
   Local. (The board also contains two management
   representatives and three outsiders. The initial
   group of outsiders was chosen jointly by labor and
   management. For the company's first 3 years, out-
   sider replacements will be alternately elected by
   the outsiders plus the management representatives
   and the outsiders plus the union representatives.
   After 1990, vacant outside board seats will be filled
   by a majority vote of the remaining board members.)
5. One hundred percent vesting after 2 years of service, including years of service with Chase. (Thus,
   95 percent of the employees were 100 percent
   vested immediately in the ESOP.)
6. Elected representatives on the ESOP Administrative Committee from the IAM, the OPEIU, management, an at-large elected representative, and an
   appointed IAM District representative.

7. A profit-sharing plan.

Substantial education programs are being developed and implemented to streamline efficiency in all areas of the company and to acquaint all employees with the new corporate governance and workplace participation methods used at North Coast.[31]

ESOPs that Restructure Employers to Preserve Labor Rates, Job Security, Participation, Dignity, and Involvement in Future Direction of Firms

United Airlines, Allegis, and TWA. The action of the Air Line Pilots Association (ALPA) in attempting to buy United Airlines from its new parent, Allegis, is the most prominent case of a new use of capital strategies by labor. ALPA concluded that United Airlines' merger with a car rental company and hotel chains to become Allegis was bad for the airline and its employees. They believed the airline was squandering resources in the auto rental and hotel businesses that were needed for reinvestment in the airline.[32]

Although the union members have not yet succeeded in their effort to purchase the airline, they have succeeded in two of their major objectives. First, the union's efforts strongly influenced the Allegis board of directors to restructure the companies so that the airline is once again a separate corporation, not being drained of its resources by the other businesses. The board sold off Hertz and the Hilton and Westin hotel chains and changed the corporation's name back to UAL, Inc. Second, a CEO whom the union found objectionable has been replaced.[33] ALPA's UAL effort built on its earlier success in siding with Carl Ichan in his effort to purchase TWA. At TWA, ALPA joined Ichan to prevent a purchase by Frank Lorenzo, who had eliminated the unions after his purchase of Continental Air Lines.[34]

EMPLOYEE OWNERSHIP AND PARTICIPATION AND THE NEW INDUSTRIAL PARTNERSHIP

The United States General Accounting Office (GAO) has been studying ESOPs, at the request of the Senate Finance Committee, almost since their inception as tax-qualified plans in 1974. In its fourth and final report, the GAO examined the following issues:

1. Do companies with ESOPS experience an improvement in corporate performance, either in terms of profitability or productivity?
2. What ESOP related factors, if any, are related to changes in performance?[35]

The report noted that:

With regard to several factors that have been suggested as likely to affect ESOP firms' performance, none that GAO examined, except employee participation, showed a statistically significant relationship with changes in either profitability or productivity. Those ESOP firms in which nonmanagerial employees have a role in making corporate decisions through work groups or committees showed more improvement in our measure of productivity than firms without such participation.

Overall, GAO concluded that ESOPS have moved in the direction of meeting their legislative goals of broadening capital ownership and providing an alternative means to finance capital growth....ESOPS also have involved some increase in employee participation in corporate management, but this has not led to control over management by nonmanagerial employees.[36]

These GAO findings support the conclusion that pursuit of the type of ESOPs preferred by labor, as described in the AFL-CIO Guidelines and in the USWA Resolution found in Exhibits 9.1 and 9.2 at the end of this chapter, which involve more employee voice and participation than many traditional ESOPs, are also the type of ESOPs most likely to produce the most increase in productivity and benefit to the corporation beyond the obvious tax advantages. This finding contrasts with the practice of most traditional ESOPs, which involve little employee voice connected to employee ownership.

CONCLUSION

Employee ownership has been used by unions for their members' benefit, and it has been used by others both for the benefit and detriment of union members. An employee ownership plan is a very flexible mechanism that can serve a wide variety of purposes. In cases where the unions and their members' rights to fair treatment have been ignored, the outcome for the company has not been beneficial. By contrast, where employee participation has been maximized, productivity has increased. Thus, a company considering proposing employee ownership in a unionized facility would do well to read and heed the guidelines of the AFL-CIO and the USWA and the GAO study. A truly participative ESOP is likely to be a worthwhile undertaking if the company is viable. But an ESOP aimed solely at tax sheltering may present considerable problems unless the concerns of the union are dealt with as a major part of the planning process.

NOTES

1   The section on Scott & Fetzer is based on material from Randy Barber, *ESOPs, Their Uses and Abuses* (Unpublished manuscript, 1985) and NCEO, "End of Scott & Fetzer ESOP Buyout to Have Major Impact on Large ESOP LBO's," *Employee Ownership* (October 1985), pp. 1, 5.

2   "End of Scott & Fetzer ESOP Buyout to Have Major Impact on Large ESOP LBO's," Employee Ownership (October 1985) pp. 1, 5.

3   29 CFR Part 2510, 53 Fed. Reg. 17,632 (1988), (to

be codified at 29 C.F.R. pt. 2510) (proposed May 17, 1988), 15 Pens. Rep. (BNA) 857 (May 23, 1988).

4 Ibid. at 859.

5 Ibid. at 861.

6 John Hoerr, "ESOPs: Revolution or Ripoff?" *Business Week* 15 April, 1985, pp. 94–97.

7 *Hartman* v. *Boulis*, No. S800100 (N.D. Ind. complaint filed February 23, 1988).

8 Telephone interview with Dennis Scott, International Representative IWA, April 26, 1981.

9 Telephone interview with Mark Hardesty, Research Department, International UAW (October 28, 1988).

10 Thomas J. Lueck, "A Noble Experiment Goes Bankrupt," *New York Times*, 3 May, 1987, sec. 3, p. 1. Lueck, "Test of Worker Owners Is Ending on Sour Notes," *New York Times*, 11 August, 1987, sec. B, p. 1.

11 Personal knowledge of author who designed and implemented the employee ownership program at Franklin Forge.

12 The section on Republic Container is based on Deborah Groban Olson, "Employee Ownership: An Economic Development Tool for Anchoring Capital in Local Communities," *New York University Review of Law and Social Change* (1986–87, pp. 234–267 and a telephone interview with Republic Container Chief Financial Officer Charlie Johnson, September 30, 1988.

13 Companies acquired by their employees when threatened with bankruptcy include Hyatt-Clark Industries and Rath Packing.

14 The association retained the author as counsel and Chuck Jacobs as business consultant to represent them in negotiations with LTV Steel and the lenders and help structure the deal. The author also assisted the union and employees in decisions

about the structure of the ESOP, the new corporation, and the revisions in their compensation package.

15 Speech by N. Green, National Association of Management and Technical Assistance Centers Annual Meeting, Washington, D.C., October 15, 1987).

16 J. Zalusky (AFL-CIO Chief Economist), "Profit-Sharing and Employee Ownership," *AFL-CIO Staff Training Institute Monograph*, October 17-21, 1988.

17 Ibid.

18 The section on Franklin Forge is based on Deborah Groban Olson, "Employee Ownership: An Economic Development Tool for Anchoring Capital in Local Communities," *New York University Review of Law and Social Change* (1986–1987), pp. 239–267.

19 Telephone interview with the President and Chief Executive Officer of Franklin Forge, November 7, 1988.

20 Telephone interview with George Andros, Representative, International United Automobile, Aerospace and Agricultural Implement Workers of America, March 5, 1987.

21 The section on McLouth Steel is based on Deborah Groban Olson, "Employee Ownership: An Economic Development Tool for Anchoring Capital in Local Communities," *New York University Review of Law and Social Change* (1986–1987), pp. 239–267.

22 In re McLouth Steel Corp., 20 Bankr. 688 (Bankr. E.D. Mich. 1982).

23 Telephone interview with Harry Lester, Director, District 29, United Steelworkers of America (March 1986).

24 Ibid.

25 Ibid.

26 Idib.

27 "Employees Buy McLouth Steel Products," *USWA District 29 Newsletter* (Summer, 1988.)

[28] The section on North Coast Brass and Copper Company is based on a press release by the company of February 23, 1988.

[29] Ibid.

[30] IAM District 54 Representative Clarence Davis, IAM Local 1108 President Jack Ruolo and Chief Steward Henry Underwood, and OPEIU Local 17 President James Loach.

[31] Telephone interview with Harry Lester, Director, District 29, United Steelworkers of America (March 1986).

[32] Air Line Pilots Association, "Allegis Names New CEO and Considers Self-Tender," *United Family News*, (December 11, 1987), p. 1.

[33] Judith Valente, "Allegis Begins Talks with Its Unions On Employee Stake in United Air Unit," *The Wall Street Journal*, (June 12, 1987)., p. 2. Telephone interview with Captain Roger Hall, 1st Vice President, Airline Pilots Association, November 9, 1988.

[34] Ibid. interview with Robert Hall.

[35] United States General Accounting Office, Report to the Chairman, Committee on Finance, U.S. Senate, ESOPs: Little Evidence of Effects on Corporate Performance (October 1987).

[36] Ibid. at 3.

Exhibit 9.1
AFL-CIO Guidelines on Employee Stock Ownership Plans*

Feasibility Studies

The legal, financial, and organizational complexities of an ESOP require that any proposals be given intense scrutiny. The condition of the firm and the industry within which it operates should be assessed by people with specific expertise in such matters. Workers should have an understanding of all potential options and be involved in the process at an early date.

Pension Plans

While ESOPs and traditional pension plans are both regulated by the Employee Retirement Income Security Act (ERISA), pension plans are guaranteed by the federal government, but the benefits of an ESOP plan are not guaranteed at all. In some situations, employees are asked to give up their pension plan as a means to provide the capital for the ESOP start-up. One of the major drawbacks to this approach is that it puts employees in the position of having their current and future security depend solely on the survival and health of a single firm. Pension plans, on the other hand, are invested in a wide variety of ways in order to protect against poor performance by a single firm or industry.

Employee Participation

Before setting up an ESOP, it is helpful to set up some mechanisms which will allow employees to participate in decision-making and information exchange in respect to the company. Each situation may require a different approach, but the workforce should be included in decision-making regarding the company from the very beginning of the effort for the ESOP to have a chance for success.

---

*Reprinted with permission of the AFL-CIO from The AFL-CIO Guidelines for Negotiating Employee Ownership, a statement by the AFL-CIO Executive Council, August 18, 1987.

Voting Power

Make sure ESOP members can vote their stock. Although there is some debate about the necessity of voting rights for worker owners, our experts all suggested that such arrangements enable members to better protect their interests and evaluate the kinds of issues they must deal with in the context of ESOP plans. Many ESOPs are created with voting structures that effectively prevent workers from exercising power or even being able to influence the activities of the ESOP. One approach suggests that voting rights should be structured on a one-person, one-vote basis and that any other approach will lessen the opportunity for participation by all segments of the workforce.

Selecting ESOP Trustees

Particularly if workers cannot vote their stock—and even if they can—they should, from the very inception of the ESOP, be represented on the ESOP board of trustees. There are frequently conflicts between workers' interests and the approach taken by management-controlled ESOP boards.

Equitable Stock Allocation

In setting up a plan, stock can be distributed in a variety of ways, including allocations by salary, tenure, hours worked, or in other ways appropriate to a given situation. This is a very important aspect of ESOP design. Over time, the allocation will determine which groups within the company will be in a position to consolidate ownership control.

Stock Distributions

It is important to work out in advance what will happen to the stock that is eventually distributed to employees. That is, when employees decide to leave the firm, how can they sell their stock and how will the price for that stock be determined? If companies are actively traded on public markets, this may not be a difficult issue. In closely held firms, however, where there may be no external market for the securities, the method by which an appropriate price for stock is determined becomes very significant.

Vesting Schedules
Most ESOP transactions place stock in trust for a period of years. It is important that workers have the right to a complete and fully vested interest in that stock within a reasonable period of time. Rapid vesting can be a useful financial goal to reward less tenured or more mobile employees.

Initial Evaluation Formula
Stock that goes into an ESOP can be evaluated in a variety of ways. In one recent case, the company not only attempted to use an ESOP to defeat the union, but was planning to sell 60 percent of the firm's stock to a few managers and financiers at an average price of about $3.30 and to sell the remainder to employees through the ESOP—at over $44 per share. In this case, on complaint of the union, ERISA administrators at the U.S. Department of Labor interceded.

Defining Employers for Purposes of the ESOP
It may be to the advantage of unionized employees to define the eligibility for ESOP participation as broadly as possible—even where that definition included nonmanagement employees that are not part of the union. Such an approach could also include part-time employees that are not part of the bargaining unit. The idea is to dilute the possibilities of managment being able to create and control a separate ESOP for noncontract employees.

Quick Implementation of Personnel Cutbacks
Many ESOPs start with the assumption that there will be cuts in the workforce at both the supervisory and production levels. Experts suggest that it is very hard to make people owners one day and to dismiss them the next. Anticipated reductions in staff should be undertaken as close to the outset of the ESOP undertaking as possible.

Exhibit 9.2
USWA Resolution on Employee Stock Ownership Plans[*]

WHEREAS, Congress has enacted favorable provisions in both corporate and personal income tax law to stimulate stock ownership by employees, and various states have similarly established programs to assist employee stock ownership plans (ESOPs) as vehicles for economic development; and

WHEREAS, employee stock ownership plans may be either "partial" ESOPs in the sense of allocating only some part of a company's total stock to employees, or "100%" ESOPs in the sense that all of a company's stock becomes employee-owned; and

WHEREAS, partial ESOPs have been used successfully by our Union in certain situations as a means by which members may invest in the future of their jobs, providing financial relief to companies in dire circumstances while also creating a means of repayment for such investments if the company survives and ultimately prospers; and

WHEREAS, 100% ESOPs may, in certain situations, be a means of preserving jobs for members whose plants might otherwise be closed or purchased by anti-union operators; and

WHEREAS, the ongoing depression which ravaged the metals industries of the United States for more than five years, largely because of the unsound economic policies pursued by the Reagan Administration and the Federal Reserve Board, has created numerous situations in which our members are forced to consider either partial or 100% ESOPs, and will create more such situations, and

WHEREAS, the labor relations laws of the United States do not consider the various unique relationships created by employee-owned companies.

[*]Reprinted with the permission of the United Steelworkers of America International Union from USWA Resolution Number 17 on Employee Ownership Adopted on August 5, 1988.

THEREFORE, BE IT RESOLVED that the following policies are herewith adopted respecting ESOPs:

(1) Any ESOP covering our members must be part of the labor agreement, and provide a continuing mechanism for repayment of any investments by our members, beyond the term of the labor agreement, if necessary.

(2) Any ESOP covering our members must provide for full pass-through of stock voting rights to the members on an equitable basis, so that our members' investments are accorded at least equal respect and influence to that accorded other comparable investments by non-employees.

(3) ESOPs must never by used as a substitute for an adequate, funded pension plan guaranteed by the appropriate governmental agency. The basic retirement incomes of our members must not be dependent on the solvency of any single business enterprise in a free market economy.

(4) Under policies established by the National Labor Relations Board, it is unlawful for the Union to make direct investments or loans to an ESOP Company and at the same time represent employees of another business in competition with the ESOP Company. Even if this were not the policy of the NLRB, it would clearly be improper for the Union to spend dues income from all of its members on such investments. It shall therefore remain the policy of the Union that none of its funds shall be directly invested or loaned to any employer, including an ESOP Company.

(5) PARTIAL ESOPS—It is only appropriate for our members to invest in a partial ESOP where the Union has performed a thorough investigation and analysis of the employer's finances and financial prospects to assess the need for such investments, the likely effect of such investments in terms of preserving job opportunities, and the potential ability of the employer to repay such investment.

Where the investigation and analysis reveal that the employer is or would be in dire circumstances threatening the stability of our members' jobs without an investment by our members and that there are reasonable grounds to expect the investments will help preserve jobs and are likely to be repaid, the Union will consider negotiating a partial ESOP. The most appropriate model for such an ESOP is the Employee Investment Program negotiated with Bethlehem Steel as part of the 1986 contract negotiations.

(6) 100% ESOPs—It is appropriate for our members to invest in 100% ESOPs only where a competent feasibility study performed by an experienced and impartial financial analyst has demonstrated that there is a reasonable prospect for the business entity to survive on a long-term basis as an employee-owned company. These feasibility studies are expensive, but they may be the only effective way of defending jobs or standards of living of our members. Accordingly, in such circumstances and where adequate joint funding by public or private sources alone is unavailable, the International Officers are authorized to advance or pay a reasonable portion of the costs of such a feasibility study. If the results of such a feasiblity study are favorable, the Union will arrange for competent independent attorneys, accountants, and, if necessary, investment bankers to advise and assist our members and their fellow employees in the complex process of negotiating for the purchase of the facilities involved and the establishment of the employee-owned business. However, these expert professional services should be provided at the expense of the newly formed ESOP Company.

BE IT FURTHER RESOLVED that to help implement the above policies, our Union shall seek the following legislative goals:

(1) Congress should be encourage to continue the favorable tax treatment for ESOPs.

(2) The National Labor Relations Act of the United States should be modified to recognize the existence of employee-owned companies and to provide for the unique collective bargaining relationship in these companies. Such modifications should fully authorize unions to represent the interests of their members, both as workers and as owners. Specifically, such modifications should:

(a) Prohibit establishment of ESOPs covering union members except through the collective bargaining process.

(b) Make both the existence of an ESOP and issues affecting the structure of the ESOP, such as stock voting rights, methods of allocating and vesting stock, valuation of stock, etc., mandatory subjects of the collective bargaining process.

(c) Authorize unions to negotiate for expert legal, accounting, and investment advice to be provided to members who are or will be owners of stock in ESOP companies, at the expense of such companies.

(3) Where they do not exist, government agencies should develop programs to help fund feasibility studies for potential ESOPs without expecting repayment from failed efforts.

Communicating the Message of Employee Stock Ownership

Shela C. Turpin-Forster

Shela C. Turpin-Forster is President and Senior Associate of ESOP/Incentive Strategies, a consulting firm specializing in employee stock ownership in Alexandria, VA. Her clients range from Fortune 500 corporations to firms with under 100 employees and cover a broad diversity of American businesses.

Shela has a background in law and behavioral sciences with a J.D. from Georgetown University where she is currently a candidate for an M.L.S. with a concentration in organizational behavior. She is on the Board of Directors of the ESOP Association of America and Chairman of its Advisory Committee on Communications and Participation.

TEN

"Now you're an owner!"

What does this message mean to the average employee who is learning, perhaps for the first time, about an ESOP at his company? Ownership is viewed positively in our culture. Owning something is usually judged to be more desirable than renting it. Most people in the United States prefer to own their homes and treat something they own with more care than something that they rent. Thus, an employee will normally have positive expectations about the message "Now you're an owner" in regard to an ESOP.

From a communicator's perspective, employee stock ownership gets everyone's attention easily. The challenge comes in communicating to employees just exactly what it means to be an owner. There is no one right way to convey this message; each company must determine its own individual ownership message.

Employee ownership holds enormous potential for improvement in attitudes and performance within most companies. However, like all potential, it has to be developed. Too many companies, whether 10 percent or 100 percent employee owned, are wasting a chance to interest and motivate their employees because they haven't decided what their expectations and intentions are for employee ownership.

This chapter sets out a framework for a company to use in analyzing what its intentions for employee stock ownership really are and, therefore, what its message should be. First, the concept of ownership and its meaning

255

in our culture, as well as the potential risk of telling employees that they are owners, will be examined. Then, a "goals" continuum to help a company place itself in terms of ESOP objectives will be explained, and some practical ways to get started will be presented.

Implied ownership contract is the core of energy waiting to be tapped in any employee ownership situation. Examining this implied contract is a first step for companies in determining what they want to accomplish through employee stock ownership.

THE IMPLIED OWNERSHIP CONTRACT

Most people work at a job with the understanding that, in return for wages and perhaps benefits, they will perform work for the organization hiring them. Their interest in the employer's well-being is assumed to focus upon continuation of their job and reasonable increases in their wages and benefits over time.

Once stock ownership is added to the equation, employees' interest in the company's financial performance usually increases. The employees' stake in the company is expanded to that of employee-investors. As stockholders, the value of their shares will depend on how well the company performs.

The implied ownership contract is composed of those images of monetary gain, control, and employee input that are conjured up when an employee hears "Now you're an owner." To a significant extent, this content is fixed by cultural context and must be addressed first before a company sets out to establish its own message of ownership.

Monetary Gain

To most people, owners of companies are the people who make "real" money—an amount sufficient to leave behind mundane cares and enjoy life. Employees, when told that they're owners, hope eventually to get some of that real money. According to the study on which the book *Employee Ownership in America* is based, the biggest plus of employee ownership for most people is the amount of value they see building in their stock accounts.[1]

The significance of the implied ownership contract is that in return for the chance to make some real money through a capital stake in the company, an employee will become fully committed to doing his part to see that results occur. This connection is the potential powerhouse of positive improvement for a company with employee ownership. An employee-owner who works late without extra compensation to revise a contract proposal or who books the most economical travel accommodations out of concern for the company's expenses does so, in part at least, for himself. When half a day's production is wasted because of inaccurate machine settings, it becomes *our* problem rather than just *their* problem.

Control

While it is true that owners are typically thought of as the people with the ability to control the company, available research indicates that most employees aren't intensely interested in voting control.[2] This research is born out by our firm's experience with surveys and focus groups in employee-owned companies. There is little indication that employees expect any automatic changes in managerial practices or operational control to occur as a result of employee ownership, although they may, in fact, wish to see such changes occur.

Employee Input

While employees do not necessarily view stock ownership as an opportunity to exert managerial control, they frequently understand the word *owner* to suggest that their voices will be heard, at least in relation to their specific jobs.[3] If they are being given the opportunity to share in their company's success, it becomes inconsistent for management to ignore what they have to say about how their work is being performed.

One of the most striking discrepancies between Japanese and American workers is the much greater number of ideas generated by the Japanese. The Japanese averaged 4 improvement ideas per worker in 1974, and they increased that number to 24 in 1987, the same year in which the average number of improvement ideas per worker in the United States was 0.14. Of course, if surveyed, many American workers would probably say they had never been asked or given the opportunity to share their improvement ideas. (Suggestion boxes don't count!)

The Paradox of Employee Ownership

Is there a paradox in the operation of an ESOP company? Employee ownership is generally expected to spread responsibility and engender a team attitude—to shift the emphasis downward in the organization. At the same time, because of the operating structures of most companies and the difficulties of large group decision making, employee ownership may require reinvigorated leadership and improved management in order to be most effective—putting more focus on the people at the top of the organization.

Thus, the implied contract of employee ownership may have a negative exposure for many companies that is ignored at some risk. Employees are quick to realize that their efforts and rewards are directly linked via their stock ownership, which may make them more responsible and committed in their individual positions. However, if they see management actions and practices that they view as wasteful and counterproductive for the company and feel that they are unable to do anything about such actions, they may actually become more cynical and negative in their attitudes (and lax in their performance) than they were before stock ownership was introduced.

An example of this can be seen in the response of one clerical manager in a company with a long-established ESOP to this question posed in a focus group: "Do you think that you or your fellow employees consider the avoidance of waste and inefficiency more important as a result of your stock ownership through the ESOP?" The employee answered that it was hard for anyone to get excited about being more careful or avoiding waste when senior management repeatedly wasted money. He cited the example of management spending over $100,000 to renovate a work area for a department that was used for less than a year before the department was moved and the renovations were torn out. The employee wasn't interested in making the decision about the renovations (he wasn't after control), but he was unwilling to meet a standard or make a commitment that he felt would be meaningless or wasted in the bigger picture of the overall attitudes and behaviors (the culture) of the company. There may, in fact, have been a completely understandable explanation for what had occurred; but in the absence of any information from senior management this employee had assumed the worst.

Such examples underline the increased importance of internal communications when employees become stock owners. It becomes obvious in many employee-owned companies that it's to everyone's advantage to maximize internal information flow on operating decisions. Not only does information sharing undermine second guesses, but it also focuses employee energies through a shared sense of what is happening in the company's performance.

In our firm's surveys of employees in ESOP companies, it is clear that most people want to be heard on issues and problems directly involving their jobs. It is equally clear that they want managers to do their jobs and can get very frustrated if they perceive that those with the greatest operational control are somehow blocking or detracting from the company's performance.

Self assurance and flexibility, two of the personal characteristics noted in managers, become even more important in an employee ownership situation. Managers may have to get accustomed to answering tough questions if they expect employees to buy into the added commitment of stock ownership.

It is, therefore, not surprising to find the greatest resistance to employee stock ownership among middle managers who, often correctly, see their burdens being increased. Not only do they have to answer to senior management, they may have to become responsive to employees reporting to them as well.

Within the context of what employee stock ownership means in general, each company must refine and spell out what its particular message of ownership will be. Establishing appropriate goals is vital to this message.

ESTABLISHING APPROPRIATE GOALS

To determine its individual goals, a company must consider several questions. These include: What does the company want to achieve through employee stock ownership? Is ownership to be viewed as just another benefit with no expectations of morale or motivation improvement? Are any changes in operating procedures planned as a result of employee ownership? Are there already in place, or does the company plan to implement, processes to tap employee's ideas and input? Is it expected that employees will be more concerned with the company's performance and their role in this performance? Do managers want the ownership to ignite the productivity of employees?

A company's view of its ESOP usually falls somewhere along the following continuum:

*	*	*
Benefit	Motivator	Part of total performance culture

ESOP as a Benefit

Clearly, not every company will be interested in making employee ownership a centerpiece of its corporate culture. Where employee ownership is a relatively small element and is viewed by management as just another benefit, it could well be harmful to oversell the company's stock program. This does not mean that the company should ignore communication about employee ownership but that its efforts should accurately reflect what the company sees as the significance of stock ownership in its particular situation.

The importance of communications in such a case is illustrated by the following example. A large publicly traded corporation decided it would be unrealistic to expect its employees to significantly improve performance as a result of stock ownership, but it did see other appropriate objectives. Management in the company is implementing a long-term, multifaceted ESOP program that is already beginning to achieve (1) a greater awareness on the part of younger employees of how the ESOP can positively affect their future (which, it is hoped, will translate into greater retention for this group) and (2) an increased sense of shared identity with the parent corporation among the geographically dispersed employees through better understanding of how their stock ownership connects their efforts. This company views the ESOP as an employee benefit but also sees the opportunity of reaping a company benefit from the unique characteristics of stock ownership.

ESOP as a Motivator

Most companies, even those in which a relatively small percentage of outstanding stock is represented in the ESOP, will see an irresistible opportunity for employee motivation and involvement. Especially when the company stock in the ESOP is expected to increase in value, it is easy to convey the opportunity that stock ownership provides to individuals.

The basic message of many companies who look upon the ESOP as a motivator can be paraphrased as follows: "We are giving you stock to interest you in the growth and success of this company; therefore, we expect you to do everything in your power to contribute to that growth and success, because it's now even more clearly in your self-interest to do so."

To communicate the motivational aspects of an ESOP can be a fairly straightforward task but relies on or requires an understanding of capital ownership by employees. Therefore, what's involved in this task usually will be different when dealing with a work force of scientists and engineers, who often already own stock, than with a work force of less educated and less well-paid employees who are not direct investors in stock. Basic information about the economy, the role of stock ownership, capitalism, and the advantages of equity ownership may be needed.

At least a minimum amount of effort must be expended by any company for the ESOP to be motivational. This fact was not understood by the corporate human resources head who came to us for assistance with the lament, "I'm tired of having employees ask every year what the ESOP is invested in!" Just as products such as Coca-Cola only became household words through frequent advertising and exposure, so stock ownership in a company will not become something readily identified as important by employees unless they are reminded of it on a regular and consistent basis.

In a fast-growing and dynamic company, an ESOP can become motivational with almost no focused communication. If the per-share value is rising by multiples of 50 percent or greater annually, word of such value is quick to flow through an organization and gain employees' attention. Of course, the danger of neglecting communication may be unwarranted expectations of constant future success and a failure to appreciate how hard won the financial success actually is.

At the other extreme, if an ESOP is put into place exclusively for financial reasons and the fact that stock will go into employees' accounts is considered an unfortunate requirement of obtaining tax benefits, then there's little point in doing anything beyond what's legally mandated in communicating the plan. One of the basic lessons of communications (despite all the political campaign evidence to the contrary) is that, despite what you say in words, people will generally know if what you are thinking contradicts what you are saying.

Most companies will doubtless fall somewhere between these extreme situations and will be well served to develop and execute an ongoing communications program in conjunction with their employee stock ownership.

ESOP as Part of a Total Performance Culture

The company that wants to be the perfect "10" or close to it clearly has the greatest challenge with its ESOP. A desire for a *total performance culture*—an environment in which both human and material resources are used to their maximum advantage—can come from a variety of sources, ranging from a financial crisis that precipitates an employee buyout to a philosophical commitment on the part of senior management that the company will be the best.

A relatively small percentage of the companies in the United States that are widely considered to be committed to a total performance culture have significant employee stock ownership. This finding tells us something important about what those companies with employee ownership can do to develop their total performance culture. The two areas that are most widely accepted as indicators of a total performance culture are quality control and employee participation. These factors are beyond the consideration of this chapter, but ESOP companies interested in a total performance culture would do well to consider them.

Communicating about employee ownership and its benefits in a total performance culture is made easier by the internal congruity of the company—most of these companies have thought long and hard about their goals and have a clear idea of what they mean by employee ownership. There are no mixed messages for the employees such as "Yes, you are an owner, but we really don't want you to say anything around here."

However, there actually may be more communications challenges in a total performance culture because this type of approach empowers a lot of people—many of whom will expect to have a voice in what is happening. Almost any executive who has been involved in moving a company from traditional management practices toward a total performance culture will quickly admit that many times everyone regretted the decision and began to doubt the wisdom of the change in the company. The early stages can be periods of continual communications crises, when the ways of the old culture constantly clash with the new. The only justification for such upheaval is attaining total performance.

GETTING STARTED

It should be very clear at this point that effective ESOP communications depend on a company's willingness to address its objectives for employee stock ownership and to develop a realistic plan to achieve those objectives. Consequently, little advantage results from offering generalized suggestions or "canned" solutions to the particular communications issues a given ESOP company may encounter.

Frequently, managers sincerely ask where they can get started. One of the most overlooked elements in getting started on a communications plan, whether for a new or established ESOP, is the very first word of the ESOP acronym—the employees themselves.

Managers, especially in the privacy of confidential interviews, are usually very good at characterizing their company's culture, both in aspects they view as flattering and as unflattering. They are much less accurate, however, in judging how employees feel about company policies and practices and in assessing workers' general attitudes toward the company and stock ownership in it. Distortion in such perceptions can lead to irrelevant efforts and ill-fated hopes when determining goals for an ESOP.

By starting with the employees, a company can gain firsthand information about both what is needed and what is attainable in communication about the ESOP. Two basic techniques are available for obtaining this important information in a reliable fashion: employee surveys and focus groups.

Employee Surveys

Employee surveys are already well known to many companies. A properly designed and administered survey can tell much about what employees understand as well as what they think. For instance, in one ESOP company, the written survey revealed that most of the employees simply didn't understand the ESOP. It had been introduced at meetings along with a new 401(k) plan. Both new plans were being explained at the same time as the elimination of a money purchase plan was taking place. The employees had never gotten a clear picture of the ESOP or what it involved. And, it was hardly surprising to find that they believed they had lost as much or more than they had gained from the changes.

Probably few things are of less value to a company than an amateurish survey. To ask a question that isn't ambiguous is a big hurdle, but to set the answer in framework so that the response will be meaningful is an even more daunting task.

Yes-and-no formats frequently fail to tell a company what it needs to know. What does a company really learn by finding out that 72 percent of its employees said yes when asked if they felt the ESOP had made a difference in their work attitudes? Even if a yes answer is assumed to mean a positive difference in attitude, the company still doesn't know what kind of attitude change is occurring. Getting more precise information on attitude changes would allow the company to relate that information to existing and future levels of job performance.

For any but the smallest companies, the compilation and correlation of survey data is an enormous task, and outside assistance is recommended. This can be especially true when open-ended questions are included and the verbatim responses must be coded before they can be tallied or correlated with other results. Useful surveys are not inexpensive. Mailed surveys typically cost from $10 to $15 per respondent.

An important factor to be considered before undertaking a written survey is what comparison of the findings will be needed. A company should consider whether it can satisfy its purposes with information from its own employees or whether it really wants to have information that it can then compare to what is available in the way of industrywide or other norms.

Focus Groups

Another way to understand the current state of employee awareness and attitudes is through the focus group. The basic approach of the focus group was originally conceived in marketing and public relations to focus the attention of the representative consumers or audience upon a topic or product. The focus group technique can function as a sample survey in an ESOP situation and has certain complementary strengths and weaknesses with surveys.

While a survey has the ability to reach all interested parties (in actual practice, when mailed to the home, between 50 and 70 percent of those contacted respond on the average), the focus group will deal with a selective sample. It becomes very important to randomize the employees selected for the groups according to age, sex, income, and other appropriate factors. On the other hand, the focus group provides a flexibility in refining the survey process that is completely unattainable when a written survey is printed. To some extent, every written survey requires that certain assumptions be made in preparing the questions used. And we all know that assumptions can be our undoing. However, in the hands of skilled facilitators, a focus group can pick up on what is actually being said by participants and discover information or relationships of factors that would never appear in the written form simply because the right questions were never anticipated.

A major potential advantage of focus groups can be illustrated by the example of one company that had gained a significant number of employees through an acquisition. The newer employees had come from a company that offered an employee stock option plan that allowed employees to buy the company's stock twice a year. Although the employees had been a part of the new company for almost 2 years, very few of them fully understood the difference between the old stock plan and the ESOP. The annual participant statements they had received served only to confuse them more. Considering the ease with which everyone involved had been confusing *stock option* and *stock ownership*, it is hard to believe that a written survey would have gotten at this basic misperception.

Both surveys and focus groups can add valuable information to the process of deciding what a company should expect from employee ownership. This information also can make communications efforts more meaningful and effective. If employees are already knowledgeable about the specifics (eligibility rules, vesting, etc.) of their ESOP, it is a waste of valuable meeting time or of an expensive video presentation to overemphasize that material.

PRESENTING THE MESSAGE

This chapter is not intended as a primer on communication skills—such information is readily available from other sources. However, a few basic points are worth mentioning here.

Selecting the right media for the message is very important. A print format, for example, is an excellent way to convey information, but it is not interactive and is less useful than other approaches for motivating employees. Written material provides a practical, relatively inexpensive, permanent record that an employee can absorb at his own pace. However, a presentation or meeting with a group allows for immediate feedback from the employees and may have more impact on them than written material, especially when audiovisual aids are included. Through a presentation, all employees are exposed to the information and are able to get questions answered or concerns addressed right away.

Most situations can very effectively combine both written and audiovisual presentations. The written material can provide the specifics, while the audiovisual presentation can provide the conceptual information and highlights.

One of the most dynamic and effective ways to communicate about an ESOP is through a video or film that conveys the company's particular story. After all, the stock of a company, whether publicly traded or privately held, represents the value of the company. How better can a company convey what employees are getting through an ESOP than to show what the company is, perhaps including its history? This customized approach also allows a company to focus on what its particular employees can do as stock owners to see profits and productivity improve. While such productions cost an average of $3,000 to $4,000 a minute, their value and cost effectiveness make them very attractive in many situations.

Creative communication is possible even for companies with small budgets. Prepackaged material, such as filmstrips, payroll stuffers, posters, and articles, is available from sources like the ESOP Association.

CONCLUSION

Communication is the ingredient that distinguishes what a company wants to do with its ESOP. It is the way to establish what employee stock ownership means in each particular situation and deserves the attention of top decision makers. Employee stock ownership, for all its considerable advantages, is not a workplace miracle. Increased productivity, improved profits, and highly energized employees do not just happen upon an ESOP's announcement. That's when the work begins—the work of communication.

NOTES

[1]   Corey Rosen, Katherine Klein, and Karen Young. *Employee Ownership in America: The Equity Solution* (Lexington, MA: Lexington Books, 1986).

[2]   Ibid.

[3]   Ibid.

[4]   John Simmons, "Quality Circles and Employee Involvement," Speech given to the ESOP Association Convention, Washington, D.C., May 1988.

Ownership, Motivation, and Corporate Performance: Putting ESOPs to Work

Corey Rosen

Corey Rosen is executive director and cofounder of the National Center for Employee Ownership, a private, non-profit research and information organization located in Oakland, California. The Center is a membership-based source of information on ESOPs and other employee ownership plans. Mr. Rosen is the principal author of *Employee Ownership in America: The Equity Solution* (Lexington Books, 1985) and coauthor of *Taking Stock: Employee Ownership at Work* (Ballinger Books, 1986).

ELEVEN

Most people are first drawn to ESOPs because of their many tax benefits. Important as these are, however, there is much more to employee ownership than rollovers, leveraging, deductions, and put options. For many companies, the real power of employee ownership is the way in which it can help respin the web of motivation, commitment, turnover, and participation that largely determines how much a company's employees contribute to corporate performance. That contribution can be substantial. Our research has shown, for instance, that the most effective employee ownership companies have annual performance rates 12 to 17 points higher per year than their competitors'.[1] The effect of that kind of difference can dwarf any tax advantages ESOPs may have.

But simply installing an ESOP is no guarantee of more motivated and effective employees. Employees will only feel and act like owners if the notion of ownership is constantly reinforced. While setting up an ESOP involves what often seems to be an endless number of complex and ever-changing rules and regulations, running an ESOP company involves concepts that are both vastly simpler to describe and much more difficult to implement. Whereas setting up an ESOP primarily requires competent counsel, running an ESOP requires constant effort on the part of management to reinforce the idea of ownership. The effort, however, is well worthwhile.

EMPLOYEE OWNERSHIP AND CORPORATE PERFORMANCE: IS THERE REALLY A RELATIONSHIP?

It seems common sense that when employees own stock, they will be more motivated and productive and the company will make more money. Unfortunately, things are not so simple. Employees may not care very much about a stock ownership plan that will not provide benefits for many years. Or perhaps they will only care if the plan is structured in a certain way. As owners, employees might want a larger role in the company than management is willing to give, ultimately leading to cynicism rather than to motivation. Employees certainly won't be more motivated if the company does not make sure they understand how the ESOP works. Even if they are motivated by their ESOP, employees' productivity may not necessarily rise. Employees may want to work harder or contribute new ideas, but may find that their work is not structured so that working harder makes any difference and that no one wants to listen to their ideas.

In fact, some people would argue that employee ownership can lead to poorer economic performance. If employees have a say in the company, they might demand that as owners they receive higher wages or benefits or that the company maintain employment even when cutbacks are needed. If they cannot demand these things, the employees may be disgruntled about not being "real owners," causing more problems, not fewer.

All of these concerns have prompted a number of researchers to investigate whether employee ownership firms do better than their competitors. A study by Michael Conte and Arnold Tannenbaum at the University of Michigan in 1978, for instance, found that employee ownership firms were 1.5 times as profitable as other firms in their industries.[2] A 1980 study reported in the *Journal of Corporation Law* found that ESOP firms had twice the average annual productivity growth rate of nonESOP firms.[3] A 1984 study by the National Center for Employee Ownership (NCEO) found that publicly traded employee ownership firms outperformed 62–75 percent of their competitors, depending on the measure being used.[4] These findings seemed to be significant.

But all of these studies shared a common problem. They looked at companies that had already set up an ESOP. Were these companies doing better because of employee ownership, or were companies that were doing better simply more likely to set up plans in the first place? What was really needed was information on how companies did before and after they set up their plans.

Recently, the NCEO completed an analysis of the employment and sales growth rates of 20 ESOP firms for 5 years before their ESOP was in place and for 5 years after the ESOP had begun.[5] Each firm studied was compared to at least five similar companies so that any effect of general changes in the company's industry could be taken into account. The results of this study are presented in Table 11.1.

Table 11.1
Change in Performance before and after ESOP
Relative to NonESOP Companies

Measure	Before ESOP %/year	Afer ESOP %/year	Change %/year	Con-fidence level
Employment Growth	3.4	6.3	2.9	.91
Sales Growth	3.7	6.3	2.9	.75

As the table makes clear, companies with ESOPs performed better than their competitors before they set up their plans and did better still afterwards. Relative to other firms in the industry, growth rates were 2.6 percent and 2.9 percent higher after the ESOPs were set up than before. Is this a significant finding? Consider that the employment growth rate for the economy in the early 1980s was only 1.5 percent per year while the GNP increased at only 2.78 percent per year. Just the institution of the ESOP, aside from anything else the companies did, contributed that much growth or more.

MAKING EMPLOYEE OWNERSHIP WORK: MOTIVATION

The impressive figures on Table 11.1 are averages, and averages can be misleading. The average daily global temperature in January is quite temperate, but people in Alaska are freezing and people in the Australian desert are broiling. Within the sample of companies with ESOPs, some do very well; others do not do so well. What improves the performance of some of these companies? Answering this question involves two issues: why employees at some companies are more enthused about their ESOPs than at others and why some companies are more successful than others at translating this motivation into better economic performance.

To study these issues, the NCEO conducted a 4-year project involving 37 ESOPs. We surveyed 2,800 employees at the companies and conducted detailed management interviews. We coupled these data with data on the companies' growth rates and those of comparable conventional firms. The results were reported in the book *Employee Ownership in America: The Equity Solution.*[6] The employees were asked to report on what they thought about their jobs, their company, their ESOP, and their participation in decision making in the firm. Managers were asked to describe the structure of the ESOP, their motivations in setting up the plans, their perceptions of the employees' role in decision making, and basic facts about the company.

Table 11.2 provides details on how employees responded to being owners. The scores are based on a 7-point scale, with "0" indicating strong disagreement and "7" strong agreement. The mean is just the average; the standard deviation tells how far above and below the mean we would have to go to include two-thirds of the employees surveyed in that range. The scores are arranged from the items on which the employees agreed most strongly to those with which they disagreed most strongly.

The results present a very clear pattern. Employees are clearly proud to be owners, and ownership makes them

Table 11.2
How Employees Respond to Ownership

Item	Percent Agreeing	Mean	Standard Deviation
Owning stock in this company makes me more interested in the company's financial performance.	84	5.61	1.40
I'm proud to own stock in this company.	75	5.42	1.40
Owning stock in this company makes me want to stay longer than I would if I did not own stock.	65	4.87	1.66
Because of employee ownership, my work is more satisfying.	50	4.31	1.73
I am more careful and conscientious in my work because I own stock in this company.	46	4.24	1.72
I work harder on my job because I own company stock.	43	4.08	1.74
Employees here have more influence in company decision making than they would if they did not own stock.	29	3.44	1.73

Source: Adapted by permission of the publisher from *Employee Ownership in America* by Corey Rosen, Katherine Klein, and Karen Young (Lexington, MA: Lexington Books). Copyright © 1986, D.C. Heath and Company.

more interested in their companies' financial performance. Ownership also makes them want to stay with the company longer. But employees give a more mixed response to whether ownership makes them work harder, although a plan that can get over 40 percent of the employees to make a greater effort is certainly accomplishing something. Employees do not believe that ownership gives them more influence, a finding that reflects the fact that only some ESOP companies use their plans to do this.

These overall data suggest that employees are reacting most strongly to the financial aspects of ownership. Comparisons between companies yield the same results. The higher a company's annual contribution to its ESOP, the more committed employees are to their company, the more satisfied they are with their jobs, and the happier they are with their ownership plan. The average ESOP company contributes 10 percent of pay per year to the plan; the 10 companies with the highest employee scores in our sample averaged 14 percent. In other words, nothing makes an employee feel more like an owner than regular, substantial contributions by the company to the ESOP.

But other factors mattered as well. The most important of these was management philosophy toward ownership. For some companies, employee ownership is primarily a tax-saving or financing mechanism. For others, it is a central part of their management philosophy and plays a major role in corporate culture and identity. This philosophy is expressed in a number of very different ways in these companies. Managers may spend a lot of time walking around the plant talking and listening to employees. Employees are often called "partners" or "associates" or even "managers." Special perquisites such as special parking spaces or lunchrooms are often eliminated. Most important, management, in its everyday dealing with employees, treats them like owners. While it is not surprising that these more committed companies are much more likely to have employees who like their ESOP, their jobs, and their companies, it is notable that this factor was the second most important thing a company could do, well ahead of several other seemingly obvious things discussed later.

In many cases, management approaches the idea of an ESOP already philosophically committed to the general notion that employees should be treated as business colleagues, not hired help. But what if an ESOP is set up in a company where these attitudes do not prevail? Can attitudes be changed? Research on organizational behavior generally shows the answer is yes.[7] If, for instance, a company sets up a substantial ESOP and accompanies it with structures that allow managers and employees to share and act upon the information, ideas, and experience that both groups have, attitudes on both sides can change. This is easier to say than to do, of course, but it can be done. And it should be done if an ESOP is to live up to its potential.

Another important factor in the success of an ESOP is employee participation. The companies with the most successful ESOPS were the ones with the highest levels of employee participation. Usually, employees are most concerned about participating at the job level. Employees very clearly wanted to have more impact on how their work is organized and performed. In a few companies, employees also wanted to have significant input at the management level, but the majority said they would be happy if management simply listened to their ideas and let them know how the company was doing (something not all companies did).

The final important factor was communication. Employees will not be enthused about being owners if they do not understand what an ESOP is all about. Making sure employees know what stock is, what the ESOP is, and what they can expect from it is crucial.

But there is more to communication than sending out a summary plan description (even one a nonattorney can understand) and an annual account balance. Even companies that do more—slide shows, small group meetings, regular ESOP reports—may not be doing as much as they can to get the most out of their plan. Ideally, communication should entail sharing of information. There is much more to communicating than just telling the employees what a great deal the ESOP is. To improve communication, a company could, for instance, advertise that it is employee owned. This may be important in terms of employee pride as well as customer reaction. The company can share financial information, something that interests employees very much. While management often fears such information will be leaked to competitors, no company that we know of that shares this information has reported any problem at all, and most think it is a very important part of their ESOP. Communication can also be improved by soliciting employee ideas and reactions at ESOP meetings, rather than limiting input to managers. All of these suggestions take some time, but companies who use these ideas find the time well spent.

While all of the factors that improved the performance of the companies with ESOPs may seem obvious, several "obvious" factors did not have the expected effect. It might seem, for instance, that more educated, senior, and higher income employees would be more open to an ESOP, since they would understand it and benefit from it more. We did not find this to be the case, however. The demographic characteristics of employees were not related to any aspect of employee ownership satisfaction. It might also seem that smaller (or larger) companies, or more capital (or labor) intensive firms would have more success. Plausible arguments could be made either way, but company size and line of business did not affect employee attitudes about ownership. The percentage of the company owned by the plan was not a factor either. Employees would rather own 20 percent of a firm contributing 20 percent of pay per year than 100 percent of a firm contributing only 5 percent of pay. Company financial success made little difference as well, unless the company was in difficulty. Employees at financially troubled firms were often concerned about their ESOP. We also tested for the effect of plan characteristics, such as vesting and allocation formulas, on employee attitudes. These characteristics were not critical. The reason a plan was established and the age of the plan (all were at least 2 years old) were also not factors.

A final factor we looked at was voting rights. Many observers of employee ownership have suggested that whether employees can vote their shares on all issues is the most important factor in determining the success of employee ownership. Employees themselves, however, usually did not see voting as a key issue. Companies with full voting rights did not have more committed, satisfied workers, and employees generally did not express any great concern with the issue. These findings will not hold in every company, of course. In some cases, such as companies in which employees have made a sacrifice to become owners, voting rights may be much more important.

This finding may give comfort to those who believe that voting rights are not appropriate in ESOPs and will inevitably lead to a kind of corporate anarchy or employee control of the company. The situation is actually not so simple. In our study of companies that allow employees to vote, the results were remarkably consistent: employees are very conservative shareholders who almost invariably support management. Even when they can elect board members, employees virtually always elect management or qualified outsiders. And boards at these companies almost always operate by consensus, whether employees are directly represented or not. So not much actually changes when employees can vote their shares. Managers at these companies are happy with the arrangement and see voting as one additional way to communicate with employees about ownership. Much of the concern about voting, both negative and positive, therefore, seems excessive.

In summary, if a company wants its ESOP to motivate employees, it should give them large, regular contributions, treat them as owners, provide opportunities for participation, and share information.

MAKING EMPLOYEE OWNERSHIP WORK: COMPANY PERFORMANCE

If a company is doing the kinds of things outlined in the previous section, chances are very good that employees will come to work in the morning ready to do a better job than they would otherwise. But some companies are better able to take advantage of this employee enthusiasm than others are. Ownership does help companies grow, but do some companies benefit more from employee ownership than other companies?

To find out, we evaluated the performance of our sample companies relative to their competitors in terms of employment growth, sales growth, and growth in sales/employees. We then compared the performance of the ESOP companies in these terms to see which companies did best. We tested for any factor that might have an impact on how the ESOP affected performance: percentage of the company owned, management philosophy, size of the contribution, participation, communication, voting rights, plan structure, and so on. The findings were very clear. Only two factors mattered: participation at the job level and management philosophy toward ownership. These two factors are actually very closely related and really are part of the same thing: a company's efforts to involve employees in decision making. Nothing else affected the relationship between ownership and performance. The results are detailed in Table 11.3, with the numbers representing the differences in growth rates between the ESOP companies and the comparison group.

All of our findings lead to a very straightforward theory of effective management of an ESOP company. Employees will be enthused about ownership if they get large annual contributions, are treated as owners, can participate in decisions, and share information about the company. Once so motivated, however, there must be channels to translate this enthusiasm and commitment into more creative and productive behaviors. This involves a lot of work but also many rewards. The companies we studied that used all of the techniques we have described had indexed growth rates 12 to 17 percent per year greater than the companies that did the least with their plans. This means that in just 4½ to 6 years these companies would be twice as large as the less effective ESOP firms.

CASE EXAMPLES

While these findings describe in general what a company can do to manage its employee ownership program effectively,

Table 11.3
Performance by Level of Employee Participation
(Percent per year)

	Participation Level		
Performance measure	Low	Medium	High
PostESOP period:*			
Employment growth	1.69	11.77	12.22
Sales growth	−0.29	12.27	16.29
Growth in sales/employee	−2.90	−1.58	8.67
Difference pre- to postESOP:*			
Employment growth	−1.38	5.11	7.93
Sales growth	−10.55	5.00	10.93
Growth in sales/employee	−3.80	5.44	3.01
Employment growth:†			
Difference pre- to postESOP	−13.99	−2.85	4.35
PostESOP period	3.69	12.79	11.30

*Controlling for comparison companies.
†Controlling for industry-wide effects.
Source: Adapted by permission of the publisher from *Employee Ownership in America* by Corey Rosen, Katherine Klein, and Katherine Young (Lexington, MA: Lexington Books). Copyright © 1986, D.C. Heath and Company.

they do not provide very specific guidelines. Other than making large contributions, what exactly can a company do to assure that its employees will feel and act like owners? Unfortunately, no magic formula ensures that each company can accomplish this goal. What will work for one company may be totally inappropriate for another. While it may seem discouraging that no simple formulas can be used, the encouraging news is that we have found that the sincerity of a company's efforts is much more important than the particulars of its approach. If a company's management makes it clear that it really cares what employees think and takes whatever opportunities it can to treat them as owners, then the chances of its program working are very good.

Nonetheless, it is instructive to look at what other companies have done as a means of getting ideas and a sense of possibilities. The cases that follow describe four businesses of different types and sizes, each of which has been very successful both financially and in motivating its employees.

Allied Plywood

Allied Plywood is a 35-employee plywood wholesaler in Alexandria, Virginia. It became 100 percent employee owned in 1982 when its ESOP completed purchase of the shares of the retiring owner. From the time its ESOP was first set up in the mid-1970s, the company has sought to involve employees in a number of ways. Each month, for instance, a figure is posted indicating the total revenues the company would need to earn a profit for that month. Once that number is reached, about half the excess is distributed equally as bonuses. At the end of the year, an additional bonus is distributed, based on a formula considering seniority, days worked, job class, and performance. Bonuses have been paid every month and every year, including years during which the industry was in a depression. Monthly bonuses can be as high as $1,200, and all bonuses often exceed the workers' salaries. These salaries are lower than those of competitors, but total compensation is much higher. The flexibility this system provides makes it possible for Allied to maintain its employment levels even when business cycles fluctuate.

While the previous owner was at Allied, participation by employees in decision making was extensive but informal. Meetings were frequent and the president's door was always open. A lot of companies claim such participation, of course, but the system was actually practiced at Allied. After the owner left, the employees took a more active role, electing the board, writing evaluations of each other, and meeting when needed to make decisions.

The current president of Allied, Bob Shaw, goes out of his way to explain to employees why he is doing things, rather than just acting on his own. Extensive employee participation, he concedes, makes it more time-consuming to make decisions, but, he points out, it makes it much easier to implement decisions. If employees understand why something is being done and have a role in making the decision, they will carry out the decision much more readily than if it is imposed on them. This is an important lesson many employee ownership companies have taught us: It is tempting to save time making decisions by making them unilaterally, but it is a false economy that will cost time later when employees need to be persuaded to enthusiastically carry out the decisions.

The employee participation at Allied has paid off. The company made profits in the late 1970s when many firms in the industry were cutting back or closing. After the employees took over entirely, employment grew from 20 to 35, while sales increased 20 percent in 1984 and 25 percent in 1985.

Fastener Industries

Fastener Industries is a larger employee-owned firm located in Cleveland. The company's 120 employees make industrial weld fasteners. When the company became employee owned in the early 1980s, many of its competitors were going out of business. But Fastener continued to make a profit and even increased its employment somewhat.

President Rich Biernacki attributes much of this success to employee ownership. Fastener's employees had the highest levels of satisfaction with their ESOP of any of the companies we studied. Part of this is a result of Biernacki's management style. He meets regularly with all employees in groups of 11 to talk about their concerns. Biernacki spends much of his time walking around the plant talking and listening to employees, as do other managers. Employees are consulted about any decisions that seem appropriate, such as buying new machines and developing new production techniques. Employees have full voting rights and elect the board (they have consistently elected company officers).

Biernacki says the "employee knows his job best," and the employee's opinion should be respected. Biernacki does not mind the pressure that can come with employee participation, saying, "If I can't convince them I'm right, then maybe I'm not right."

Quad / Graphics

Quad/Graphics is a Wisconsin-based printing firm that has had a compound annual growth rate of 50 percent for the last 10 years. It now employs over 2,000 "partners" (not employees).

The company's corporate philosophy as expressed in their 1984 annual report, puts people first:

> Our emphasis is not on the numbers, but rather on people who are caring and sharing in common values; people who have stretched their minds and broadened their horizons to bring printing from the craft of the Middle Ages to the technology of the Space Age; and people—ordinary people—who have achieved this extraordinary result through the Quad philosophy of people helping people to become more than they ever hoped to be.

New employees at Quad/Graphics are put through what Quad/Graphics' president Harry Quadrucci calls "boot camp." They are assigned a mentor, go to the Quad/Graphics school (the school, housed in a former school building, was an employee idea), and are treated in a traditional, authoritarian way until they can demonstrate they can handle the company's participative management style. But after that testing period, employees are given considerable responsibility, including setting disciplinary standards for their peer groups, developing new products and processes, and being able to communicate directly with anyone else in the company.

Quadrucci tells his managers that they should not be supervisors but coordinators, seeking out people's ideas and talents, not telling them what to do. The ultimate symbol of this is the "spring fling" when all the managers take off for a retreat and the employees run the company. A lot could go wrong that day—an ink hue miscalculated, a customer turned away, an order filled improperly—but Quadrucci says it is well worthwhile. It reminds people that trust, not authority, is what makes the company work. This philosophy obviously has merit: Aside from their spectacular growth, the company has won numerous awards, Quadrucci has been the cover story of *Inc.* magazine, and the company is widely regarded as the industry's most innovative firm.

Weirton Steel

Weirton Steel presents what may be an even more dramatic case example. Bought by its 7,000 employees in 1984 to save the plant from closing, Weirton was considered to be just another doomed steel mill. But from 1984 through this writing, Weirton has made a profit in every quarter and has made a better return per ton sold than any steel company in America. While the steel industry was laying off over 90,000 workers in 1985 and 1986, Weirton was hiring another 1,400.

Part of Weirton's success can be attributed to the fact that, as owners, workers were willing to take an 18 percent pay cut. Even without that, however, Weirton would still be profitable, and given recent cuts at other mills, its total wage costs are fairly close to its competitors'. That is especially true when one considers that Weirton did something in early 1986 that no other large steel maker could have done; it distributed profit-sharing checks worth about $2,200 to each of its employees.

The real story behind Weirton's success is the way it has used its employee ownership plan as a springboard to create a more participative company. Employee representatives are on the board, and the union's leadership meets with management regularly to discuss future strategies. The company's president, Robert Loughhead, regularly tours the plant with the union president, Walter Bish, to listen to employee ideas and keep employees informed on current developments. Employees throughout the plant have been organized into employee participation groups, and a growing number of employees are being trained in statistical process control techniques to help assure efficient production. The participation groups saved $13 million dollars in the first year alone.

Participation is backed up with information sharing. A weekly Weirton video news program is carried on 80 VCRs throughout the plant. An employee-edited newspaper provides detailed and sometimes critical reports about how the company is doing. Public relations director Charles Cronin says the newsletter is the most thorough he has seen. "There are no bowling scores in the newsletter," he says with pride. A detailed annual report is sent to employees, although as a now 100 percent employee-owned firm, there is no obligation to share that kind of information. Far from seeing all of this as risky, Cronin contends that not sharing it would be risky.

The four companies we have described are very different, and the ways they involve employees are different. But they all share in common one very important thing: a president of the company who deeply believes that employees must be treated as owners of the company, not just at the end of the plan year when a statement is sent out, but every working day.

CONCLUSION

Although the tax and financial planning aspects of an ESOP are crucial, it is important to remember that the first word in ESOP is "employee." When considering whether to leverage or not, or how to deal with breaks in service, or what vesting schedule to use, a company should consider as well how the new owners of the company can be made to feel like owners. The results, whether measured in the satisfaction of going to work with more committed, involved people, or in the black and white of bottom lines, are likely to be worth the effort.

NOTES

[1]   Corey Rosen and Michael Quarrey, "How Well Is Employee Ownership Working?" *Harvard Business*

Review, 65, no. 5 (September/October 1987), pp. 126–30.

2 Michael Conte and Arnold Tannenbaum. *Employee Ownership* (Ann Arbor, MI: Survey Research Center, University of Michigan, 1980).

3 Thomas Marsh and Dale McAllister, "ESOPs Tables: A Survey of Companies with Employee Stock Ownership Plans," *Journal of Corporation Law*, 6, no.3 (1981), pp. 551–623.

4 Ira Wagner, *Report to the New York Stock Exchange on Employee Ownership and Corporate Performance in Public Companies* (Oakland, CA: NCEO, 1984).

5 Rosen and Quarrey, "How Well Is Employee Ownership Working?" pp. 126–30.

6 Corey Rosen, Katherine Klein, and Karen Young, *Employee Ownership in America: The Equity Solution* (Lexington, MA: Lexington Books, 1986).

7 See Fred Luthans, *Organizational Behavior* (New York: McGraw-Hill, 1973) for a general discussion of this issue. On the specific issue of the impact of ESOPs on attitudes, see Rosen, Klein, and Young, *Employee Ownership in America*.

APPENDIX A

Major Federal and State Laws

Compiled by William W. Merton,
Alan J. Hawksley, and
Helen H. Morrison*

* William W. Merton and Helen H. Morrison, with the law offices of Keck, Mahin & Cate in Chicago, and Alan J. Hawksley with the law offices of Mc-Dermott, Will & Emery, adopted the material in this appendix with permission from Corey Rosen and William Foote Whyte, *Legislative Guide to Employee Ownership* (1986), National Center for Employee Ownership.

APPENDIX A

FEDERAL LAWS

1. Regional Rail Reorganization Act of 1973. This was the first statute to mention "ESOPs." It required a feasibility study of the use of an ESOP for the reorganization of the Midwest and Northeast freight rail system into Conrail. The study eventually recommended against the idea.

2. Employee Retirement and Income Security Act of 1974 (ERISA). This law created a specific statutory framework for ESOPs and carefully exempted them from certain requirements applicable to other plans (such as pension and profit-sharing plans). The act thus provided ESOPs with the unique authority among employee benefit plans to borrow money. It also required ESOPs to invest primarily in employer securities, whereas other employee benefit plans cannot invest more than 10 percent of their assets in employer securities unless they can demonstrate that to do so is fiduciarially sound. ESOPs were defined as "qualified employee benefit plans," meaning that contributions to them are tax deductible (within limits) and that they must abide by the allocation, vesting, and other rules ERISA applies to qualified benefit plans.

3. Trade Act of 1974. This act created an authority within the Department of Commerce to make certain kinds of assistance available for areas suffering adverse effects

from foreign trade. The act contained provisions providing a preference for firms with ESOPs, but they were never effectively implemented.

4. Tax Reduction Act of 1975.   This act created the "TRA SOP"—the Tax Reduction Act Stock Ownership Plan. Under the act, a company could get an additional 1 percent credit over and above the 10 percent investment tax credit if an amount equal to at least 1 percent of the qualifying investment were contributed to an ESOP meeting the special rules of this act (including immediate vesting, allocation according to salary, etc.).

5. Tax Reform Act of 1976.   This act extended the life of TRASOPs through 1980 and added a provision that allowed the employer an additional ½ percent credit if an employee contribution equal to ½ percent of the qualifying investment were matched by the employer. The act contained an unusual congressional directive to the IRS to rewrite rules it had drafted earlier that Congress considered unfair to ESOPs.

6. Revenue Act of 1978.   TRASOPs were extended to 1984 (this was later changed) and allocation and other rules for TRASOPs were tightened. This act also required leveraged ESOPs to offer employees a put option in cases where the stock was not publicly traded. A full pass-through of voting rights on all allocated shares was made mandatory for publicly traded companies, while closely held firms were required to pass-through voting rights on issues that required more than a majority vote. These voting right rules applied to all ESOPs and, in closely held companies, to all qualified employee benefit plans investing more than 10 percent of their plans' assets in employer securities. Finally, the act created the General Stock Ownership Corporation, a special kind of statewide corporation in which all state residents could automatically become shareholders

in state economic ventures. The idea was intended for Alaska but never used.

7. United States Railway Association Authorizations of 1979. This act authorized an additional $2 million in loans to the Delaware and Hudson Railroad, provided the company set up an ESOP.

8. Technical Corrections Act of 1979. This act made a number of technical corrections to laws governing TRASOPs.

9. Miscellaneous Revenue Act of 1980. This act further extended the TRASOP credit and made a variety of technical corrections to ESOP law. The act also made various technical changes in rules for employee contributions to TRASOPs.

10. Small Business Employee Ownership Act. Prior to this act, the Small Business Association (SBA) would not guarantee loans to ESOPs, and their rules for loans in other employee ownership situations were very restrictive. This act provided statutory authority for the SBA to make loan guarantees to ESOPs and made their rules for loans to employee ownership situations more liberal.

11. Chrysler Loan Guarantee Act of 1980. As a part of the government's loan guarantee to Chrysler, the company was required to set up an ESOP and contribute $162.5 million worth of company stock to it by 1984.

12. Economic Recovery Tax Act of 1981. This act contained several important provisions. First, it phased out TRASOPs and replaced them with the "PAYSOPs"—Payroll Based Stock Ownership Plans. Under this act, a company could receive a tax credit equal to ½ percent of payroll for contributions to a PAYSOP of at least that amount in 1983

and 1984, increasing to ¾ percent in 1985–1987. Generally, PAYSOPs must follow the same rules that applied to TRASOPs, but with somewhat stricter allocation rules. Second, the act raised the limits on how much can be deducted for contributions to a leveraged ESOP. Under previous law, these deductions were limited to 15 percent of payroll; under the new law they were raised to 25 percent of payroll to cover the principal part of the repayment and an unlimited amount for the interest portion. Third, the act allowed companies that are substantially employee owned to require that departing employees take cash for the fair market value of their stock, rather than the stock itself, when receiving their ESOP distribution. Finally, the act broadened the put option requirement to include non-leveraged ESOPs.

13. Tax Equity and Fiscal Responsibility Act of 1982.
This act tightened provisions for all employee benefit plans in an effort to address abuses occurring in some plans. "Top- heavy" plans, plans in which 60 percent of the benefits go to officers, highly compensated employees, and top shareholders, were required to set up faster vesting schedules and follow other rules designed to get more benefits to other employees. New limits were imposed on how much a company can deduct when it has more than one qualified employee benefit plan, and the dollar limit on annual additions to a participant's account was lowered from $47,475 to $30,000, adjustable for inflation after 1985.

14. Trade Adjustment Assistance Act. This act reauthorized the program that can provide loans, loan guarantees, and technical assistance to firms adversely affected by foreign trade. The amendments provide that preference will be given to companies that channel at least 25 percent of the assistance they receive through an ESOP.

15. Deficit Reduction Act of 1984. This act contains the most significant incentives for employee ownership. They include:

A provision allowing an owner of an independent business to defer taxation on the gains made by a sale of stock to an ESOP or worker cooperative by reinvesting the gains within 12 months in the stock or stocks of other companies. When that new stock is sold, capital gains taxes would be due. At least 30 percent of the ownership of the firm must be held by the ESOP or cooperative after the transaction for the provision to be effective.

A provision allowing commercial lending institutions to deduct 50 percent of the interest income they receive from a loan to a company for the purpose of acquiring stock through an ESOP. (The loan can be directly to the ESOP, or to the company if the company contributes an amount of stock equal to the principal portion of the loan to the ESOP.)

A provision allowing an ESOP company to deduct dividends paid directly to ESOP participants.

A provision allowing an ESOP or workers' cooperative to assume the estate tax liability of the estate of an owner of a business in return for a stock contribution from the estate worth at least as much as the tax liability.

16. Tax Reform Act of 1986. This act made a number of technical changes in ESOP law, as well as adding several new incentives for ESOPs and a number of new regulations.

New Incentives:

Fifty percent of the income from the sale of stock to an ESOP or a worker cooperative is excluded from the total taxable income to an estate. The provision expires at the end of 1992.

Dividends contributed to an ESOP can be used to repay an ESOP loan. Dividends do not count against the 25 percent of covered compensation limit that normally can be deducted to repay the principal part of an ESOP loan.

Companies terminating a pension plan and placing the assets in an ESOP will not be subject to the 10 percent excise tax other pension plan rollovers must pay. The exclusion expired at the end of 1988.

New Regulations:

If requested by the employee, ESOPs are required to distribute up to 25 percent of account balances to employees over age 55 with 10 years of ESOP participation and up to 50 percent for employees at age 60 with 10 years of ESOP participation.

Independent, outside appraisals must be performed for all ESOP companies at least annually.

Stock bonus plans must offer put options for departing employees (ESOPs were already required to do so).

After 1989, employees receiving their ESOP distributions before age 59½ must pay a 10 percent excise tax on the amount unless they roll it over into an IRA or have it paid in a life annuity.

Companies must begin distributions of account balances to employees who leave before retirement within 6 years of departure.

Vesting must be complete in 7 years if gradual or 5 years if vesting does not start until the fifth year.

The percentage of employees who must be covered by a plan and the rules for seeing if a plan discriminates in favor of highly compensated people have been tightened.

GENERAL STATE LAWS

Oregon, Delaware, and Maryland have passed laws declaring it the policy of the state to promote employee ownership, and these states require state agencies to issue reports on what they have done to comply. See the Oregon Employee Ownership Opportunity Act and Employee Corporation Act, ORS 59.025 (1987), the Delaware Employee Ownership Act, 63-35 (1981), and the Maryland Broadened Ownership Act, SB Section 131 (1979).

STATE COOPERATIVE STATUTE LAWS

Connecticut, Maine, Massachusetts, New Hampshire, New York, and Vermont have each passed identical legislation establishing a state worker cooperative incorporation statute. The laws, modeled after the Massachusetts Employee Cooperative Corporations Act, (chapter 104, Massachusetts General Laws, 1982), make it clear that companies can incorporate as worker cooperatives, use an internal account system similar to profit sharing, be based on the membership of workers, follow one-member-one-vote rules, and use the word *cooperative* in their corporate name.

LAWS PROVIDING FINANCIAL AND TECHNICAL ASSISTANCE SUPPORT

California, Connecticut, Illinois, Michigan, New Jersey, New York State, New York City, Oregon, Pennsylvania, West Virginia, and Wisconsin have each passed laws providing loans and/or loan guarantees for worker buyout efforts, funds for technical assistance in buyout efforts and programs for general outreach on employee ownership (not limited to buyouts).

California's law empowers the Department of Economic and Business Development to provide technical assistance and bond-backed financing for buyout efforts. Buyouts must result in companies that will be majority employee owned. Employees attempting a buyout can continue to receive unemployment insurance even though they are not actively seeking another job.

Connecticut's law directs the Department of Ecomonic Development to help fund both feasibility studies and provide financing for employee buyouts of plants that would otherwise be closed or sold to out-of-state companies. Eight million dollars has been appropriated for the program.

The Illinois law provides authority for the Department of Commerce to assist buyouts. Bond-backed financing can be used for low-interest loans with a limit of $250,000 or 25 percent of purchase price (whichever is lower). The company must have at least 60 percent of its voting stock owned by employees. The department can also conduct outreach programs and provide technical assistance for buyout efforts.

Michigan has passed five laws in this area. The first, passed in 1979, provides the Department of Labor with the authority to provide technical assistance for buyout efforts. The second, passed in 1981, provides the Michigan Economic Development Authority with the authority to make bond-backed funding available for economic conversion projects, including employee buyouts. Loans generally cannot exceed $100 million per deal and must create or retain at least 100 jobs. Employees must end up with at least 60 percent of the voting stock. The last three laws, passed in 1985, create the most comprehensive state employee ownership program in the United States. They provide specific authorization for the state Department of Labor to promote employee ownership through workshops, education, publications, and so on; to help employee groups fund feasibility studies and obtain financing; and to help finance employee buyouts at below market rates. Unlike other state laws, the Michigan laws make this assistance available to all employee ownership efforts in which employees obtain or will obtain a majority of the voting stock of the company, not just to employee buyouts of troubled firms.

The Employee Stock Ownership Plan Act of 1984 provided the New Jersey Department of Commerce with the authority to assist employee buyouts through technical assistance and loans, loan guarantees, and direct interest subsidies. Requests must come through municipal governments, and employees must end up with 100 percent of the stock. No specific funds were appropriated for the program.

The department was also authorized to do research, hold conferences, and issue publications on employee ownership.

New York's Employee Ownership Assistance Act of 1983 provides the Department of Commerce with authority to promote the idea of employee ownership generally and to provide technical assistance for employee buyout efforts. The Job Development Authority can also issue bonds to provide loans for employee buyout efforts, with limits of 40 percent of project costs or $10,000,000, whichever is lower. Employees must end up with a majority of the voting stock.

In 1984, New York City passed an amendment to its charter authorizing the city to assist employee ownership efforts. The city, through its economic development program, can now make technical and financial assistance to employee buyouts and sponsor educational efforts to make New York City businesses more aware of employee ownership.

Oregon's law provides $2 million for employee buyout assistance, to be administered by a nonprofit agency to be designated by the state Department of Development. Part of the funds can be used to finance feasibility studies.

Pennsylvania's Employee Ownership Assistance Program, passed in 1984, is the most ambitious of these laws. Over 3 years, $15 million dollars is allocated—$3 million dollars is available for technical assistance for buyouts and $12 million for loans. The technical assistance portion is limited to 50 percent of the cost of a feasibility study and is in the form of a loan. If the study is negative, the loan does not have to be repaid. Project loans are limited to 25 percent of project costs or $1.5 million, whichever is lower. At least two-thirds of the employees must make an equity investment worth 10 percent of the purchase price. Employees must end up with a majority of the company's voting stock.

West Virginia's Employee Ownership Assistance Program, passed in 1986, provides technical assistance and loans for feasibility studies for employee ownership efforts in distress or business transfer situations and financial assistance for distress buyout efforts. The state may provide subsidies on the loan.

Wisconsin's Employee Ownership Act, passed in 1983, gives the Wisconsin Department of Development authority to provide technical assistance for employee buyouts and other employee ownership efforts and to conduct educational and research programs to help promote employee ownership. A "Council on Employee Owned Businesses" was created as part of the act to oversee its implementation and will consist of members from labor, business, government, academia, and the public. No specific funds were set aside for the program, and it does not disperse funds to support employee ownership efforts.

OTHER STATE LAWS

Assembly Bill 2271 (untitled, 1982) in California amended state securities laws to exempt ESOPs from requirements that would have, in effect, made leveraged ESOPs almost impossible. Maryland HB 237 in 1979 also exempted ESOPs from state security laws.

The New Hampshire Community Development Finance Authority Act of 1983 created a system of tax credits to fund a state economic development agency to assist community development corporations and worker-owned cooperatives. The program can provide both technical assistance and financing.

In 1984, Hawaii passed An Act Relating to Employee Stock Ownership. The law requires the state to study what approaches could best promote employee ownership in Hawaii and report back to the legislature in anticipation of more comprehensive legislation. In 1986, the act was amended to continue through 1988 and specified that the state should provide educational and promotional services for employee ownership.

SB–659 (1983, untitled) provides that under West Virginia tax laws, contributions to repay a loan through an ESOP are fully deductible.

APPENDIX B

Key Organizations

Compiled by Corey Rosen*

*Corey Rosen is the Executive Director of the National Center for Employee Ownership, located in Oakland, California.

APPENDIX B

Action Resources West
1218 South 1200 West
Salt Lake City, Utah 84104
(801) 378-2664

Consulting on workplace participation programs, especially in
employee ownership settings. Contact Warner Woodworth or
Chris Meek.

Association for Workplace Democracy
1714 Connecticut Ave., NW
Washington, DC 20009
(202) 265-7727

Journal on workplace democracy; regional chapters of active
volunteers interested in workplace democracy.

Center for Community Self-Help
P.O. Box 3259
Durham, NC 27705
(919) 683-3019

Technical assistance for employee buyout efforts, cooperatives, and other matters related to plant closing and worker
ownership in the North Carolina area. Operates credit union
and loan fund to assist employee ownership effort. Contact
Martin Eakes.

Industrial Cooperative Association
249 Elm Street
Somerville, MA 02144
(617) 628-7330

Technical assistance, information and loan fund for worker cooperatives, democratic ESOPs, employee buyouts, and community development. Contact Steve Dawson.

Michigan Employee Ownership Center
3163 Penobscot Building
Detroit, MI 48226
(313) 964-5040

Nonprofit local support group focusing on assistance to unions and small businesses. Contact Deborah Groban Olson.

National Center for Employee Ownership
426 17th Street
Suite 650
Oakland, CA 94612
(415) 272-9461

Private nonprofit research and information organization. Services include conferences and workshops, publications, referral service for members, clipping service, and special projects for members. Contact Corey Rosen.

New York Interface
251 Park Avenue South
12th Floor
New York, NY 10010

Research, workshops, and technical assistance for employee ownership in the New York area. Contact Marilyn Ondrasik.

Philadelphia Association for Cooperative Enterprise
1321 Arch Street, Room 806
Philadelphia, PA 19107
(215) 561-7079

Technical assistance for employee ownership, focusing on cooperatives and employee buyouts. Contact Sherman Kreiner.

Program for Employment and Workplace System
School of Industrial and Labor Relations
Box 1000, Ives Hall
Cornell University
Ithaca, NY 14853

Organizational assistance and research on employee ownership and labor–management cooperation programs. Contact William Foote Whyte.

Social Economy Program
Department of Sociology
Boston College
Chestnut Hill, MA 02167

Newsletter on workplace democracy and related topics; graduate education in workplace democracy, employee ownership and related topics. Contact Charles Derber.

Study Group on Worker Ownership and Participation
129 Vanserg, 10 Divinity Lane
Harvard University
Cambridge, MA 02138
(617) 495-3436

Research and speakers series on employee ownership. Contact Joseph Blasi.

Twin Streams Educational Center
243 Fleminton Street
Chapel Hill, NC 27514
(919) 929-3316

Educational programs for workers in employee ownership efforts. Contact Wes Hare.

Utah State University Business and Economic Development Services
UMC 35, P.O. Box 95923
Logan, Utah 84322
(801) 750-2283
Research and information on plant closings, employee ownership, and related issues. Contact Gary Hansen.

Work Books
P.O. Box 587
Gatesville, NC 27938

Books on employee ownership, workplace democracy, and related topics. Contact Frank Adams.

APPENDIX C

Suggested Readings

Compiled by Corey Rosen*

* Corey Rosen is the Executive Director of the National Center for Employee Onwership, located in Oakland, California.

APPENDIX C

LEGAL AND PRACTICAL GUIDES

Clark, Dennis, and Merry Guben. *Future Bread*.
Philadelphia: O & O Investment Fund, 1983.

Describes how the "O & O" (owned and operated)
worker-owned supermarkets were established in
Philadelphia, and provides detailed, step-by-step
guidance on how to form a worker cooperative.

Ellerman, David. "What Is a Workers' Cooperative?" Available from the Industrial Cooperative Association, 249
Elm Street, Somerville, MA 02144

A good brief discussion laying out the ICA's innovative
cooperative structure model.

Frisc, Robert. *ESOPs for the 80's*. Rockville Center, NY:
Farnsworth Publishing, 1981.

A detailed look at ESOPs presented in layman's language.

Industrial Cooperative Association. *ICA Model By-Laws for
Worker Cooperatives*. Available from author, 249 Elm
Street, Somerville, MA 02144

A detailed guide for setting up a worker cooperative.

Larson, Daniel, Darrol Stanley, and James Warren. "ESOP Valuations of Closely Held Company Stock." *Financial Planner*, January, 1981, pp. 2–6.

Ludwig, Ronald, and Jared Kaplan. *ESOPs*. Washington, D.C.: Bureau of National Affairs, Tax Management Subsidiary.

A detailed explanation of ESOPs, containing technical explanations of legal issues, required legal forms, and a list of ESOP regulations and statutes.

National Center for Employee Ownership (NCEO). *An Employee Buyout Handbook*. Available from author, 426 17th Street, Suite 650, Oakland, CA 94612.

A detailed, step-by-step explanation of the steps necessary to evaluate whether an employee buyout is worth pursuing, including a variety of financial questions and guidelines.

NCEO. *A Model Employee Stock Ownership Plan*. Available from author, 426 17th Street, Suite 650, Oakland, CA 94612.

A 100-page compilation of the legal language for an ESOP, a plain English explanation of each provision, a suggested model for an employee handbook, a list of consultants, and other material. Contains several different options for tailoring plans to specific needs.

Sellers, Robert. "Banks as Employee Stock Ownership Plan Sponsors and Lenders." Washington D.C.: American Bankers Association, 1983.

Introduction to the role of banks in ESOPs.

CASE STUDIES

Barnes, Peter. "Confessions of a Socialist Entrepreneur."
Available from the NCEO (members only), 426 17th
Street, Suite 650, Oakland, CA 94612.

The best article on what it actually is like to organize
and run an employee-owned business, from the founder
of the Solar Center.

Berman, Katrina. *Worker Owned Plywood Companies.*
Pullman, WA: Washington State University, 1967.

A pioneering study of worker plywood cooperatives.

"ESOPs: A Capital Idea." *Inc.*, April 1982, pp. 36–46.

One of the best articles on how ESOPs are actually
used.

Long, Richard. "Job Attitudes and Organizational Performance Under Employee Ownership." *Academy of
Management Journal*, December 1980, V. 23, No. 4,
726–37.

Examines effects of employee ownership on job attitudes in three firms and finds that positive impact is
greatest when amount owned is highest and participation strongest.

Miller, Marc. "Workers' Owned." *Southern Exposure*, v. 8,
Winter 1980, pp. 12–21.

Case study of co-op formed by low-income people in
North Carolina.

Rowe, Jonathan. "Weirton Steel: Buying Out the Bosses."
Washington Monthly, January 1984, pp. 34–38.

Good discussion of the Weirton buyout.

Simmons, John, and William Mares. *Working Together*. New York: Alfred Knopf, 1983.

Excellent account of over 50 companies using employee ownership or quality of worklife programs.

Whyte, William F., Tove Helland Hammer, Reed Nelson, Chris Meek, and Robert Stern. *Worker Participation and Ownership*. Ithaca, NY: Cornell University, 1983.

An outstanding look at several employee buyout cases and the Jamestown Area Labor–Management Committee program.

Wintner, Linda. *Employee Buyouts: An Alternative to Plant Closings*. New York: The Conference Board, 1983.

A detailed look at several employee buyouts.

GENERAL STUDIES

Conte, Michael, and Arnold Tannenbaum. *Employee Ownership*. Ann Arbor: Survey Research Center, University of Michigan, 1980.

A comprehensive study of the effects of employee ownership on profitability which finds that employee ownership firms are 1.5 times as profitable as conventional firms.

Frieden, Karl. *Productivity and Workplace Democracy*. Washington, D.C.: National Center for Ecomonic Alternatives, 1980.

Summarizes the literature in this field.

Robert Jackall and Henry Levin, Eds. Worker Cooperatives in America. Berkeley: University of California Press, 1985.

A reader on worker cooperatives that brings together in one volume most of the best writings on the subject.

Kelso, Louis, and Mortimer Adler. *The Capitalist Manifesto*. New York: Random House, 1958.

The basic book explaining Kelso's philosophy of broadened ownership.

Kelso, Louis, and Patricia Hetter. *Two-Factor Theory: The Economics of Reality*. New York: Random House, 1967.

A briefer explanation of Kelso's theory.

Kruse, Douglas. *Employee Ownership and Attitudes: Two Case Studies*. Norwood, VA: Norwood Editions, 1984.

Discusses two detailed case studies and the general philosophy of employee ownership.

Kurland, Norman. "Beyond ESOPs: The Kelso-Adler Theory of Ecomomic Justice." Available from the NCEO (members only), 426 17th Street, Suite 650, Oakland, CA 94612.

A complete bibliography on the philosophical writings on the theory of ESOPs and broadened ownership, briefly annotated.

Marsh, Thomas, and Dale McAllister. "ESOPs Tables: A Survey of Companies with Employee Stock Ownership Plans." *Journal of Corporation Law*, v. 6, no. 3, Spring 1981.

A survey of 229 companies with 10 or more employees. The best study available on the structure, performance, and characteristics of ESOP firms. It concludes with the finding that these companies are much more productive than their conventional counterparts.

NCEO. *Employee Ownership: A Bibliography*. 77 pp., partly annotated. Available from the author, 426 17th
Street, Suite 650, Oakland, CA 94612.

NCEO. *An Employee Ownership Reader*. Available from
the author, 426 17th Street, Suite 650, Oakland, CA
94612.

A comprehensive introduction to employee ownership,
containing practical articles on ESOPs and cooperatives, case studies, suggestions on organizational
development and legal structure, and more.

Olson, Deborah Groban. "Some Union Experiences with Issues Raised by Worker Ownership in the U.S.: ESOPs,
TRASOPs, Co-ops, Stock Plans and Board Representation." *Wisconsin Law Review*, December 1982.

An excellent review of unions' concerns and possibilities on these issues.

Rosen, Corey, and Katherine Klein. "Job-Creating Performance of Employee Ownership Companies." *Monthly
Labor Review*, August 1983.

Reports a study of majority employee owned companies
that showed that they created three times more new
jobs per year than comparable conventional firms.

Wagner, Ira. "Report to the New York Stock Exhange on
the Performance of Publicly Held Companies with
Employee Ownership Plans." Arlington, VA: NCEO,
1984. Available from the NCEO, 426 17th Street,
Suite 650, Oakland, CA 94612.

Report of a study of 13 publicly held companies at least
10 percent employee owned, which finds that they out-
perform their conventional counterparts.

FILMS

Bill Moyers Journal. *It's Not Working*. WNET, 1980, 25 minutes, 16 mm, color. Available from California Newsreel, 630 Natoma St., San Francisco, CA 94103

Examines closing of Youngstown steel mill and workers' efforts to buy it.

The Mondragon Experiment. 58 minutes, BBC. Available from California Newsreel.

An outstanding film on the Mondragon cooperatives, the largest and most successful worker-owned business network in the world.

CLIPPING SERVICE

The NCEO maintains a complete file of newspaper and other print media clippings from over 9,000 U.S. publications. Clipping service subscribers receive a bimonthly compilation of the clips.

Index

A

Accounting for ESOP transactions,
   excess contributions to
      defined contribution
      plan, 156
      assets, 156-58
      dividends, 161
      earnings per share, 161-62
      equity, 158-59
      liabilities, 158
      profit/loss, 159-61
   leveraged buyouts, 162
      assets, 162-63
      earnings per share, 165
      equity, 163-64
      liabilities, 163
      profit/loss, 165

mirror loan transactions,
   152-53
for nonleveraged ESOP,
   165-66
traditional leveraged ESOP
   rules, 144-45
   assets, 145
   dividends, 149-50
   earnings per share, 150-51
   equity, 145-49
   footnote disclosure, 151
   liabilities, 145
   profit or loss, 150
two-step ESOP loan trans-
   actions, 153-56
*Accounting Principles Board
   Opinion 25*, 163

Acquisitions, 208-14
Action Resources West, 305
Adequate consideration, 24
Adler, Mortimer, 4
Administration
　contribution/deduction
　　limits, 179
　employee contributions, 192
　existing retirement plans,
　　190-91
　general qualification re-
　　quirements, 169-70
　　average benefit percent-
　　　age test, 172
　　benefit limitations, 173-
　　　74, 182
　　cost basis of stock, 188-89
　　distribution options, 183-
　　　87
　　fiduciary standards, 178
　　investment diversifica-
　　　tion, 182-83
　　participation, 170-71
　　percentage test, 171
　　ratio test, 171-72
　　reporting requirements,
　　　176-78
　　top-heavy status, 174-76
　　vesting, 173
　　voting of ESOP stock, 187-
　　　88
　release of collateral, 179-82
　repayment terms of loan,
　　191-92
　repurchase liability, 192-93
　required reports
　　annual return report of
　　　employee benefit plan,
　　　Form 5500, 177

employee benefit state-
　ment, 177
Form 1099, W2P, 178
summary annual report,
　177
summary description of
　material modification
　of plan, 177
summary plan descrip-
　tion, 176
updated summary plan
　description, 177
AFL-CIO, 219
　guidelines for employee
　　stock ownership plans,
　　245-47
　defining employers for
　　purposes of ESOP, 247
　employee participation,
　　245
　equitable stock allocation,
　　246
　feasibility studies, 245
　initial evaluation formula,
　　247
　pension plans, 245
　quick implementation of
　　personnel cutbacks,
　　247
　selecting ESOP trustees,
　　246
　stock distributions, 246
　vesting schedules, 247
　voting power, 246
AICPA Statement of Position
　76-3, 143, 204
Air Line Pilots Association
　(ALPA), 239

Allegis, attempted employee ownership at, 239

Allied plywood, employee ownership at, 284-85

Amalgamated Clothing and Textile Workers Union (ACTWU), 220-21

A mergers, 212-14

Annual return report of employee benefit plan, Form 5500, 177

Appraisal
assumptions underlying, 80
effective date of, 79

Assessment of employee awareness/attitudes
through employee surveys, 265-66
through focus groups, 266-67

Asset-based financing, target rate of return for, 119

Asset-based lending, 125-26

Assets
in defined contributed plan, 156-58
in leveraged buyouts, 162-63
in leveraged ESOP, 145

Association for Workplace Democracy, 305

Average benefit percentage test, 172

B

Back-to-back loans, 98, 101-2

Bait and switch, 120

Benefit, ESOP as, 260-61

Benefit limitations, in ESOP, 173-74, 182

Biernacki, Rich, 285

Bish, Walter, 287

Blue Bell, 221

B merger, 214

Bonn, Karen, 168

Brown, Gregory K., 10

Business judgment rule, 40

Buy-sell plans, coordinating ESOP with shareholder estate and, 67-69

C

Cable, Mike, 225

Capitalist Manifesto (Kelso & Adler), 4

Capital stock accounts, annual adjustments for, 158-59

Capitol Manufacturing, 228-29

Carefree of Colorado, 220

Cash flow ESOP leveraged buyout, 126-27
method for, 128-30

Cash reserve, use of sinking fund approach to develop, 63

Center for Community Self-Help, 305

Chrysler Loan Guarantee Act (1980), 295

C merger, 214

Collateral
ESOP shares as, 105-6
release of, for ESOP, 179-82

Communications

developing plan for, 264-67

establishing appropriate goals, 260-64

as factor in motivating employees in employee ownership, 279

implied ownership contract, 256

control, 257

employee input, 257-58

monetary gain, 256-57

paradox of employee ownership, 258-60

presenting message, 267-68

Conte, Michael, 274

Contra equity account, 147, 148, 158

Contribution/deduction limits, for ESOP, 179

Corporate finance

use of ESOP for, 197

debt financing, 199-204

equity financing, 205-208

improving liquidity, 198-99

mergers, 208-14

tax advantages of ESOPs, 197-98

Corporate performance, and employee ownership, 274-75

Cost basis, of stock, 188-89

D

Dan River Co., 221

Davis, Clarence, 234-35

Debt coverage ratios, 131

Debt financing, 13, 199-204

Deficit Reduction Act (1984), 33, 297

Defined contribution plan

excess contributions to, 156

top-heavy, 174-76

limit on compensation, 176

minimum contributions, 175-76

minimum vesting restrictions, 175

de minimis exception, 190

Direct loan, 97-98, 200

Distribution options, for ESOPs, 186-87

Distributions, timing and form of, 15-16, 38, 60

Diversification, 18-19

Dividend deduction, 32-33

Dividends

in defined contribution plan, 161

in leveraged ESOP, 149-50

Donovan v. *Cunningham*, 24-25, 79, 80

E

Earnings per share

in defined contribution plan, 161-62

in leveraged buyout, 165

in leveraged ESOP, 150-51

Eaves v. *Penn*, 22

Economic Recovery Tax Act (1981), 295-96

Emerging Issues Task Force (EITF), 143-44

Issue No. 85-11, 163

Issue No. 86-27, 149, 156, 159-60, 162

Emerging liability study, 63

Employee benefit statement, 177

Employee contributions, 61, 192

Employee coverage, under ESOP, 59-60

Employee ownership, 219
  and company performance, 281-83
  and corporate performance, 274-75
  general accounting office study of, 240-41
  motivation for success, 276-81

Employee participation, as factor in success of ESOP, 170-71, 279

Employee Retirement Income Security Act (1974) (ERISA), 293
  definition of ESOP in, 169
  exclusive benefit rule of, 20-23, 40
  fiduciary prudence, 20-23
  recognition of leveraged ESOPs in, 5
  special ESOP considerations under, 19-29

Employee stock ownership plans (ESOPs)
  administration of. *See* Administration
  as a benefit, 260-61
  communicating message of, 255-68

conversion of retirement plan to, 57-58

coordinating
  with other retirement plans, 57-59
  with shareholder estate and buy-sell plans, 67-69

corporate and employee tax considerations, 37-39

and corporate law considerations, 40-42

definition of, 11, 169

designing, 59-61
  allocation of financed shares, 60
  employee contributions, 61
  employee coverage, 59-60
  responsibility of plan administrator for, 61
  responsibility of trustee for, 61
  timing of distributions, 60
  vesting schedule, 60

development of, 3-5

distributions, 12, 15-16

and diversification, 18-19

dividend deduction, 32-33

dual role of, 5-6

elements of successful, 56-57

and employee ownership, 6

employer securities, 17

establishment of, as poison pill, 22-23

estate tax exclusion, 33-35

exemption from prohibited transactions, 24-25

exempt loans for, 25-29
financing, 115
   arranging, 117
   complexity of, 118
   cost of, 119-20
   expectations from lender,
      120-21
   expectations of lender,
      121-25
   parties in secured financ-
      ing, 125-26
   sources of financing, 115-
      16
flexibility of, 3
floor-offset arrangements,
   46-47
independent appraiser, 17-
   18
legal treatment of, 6
leveraged, 12-15, 56
   traditional accounting
      rules for, 144-45
   use of, to reduce cost of ser-
      vicing debt, 198-99
   use of exempt loan
      provisions by, 28-29
leveraged buyout, 106-7
   advantage of, 127
   approaching lenders, 136-
      40
   pricing ESOP loan, 130-36
   unsecured financing, 126-
      30
loans
   lender's interest exclu-
      sion, 95-103
   practical implications of,
      103
      amount of loan, 103

assurance of posttran-
      saction solvency, 106-
      7
   ESOP shares as col-
      lateral, 105-6
   interest rate risk, 104-5
   purchase price for
      employer securities,
      103-4
   securities law risks, 107-
      8
pricing, 130-36
statutory framework for,
   95-103
as motivator, 261-63
nondiscriminatory coverage
   rules for, 11
origin of concept, 4-5
partial interest exclusion
   for, 29-30
as part of total performance
   culture, 263-64
and plan disqualifications,
   47-48
popularity of, 95
prohibited transactions, 23-
   24
put options, 16
as qualified plan, 11-12, 97
recognition of leveraged, 5,
   6
resales by plan participants,
   43-44
securities law considera-
   tions, 42-46
shares in, as collateral, 105-
   6
special considerations
   under ERISA, 19-29

special incentives, 29-37
statutory framework for
  eligible lenders, 96
  ESOP as a qualified plan,
    97
  use of proceeds, 96-97
steps in process, 55-56
tax advantages of, 197-98
tax-free rollover, 30-32
transfers of reversions, 35-
  37
types of, 12-15
unique role of, in corporate
  finance, 3
uses and applications of, 12
USWA resolution on, 248-
  51
valuation, 73
  assumptions underlying
    appraisal, 80
  effective date of appraisal,
    79
  fair market value defined,
    74-76
  fairness, 88-90
  importance of reasonable
    judgment and quan-
    titative support, 76-78
  relative levels of value, 80-
    87
  requirements for inde-
    pendent appraisal, 73-
    74
  securities acquisition
    loans, 97-98
vesting schedules, 11
as viewed favorably by
  labor, 224-40

as viewed unfavorably by
  labor, 220-24
voting, 16-17, 187-88
Employee surveys, assessing
  employee awareness/at-
  titudes through, 265-66
Employer securities, 17
  purchase price for, 103-4
Equity
  in defined contribution
    plan, 158-59
  in leveraged buyouts, 163-
    64
  in leveraged ESOP, 145
Equity financing, use of
  ESOP, 205-208
Equity kicker, 127
ERISA. *See* Employee Retirement Income Security Act
  (1974)
Estate tax assumption, 68
Estate taxes, reduction or
  elimination of through
  ESOP, 198
Estate tax exclusion, 33-35,
  68-69
Excess contributions to
  defined contribution plan,
  156
Exclusive benefit, 20-23, 40
Exempt loans for ESOPs, 25-
  29
  requirements for, 102-3
Fair market value
  definition of, 74-76
  of marketable minority in-
    terest, 81

Fastener Industries, employee ownership at, 285

Federal Reserve Board, Regulation U, 45

Fiduciary
definition of, 19
ERISA requirements for, 19-20
procedural prudence of, 25
prohibited actions of, 23-24

Fiduciary prudence, 20-23

Financed shares, allocation of, 60

Financial Accounting Standards Board (FASB), organization of Emerging Issues Task Force by, 143

Financing, sources of, 115-16

Fixed-rate senior and subordinated debt, 119

Flexibility, importance of in employee ownership, 259

Floor-offset arrangements, 46-47

Focus groups, assessing employee awareness attitudes through, 266-67

Footnote disclosure, in leveraged ESOP, 151

Fort Vancouver Plywood, employee ownership at, 222-23

401(k) feature, adding, to ESOP, 192

Fractional method, 179, 180-81

Franklin Forge, 224

employee ownership at, 228-31

Front-end loan, 98

Future net cash flows, discounting, 77-78

G

GAAP approach, 164, 165

GAAP position, 150

Goals, establishing appropriate in ESOPs, 260-64

Goldstein, Alex, 236

Green mail payment, 41-42

H

Harsco Corporation, 229

Hedging, 122

Highly compensated employee
definition of, 170-71
identification of, 14

Hostile takeover
establishing ESOP in light of, 40-41
and purchase of shares during, 21-22

Hyatt Clark, employee ownership at, 224

I

Ichan, Carl, 239

Immediate allocation loans, 203-4

Implied ownership contract, 256

Independent appraisal, requirements for, 73-74

Independent appraiser, 17-18

Industrial Cooperative Association (ICA), 230, 306
Interest rate risk, 104-5
Internal Revenue Code (IRC)
  Section 133, 132-36
  Section 404(k), 32
  Section 415, 35
  Section 1042, 205
  Section 2057, 33-34
  Section 4980, 35, 36, 156
Internal Revenue Service
  Form 1099, W2P, 178
  Revenue Ruling 5960, 18, 24, 74, 76, 79
  Revenue Ruling 76-25, 47
International Association of Machinists (IAM), 234
International Automobile, Aerospace, and Agricultural Implement Workers of America (UAW), 229
International Woodworkers of America (IWA), on ESOPs, 223
Investment diversification, for ESOPs, 182-83
IRS *General Counsel Memorandum 39744*, 36

J
Japan, and use of improvement ideas, 258

K
Kalish, Gerald I., 54
Kelso, Louis, 4-5
Key employee, identification of, 174-75

L
Labor
  ESOPS viewed favorably by, 224-40
  ESOPs viewed unfavorably by, 220-24
Labor, U.S. Department of
  and fair market value, 75
  and independent appraisal requirements, 18
  and payment of control premium, 85-86
Laskowski, Jack, 229
Legislation
  federal, 293-98
  state, 298-302
Lenders
  approaching for ESOP financing, 136-40
  interest exclusion for, 95-103
Lester, Harry, 231
Leveraged buyouts. *See under* Employee stock ownership plans
Leveraged ESOPs. *See under* Employee stock ownership plans
Liabilities
  in defined contribution plan, 158
  in leveraged buyouts, 163
  in leveraged ESOP, 145
Liquidity, improving, 198-99
Loan suspense account, release of shares from, 14
Lock-up provision, 86
Long, Russell, 5

Lorenzo, Frank, 239
Loughhead, Robert, 287
Lump-sum distribution,
from an ESOP, 38-39
Lyon Metal Products, ESOP
leveraged buyout of, 86-
87, 88

M
McLouth Steel, employee
ownership at, 231-33
Mergers, 208-14
Mezzanine financing, 119
Michigan Employee Owner-
ship Center (MEOC),
229-30, 306
Miller, Herman Company,
employee ownership at,
228
Miller, Rebecca J., 142
Minority shareholder
rights, 211
Mirror loans, 98, 152-53,
161, 203
Miscellaneous Revenue Act
(1980), 295
Motivation, as factor in
employee ownership, 276-
81
Much, Paul J., 72

N
National Center For
Employee Ownership,
306
Net unrealized apprecia-
tion, 39
New York Interface, 306

Nonleveraged ESOP, ac-
counting for, 165-66
Non-qualified plan, using a,
59
North Coast Brass and Copper Company,
employee ownership at,
234-39
Notice 87-13, 34-35
Notice 88-58, 36

O
Olson, Deborah Groban, 218

P
Partial interest exclusion,
29-30
Parties in interest, 23
Payroll Based Stock Owner-
ship Plans (PAYSOPS),
34, 295-96
Percentage test, 171
Performance, as factor in
employee ownership, 281-
83
Philadelphia Association for
Cooperative Enterprise,
307
Plan administrator, respon-
sibility of,
for designing ESOP, 61
Plan disqualification, and
ESOPs, 47-48
Plan participants, resales
by, 43-44
Plan sponsor, accounting
for ESOP
transactions by, 143-66

Poison pill, establishment
of ESOP as, 22-23
Posttransaction solvency, assurance of, 106-7
Pricer, R. W., 196
Principal only method, 179,
181-82
Procedural prudence, 25
Profit/loss
in defined contribution
plans, 159-61
in leveraged buyouts, 165
in leveraged ESOP, 150
Profit-sharing plans, allocations under, 60
Program for Employment
and Workplace System,
307
Prohibited allocation rule,
32
Prudence rule, application
of, to acquisitionof
employer stock, by
ESOP, 22
Put options, 16, 186

Q
Quad/Graphics, employee
ownership at, 286-87
Quadrucci, Harry, 286-87
Qualified plan, ESOP as a,
97
Qualified replacement
property, purchase of, 30-
31

R
Ratio test, 171-72
Raymond Co., 221

Reasonable judgment and
quantitative support,
importance of, 76-78
Regional Rail Reorganiza-
tion Act (1973), 293
Registration-type class of
securities, 187
Republic Container,
employee ownership at,
225-27
Repurchase liability, 192-93
definition of, 61-62
measuring, 62-63
planning for, 61-64
Repurchase liability study,
63
Retirement plans
conversion of, to ESOP, 57-
58
coordinating ESOP with
other, 57-59
maintaining an existing,
58-59
Revenue Act (1978), 294-95
Revenue Act (1987)
modification of ERISA
under, 47
and timing of pension
plan terminations, 36
Right of first refusal, 187
Risk protection, importance
of, 122
Rosen, Corey, 272

S
Scott & Fetzer Company,
employee ownership at,
220-21

SEC *Release 33-6188*, 42, 43-44

SEC *Release 33-6281*, 43, 44

SEC Rule 144, 43, 44

Secured financing
advantages of, 118
parties in, 125-26

Secured transaction
complexity of, 118
parties in, 118

Securities acquisition loans, 29, 97-98
back-to-back loans, 98, 101-2
direct loan, 97-98
front-end loan, 98
immediate allocation loan, 98
mirror loan, 98, 152-53, 161, 203

Securities Act (1933), 42-43

Securities Exchange Act (1934), 44-45
and voting rights, 16

Securities law risks, 107-8

Self-assurance, importance of in employee ownership, 259

Senior bank debt, 119

Seven-year term issue, 98, 101

Shareholder estate, coordinating ESOP with, and buy-sell plans, 67-69

Shaw, Bob, 284

Sinking fund approach, use of, to develop cash

reserve, 63

Small Business Employee Ownership Act, 295

Smiley, Robert W., Jr., 114

Social Economy Program, 307

South Bend Lathe (SBL), employee ownership at, 222

State cooperative statute laws, 299

Statement of Financial Accounting Standards No. 88, 160-61

Statement of Position 76-3, 144, 145, 149, 150, 152, 155, 159, 161, 162, 163

Statutory framework, 95-96

Stock, cost basis of, 188-89

Stock bonus plans, 12, 13

Study Group on Worker Ownership and Participation, 307

Subsidiary, use of, to accomplish equity financing, 206-7

Summary annual report, 177

Summary description of material modification of plan, 177

Summary plan description, 176

Suspense account
release of stock held in, 179-82
voting of, 188

T

Tang, Cyrus, 231-32

Tannenbaum, Arnold, 274

Tax advantages, of ESOPs, 197-98

Tax Equity and Fiscal Responsibility Act (1982), 296

Tax-free rollover, 30-32, 64-67, 190

Tax Reduction Act (1975), 294

Tax Reform Act (1976), 294

Tax Reform Act (1984), 95
  and pricing of ESOP loans, 132-33

Tax Reform Act (1986), 33-34, 297-98
  and administration of ESOPs, 192
  and benefit limitations, 173
  and deduction of dividends to repay ESOP acquisition, 26, 32-33
  definition of highly compensated employee in, 170-71
  diversification requirement under, 18-19
  and establishment of types of ESOPs, 12-13
  and general qualification requirements for ESOPs, 172
  and independent ap-
  praisal, 17-18, 73-74
  and investment diversification, 182-83
  and pricing of ESOP loans, 132-33
  and repurchase liability, 62, 193
  and transfer of reversion to ESOP, 156
  use of net operating loss and carry forwards, 37

Tax shield, 132

Technical Corrections Act (1979), 295

Top-heavy status, 174-76

Total performance culture, ESOP as part of, 263-64

Trade Act (1974), 293-94

Trade Adjustment Assistance Act, 296

Transfers of reversions, 35-37

TRASOPS, 34, 227-28, 295-96

Treasury stock method, 155, 160

Trustee, responsibility of, for designing ESOP, 61

Turpin-Forster, Shela C., 254

TWA, and attempted ESOP at, 239

Twin Streams Educational Center, 308

Two-step ESOP loan transaction, 153-56, 161

U

U.S. Railway Association
   Authorizations (1979),
   295
United Airlines, attempted
   ESOP at, 239
United Auto Workers
   (UAW), on ESOPs, 223-
   24
United Steel Workers of
   America (USWA), 219,
   222
   on ESOPs, 225, 248-51
Unsecured deal, complexity
   of, 118
Updated summary plan
   description, 177
Utah State University Busi-
   ness and Economic
   Development Services,
   308

V

Value, relative levels of, 80-
   87
Vesting, in ESOP, 60, 173
Voting
   of ESOP shares, 16-17
   of ESOP stock, 187-88
Voting rights, as motivating
   factor in ESOP, 280-81

W

Weirton Steel, employee
   ownership at, 287-88
Work Books, 308